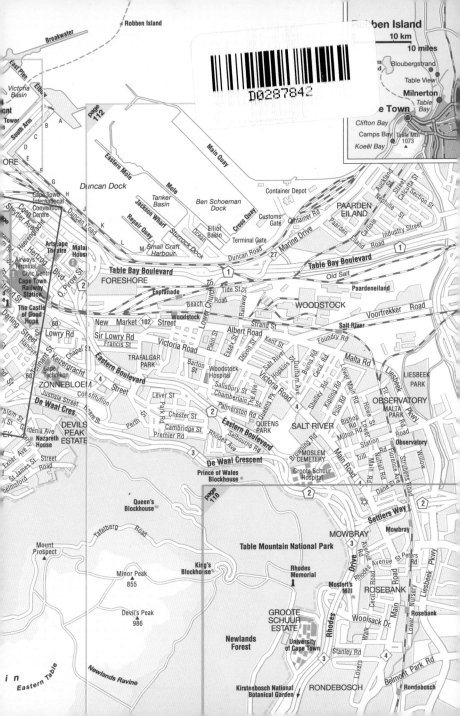

INSIGHT CITY GUIDE

Cape Town

APA PUBLICATIONS
Part of the Langenscheidt Publishing Group

※ INSIGHT GUIDE
CapeTown

Editor
Dorothy Stannard
Art Director
Klaus Geisler
Picture Editor
Hilary Genin
Cartography Editor
Zoë Goodwin
Production
Kenneth Chan
Editorial Director
Brian Bell

Distribution

UK & Ireland
GeoCenter International Ltd
The Viables Centre, Harrow Way
Basingstoke, Hants RG22 4BJ
Fax: (44) 1256-817988

United States
Langenscheidt Publishers, Inc.
36-36 33rd Street 4th Floor
Long Island City, New York 11106
Fax: (1) 718 784-0640

Canada
Thomas Allen & Son Ltd
390 Steelcase Road East
Markham, Ontario L3R 1G2
Fax: (1) 905 475 6747

Australia
Universal Publishers
1 Waterloo Road
Macquarie Park, NSW 2113
Fax: (61) 2 9888 9074

New Zealand
Hema Maps New Zealand Ltd (HNZ)
Unit D, 24 Ra ORA Drive
East Tamaki, Auckland
Fax: (64) 9 273 6479

Worldwide
**Apa Publications GmbH & Co.
Verlag KG (Singapore branch)**
38 Joo Koon Road, Singapore 628990
Tel: (65) 6865-1600. Fax: (65) 6861-6438

Printing

Insight Print Services (Pte) Ltd
38 Joo Koon Road, Singapore 628990
Tel: (65) 6865-1600. Fax: (65) 6861-6438

©2005 Apa Publications GmbH & Co.
Verlag KG (Singapore branch)
All Rights Reserved

First Edition 2005

ABOUT THIS BOOK

This guidebook combines the interests and enthusiasms of two of the world's best-known information providers: Insight Guides, whose titles have set the standard for visual travel guides since 1970, and Discovery Channel, the world's premier source of nonfiction television programming.

The editors of Insight Guides provide both practical advice and general understanding about a destination. Discovery Channel and its Web site, www.discovery.com, help millions of viewers explore their world from the comfort of their own home.

How to use this book

The book is carefully structured to convey an understanding of the city:

◆ To understand Cape Town today, you need to know something of its past. The first section covers the city's people, history and culture in lively essays written by specialists.

◆ The main Places section provides a full run-down of all the attractions worth seeing. The main places of interest are coordinated by number with full-colour maps.

◆ Photographic features focus on important aspects of the city, such as the former high security prison on Robben Island, where Nelson Mandela was incarcerated, the city's great sporting events and venues, and the wonderful flora of the Cape Peninsula.

◆ Photographs are chosen not only to illustrate geography and buildings but also to convey the moods of the city and the life of its people.

◆ The Travel Tips listings section provides a point of reference for information on travel, hotels, shops and festivals. Information

may be located quickly by using the index printed on the back cover flap – and the flaps are designed to serve as bookmarks.

The contributors

Insight Guide: Cape Town was put together by Insight Guides' Executive Editor, **Dorothy Stannard**, using writers and photographers based in Cape Town or with specialist knowledge of the destination.

Her main author for the book was **Paul Duncan**, the editorial director of Condé Nast South Africa, who had previously written *Insight Pocket Guide: Cape Town*. Duncan, who has also lived in London and Paris, eventually returned to his native South Africa in search of a quieter life – only to find Cape Town humming with activity. The Mother City had shaken off the shackles imposed by the

Apartheid years and had joined the ranks of those other places defined by their shops, festivals, restaurants, social life, beaches and sunshine-on-the-body-beautiful. As well as writing most of the Places chapters in this guide, Duncan, an enthusiastic patron of Cape Town's excellent restaurants, also wrote the feature on food and wine, compiled the restaurant listings, and wrote the short feature on architecture.

Duncan recommended two other contributors to this guide. The first **Mary Armour**, a feature writer and editor who also works for Condé Nast, wrote the history chapters, Cape Communities and the text for the picture story on sport. The second, **Sally Munro**, an assistant editor at Condé Nast, compiled the travel tips.

Other contributors include **Brent Meersman**, a Cape Town arts critic for the Johannesburg-based *Mail & Guardian*, who wrote the Creative Cape Town chaper and the small box on the city's Art Deco buildings, in which he has a special interest, and **Philip Briggs**, who wrote the Further Afield chapter. Briggs, an expert on African travel, has also contributed to *Insight Guide: South Africa*, *Insight Guide: Tanzania and Zanzibar* and *Insight Guide: East African Wildlife*.

Many photographers contributed images to the book, including **Bill Wassman**, **Ariadne van Zandbergen**, **Richard Nowitz** and **David Sanger** (a full credits list can be found on page 251). The book was proofread by **Neil Titman** and indexed by **Penny Phenix**, who also edited the Travel Tips section.

CONTACTING THE EDITORS

We would appreciate it if readers would alert us to errors or outdated information by writing to:

Insight Guides, P.O. Box 7910, London SE1 1WE, England.
Fax: (44) 20 7403-0290.
insight@apaguide.co.uk

Contents

Introduction

The Best of Cape Town 6
The Mother City.......................15

History

The Making of Cape Town..........17
From Apartheid to Democracy ..23
Decisive Dates 32

Features

Cape Communities 37
Cooking up a Feast 47
Creative Cape Town..................53

Places

Introduction 67
The City Centre 69
The Victoria & Alfred Waterfront..91
Bo-Kapp 105
The Townships 111
The Southern Suburbs............117
Table Mountain National Park ..137
The Cape Peninsula 149
Further Afield 171
The Garden Route 191

Photo Features

Sporting Cape Town 44
Robben Island 102
Cape Town in Bloom 146

Information panels

Wine 51
Architecture.............................59
What's On on the Waterfront.....96
Conserving Table Mountain
    National Park.....................140

Maps

Map Legend **239**
Street Atlas **240–247**
Street Atlas Index **248**

Cape Town **64 and inside front cover**
City Centre **70**
Victoria and Alfred Waterfront **94**
Robben Island **103**
Bo-Kapp 106
The Townships **112**
Southern Suburbs **118**
Kirstenbosch National Botanical Gardens **127**
Constantia Valley **129**
Table Mountain National Park **138 and Inside back cover**
Cape Peninsula **150**
Simon's Town **160**
Excursions from Cape Town **172**
Stellenbosch **174**
The Garden Route **192**

Travel Tips

TRANSPORT

Getting There **202**
By Air **202**
By Rail **202**
By Bus **202**
By Car **203**
By Ship **203**
Getting Around **203**
Taxis **204**

ACCOMMODATION

Choosing a Hotel **205**
City Centre and the City Bowl **206**
Victoria & Alfred Waterfront **208**
Southern Suburbs **210**
Atlantic Seaboard **211**
False Bay **212**
Further Afield **213**
The Garden Route **215**

ACTIVITIES

Theatre, Ballet & Classical Music **216**
Buying Tickets **217**
Nightlife **218**
Children's Activities **222**
Festivals **223**
Shopping **224**
Sports **226**
Sightseeing Tours **226**

A–Z: PRACTICAL INFORMATION

Admission Charges **227**
Budgeting for a Visit **227**
Business Hours **228**
Climate **228**
Clothing **228**
Crime & Safety **228**
Customs Regulations **229**
Disabled Travellers **229**
Electricity **230**
Embassies & Consulates **230**
Emergency Numbers **230**
Entry Requirements **230**
Gays and Lesbians **231**
Health & Medical Care **231**
Helplines **232**
Internet **232**
Libraries **232**
Lost Property **232**
Media **232**
Money **233**
Postal Services **233**
Public Holidays **233**
Public Toilets **233**
Religious Services **233**
Student Travellers **234**
Telephones **234**
Tiime Zone **235**
Tipping **235**
Tour Operators **235**
Tourist Offices **235**
Websites **236**
What to Read **237**

THE BEST OF CAPE TOWN

Setting priorities, saving money, unique attractions...
here, at a glance, are our recommendations, plus some
tips and tricks even the locals won't always know

CAPE TOWN FOR FAMILIES

These six attractions are popular with children,
though not all will suit every age group.

● **Two Oceans Aquarium**
Imaginative displays, two-storey tanks and a hands-in touch pool make this a perennial hit with children of all ages. *See page 97.*

● **The Cable Car**
For most children, being whisked up Table Mountain in a revolving pod beats hiking up any day. *See page 139.*

● **Seals and Penguins**.
Watch seals playing in the harbour and see penguins at Boulders Beach on the Cape Peninsula.
See pages 158.

● **Whale-watching**
May–November is the whale-watching season. Hermanus is the best place for land-based whale-watching and is a

convenient springboard for boat excursions. *See page 180.*

● **Scratch Patch**
Children (and adults) can learn more about South Africa's glittering gemstones at Scratch Patch on the Waterfront and in Simon's Town. *See page 98.*

● **The IMAX**
If you don't manage to visit a game park while you are in South Africa, the next best thing is a 3-D safari at the BMW Pavilion's IMAX on the Waterfront. *See page 93.*

For further ideas, see page 222 of the Travel Tips section.

BEST VIEWS

● **Table Mountain**
Nothing beats Table Mountain for appreciating Cape Town's stupendous location. *See page 138.*

● **Chapman's Peak Drive**
For truly scenic motoring, drive to Noordhoek via the Atlantic Seaboard and Hout Bay. The best views unfold as you enter Chapman's Peak Drive. The road soars up the cliff face, defying the vertiginous drop to

the sea below. *See page 156.*

● **Tafelberg Road**
Another fantastic drive, this runs around the base of Table Mountain. It is best at night when the mountain is floodlit. *See page 138.*

● **Best hotel views**
For a room with a great view, book into the Table Bay on the Waterfront, or the Twelve Apostles on Victoria Road between Bakoven and Llandudno. *See pages 208 and 211.*

BELOW: Cape Town is a city of spectacular views.

BEST MUSEUMS

- **The District Six Museum**
Memorabilia, documents, personal accounts and recreations of homes and businesses evoke the flavour and culture of this characterful area, famously destroyed by apartheid's Group Areas Act. *See page 73.*

- **Bo-Kaap Museum**
Also in a fine period townhouse, this museum documents the Muslim contribution to the development of the city. *See page 108.*
- **Groot Constantia**
This old Dutch manor house belonged to one of the first governors of the Cape Colony. *See page 129.*

ABOVE: learn about the San, the original inhabitants of the Cape, in the South African Museum.
LEFT: inside the District Six Museum.
BELOW: participants in the annual Jazzathon.

FUN FESTIVALS AND EVENTS

- **New Year**
The year kicks off with the Cape Town Minstrel Festival. *See page 107.*
- **Jazzathon**
A four-day international jazz festival in January. *See page 96.*

- **V&A Waterfront Winter Food Fair**
August. *See page 96.*
- **Kite Festival**
Catch the Cape's southeaster at Muizenberg in September. *See page 164.*

- **The Castle of Good Hope**
Worth at least half a day's visit, this is where Cape Town's history began. It contains the military museum and the William Fehr Collection of paintings of early Cape Town. *See page 71.*
- **Koopmans de Wet Museum**
This elegantly furnished 18th-century townhouse conveys a vivid sense of the comfortable lifestyle of wealthy early European settlers. *See page 75.*

- **Irma Stern Museum**
Visit this museum in the Southern Suburbs for an almost private view of the painter's home and studio. *See page 119.*
- **Anglo-Gold Museum**
A dazzling display of traditional gold jewellery and ceremonial objects from West and South Africa. *See page 86.*
- **The South African Museum**
Come here to learn more about the San, the original bushmen of the area, in particular their mysterious rock art. *See page 81.*

BEST BEACHES

- **Clifton**
Clifton's four beaches, backed by the Twelve Apostles, are the most beautiful and good for people-watching. *See page 152.*
- **Muizenberg**
The best beach for swimming is not Clifton, but Muizenberg, on the False Bay coast, where the water temperatures are warmer. *See page 164.*

- **For Surfers**
Llandudno on the Atlantic Seaboard is considered one of the best places for experienced surfers. *See page 154.*

- **Camps Bay**
If the après-beach means more to you than swimming (which is freezing here) come to Camps Bay for its swathe of swish café-bars. *See page 153.*
- **Cape Point Nature Reserve**
This is the best place for a remote picnic. There are no buildings, few people and if you're lucky, you may see deer wandering on the beach. *See page 157.*
- **For Children**
Strong currents make swimming inadvisable on many beaches, but there are tidal pools where children can splash about safely. St James, renowned for its colourful beach huts, is one of the best places for tidal pools. *See page 164.*

LEFT AND ABOVE: Llandudno is good for surfing, and St James, with its brightly coloured beach huts, is best for bathing.
BELOW LEFT: Table Mountain National Park has many wonderful hiking trails to suit all ages and abilities.

BEST WALKS

- **Lion's Head**.
For a short but dramatic walk, follow the path spiralling up to the summit of Lion's Head. It offers a 360° panorama of the ocean, mountain and city. *See page 141.*
- **Platteklip Gorge**
For a sense of achievement, ascend Table Mountain on foot via this fairly simple zig-zag route of 3km (2 miles). *See page 141.*
- **Kirstenbosch**.
As well as offering botanical trails, Kirstenbosch is a springboard for hikes into the Table Moun-

tain National Park. Skeleton Gorge is one of the most popular. *See page 125.*
- **Noordhoek**
For a long bracing walk on the beach it is hard to beat Noordhoek, but take care here because it is also one of the Peninsula's remotest spots. *See page 156.*
- **Hoerikwaggo Trail**.
For serious hikers, this five-day organised hike, designed by the Table Mountain National Park, runs from the city to Cape Point. Accommodation is available en route. *See page 142.*

BEST DINING

- **95 Keerom**
  In an early Cape build-
  ing in the heart of the
  city, this Italian eatery is
  smart, cool and fashionable. *See page 88.*
- **Uitsig Restaurant**
  A superb dining expe-
  rience in a vineyard
  setting in the Southern
  Suburbs. *See page 133.*
- **La Colombe**
  French country cook-
  ing, again in the
  Southern Suburbs. *See
  page 133.*
- **Willoughby & Co**
  An inexpensive venue
  in busy Victoria Mall
  on the Waterfront

serving some of the
best fish in town.
See page 101.
- **Moyo**
  For a pan-African
  dining experience this
  restaurant in Spier is
  second to none.
  See page 186.
- **Olympia Cafe**
  Great food beside the
  seaside in laid-back
  Kalk Bay. *See
  page 163.*
- **Cape Colony**
  In the Mount Nelson
  Hotel, this restaurant
  has one of the best
  wine lists in town. *See
  page 87.*

ABOVE: a room with a view overlooking Camps Bay.
BELOW LEFT: for old maps, second-hand books, curios and
interesting Africana check out the antiques and junk shops on
Long Street and Church Street in the city centre.

TOP SHOPPING

- **The V&A
  Waterfront**.
  If you're after gifts,
  books, maps and jew-
  ellery, the Waterfront is
  best. *See page 93.*
- **Long Street**
  For vintage clothing,
  first-edition books or
  old china, visit the
  south (top) end of Long
  Street, which is
  crammed with bou-

tiques, bric-a-brac
shops and antique
stores. Neighbouring
Church Street is
especially good for
antiques. *See page 84.*
- **Canal Walk and
  Cavendish Square**
  This is where Cape-
  tonians go if they want
  to shop for lifestyle and
  home accessories.
  See page 223.

MONEY-SAVING TIPS

Cape Town Pass

In spite of talk of raising admission
fees for foreign visitors, at present
entry to museums and other attractions is low compared with major
European and American cities.

However, organised tours to the
Winelands and along the Cape Peninsula, although plentiful (pick up
assorted leaflets from the Tourism
Office on Burg Street or in the Clock
Tower Precinct at the Waterfront) are
fairly expensive. An alternative, if you
don't have your own transport, is to

buy the 6-day Cape Town Pass for
R750 (you can also get cheaper 1-
day, 2-day and 3-day passes), which
offers free entrance to over 50 of
the best attractions, a tour of the
Winelands and a day exploring
the Peninsula.

Some activities are included too,
such as horse-riding on the beach,
sand-boarding and a harbour cruise.
If you order on-line before you go,
(www.capetownpass.co.za), you can
have the pass delivered directly to
your hotel and will also be given a
cell phone to use for the duration
of your stay.

Getting Around
Sedan taxis are relatively expensive, but due to the skeletal public
transport system essential for anyone without their own vehicle. If you
take a taxi to somewhere such as
Table Mountain or Kirstenbosch, you
can ask the taxi driver to wait, as
there is no charge for this (though it
is sensible to double-check).

If you want to explore the False
Bay coast of the Cape Peninsula,
consider going by train (a direct service runs from Cape Town Railway
Station), but for safety reasons be
sure to travel in the restaurant car.

THE MOTHER CITY

It was once a magnet for all manner of European migrants, from fortune-hunters to political refugees. Things have certainly changed: today Cape Town is the focus of South Africa's tourism, attracting 80 percent of its visitors

Called the Mother City, Cape Town was the first white settlement in South Africa, from which colonialism spread north through southern Africa and beyond. Its position near the tip of Africa had undeniable strategic value, as did its sheltered bay, but another irresistible draw must have been its iconic flat-topped mountain, so mysterious when seen from the sea. A beacon to early mariners, in Xhosa legend it was Umlindi Welingizunu, the "Watcher of the South". To this day, in spite of the hustle and bustle of modern city living, Table Mountain's majestic and ancient presence impinges on the consciousness, whichever way one turns. For visitors it is the symbol of South Africa, more potent than wine, rugby or cricket, more famous than the Kruger National Park.

Come to the city to see the mountain, the beaches, the Winelands and the unique flora, and to experience life in the townships, which embody such a rich chunk of South Africa's cultural, historical and political identity. But come too to eat in the city's superb and very reasonably priced restaurants and to explore colourful Bo-Kaap, the traditional Muslim quarter on the slopes of Signal Hill. Also see the colonial architecture that developed at the time Cape Town was probably no bigger than a very small country town in Europe. The Cape Dutch heritage is unique, and Cape Town is the best place to experience it, though you'll also see fine examples in nearby Stellenbosch.

The city is also full of interesting diversions provided by its creative and entrepreneurial inhabitants. It has first-class bookshops and antique shops, vintage clothing stores and many excellent and stylish hotels and guest-houses run with pride and care. Active churches, mosques and synagogues reflect the city's rich cultural heritage, just as its full calendar of festivals celebrates modern Capetonians' diverse leisure interests, from food, wine, art and music to antiques, cars and flowers.

And should you grow tired of Cape Town and the Peninsula, hire a car and venture a little further afield, to the West Coast National Park or the Overberg (for whale-watching). You could also follow the famous Garden Route through a stunning landscape of coastal lagoons, fynbos and rainforest beginning from Mossel Bay. ❑

PRECEDING PAGES: city overview; False Bay from Boyes Drive.
LEFT: Table Mountain from Bloubergstrand on the West Coast north of Cape Town.

THE MAKING OF CAPE TOWN

Cape Town began as a refreshment station for European ships sailing to the east, but by the early 19th century it had become a focus for conflicting Dutch and British interests, a rivalry that gradually escalated into the Anglo-Boer War

The history of Cape Town is first of all a history of the singular mix of people who shaped the city, their conflicts and their struggle to live together. It is also the history of an extraordinary place, of prime strategic value, with its narrow peninsula, two oceans and distinctive flat-topped mountain.

Stone-age hunter-gatherers

The earliest evidence of man on the Cape is of Early Stone Age hunter-gatherers, who inhabited the area around 600,000 years ago. Tools belonging to such people have been found near the Cape of Good Hope. More widespread are finds from the Middle Stone Age period (200,000–40, 000 years) and of the Late Stone Age (from around 21,000 years ago). The San, or Bushmen as they are also known, were hunter-gatherers who lived in caves around the Cape Peninsula and foraged on the beaches. Their rock paintings have been found in caves throughout the Cape and elsewhere. In fact, South Africa has the largest collection of Stone Age art in the world.

About 2,000 years ago the San were displaced by the Khoikhoi (Khoi), who migrated to the Cape from the north. It was the Khoi whom the Europeans encountered when they sailed into Table Bay in the 15th century. As the colony developed and settlement fanned northwards, they also encountered the San.

Early discovery

Europeans inadvertently discovered the Cape of Good Hope as a result of Portuguese voyages in search of a sea route to India. In 1487 the explorer Bartolomeu Dias made a perilous journey around the Cape, which he named the "Cape of Storms" on account of its fierce weather. On hearing Dias relate the story of his voyage, King João II of Portugal renamed it the Cape of Good Hope, believing that its successful navigation would bring the riches of India within Portugal's reach at last

But it was a full 10 years after Dias's historic journey that Vasco de Gama became the first explorer to land on Indian soil via

---

LEFT: the Dutch East India ship *Noordt Nieuwlandt* sailing into Table Bay in 1762.
RIGHT: San Hunters, from a painting by Samuell Daniell (1830).

A FORT AND A GARDEN

Van Riebeeck's brief in 1652 was to establish a "fort and a garden". Both can be seen today as the Castle on the Foreshore and the Company Gardens above Adderley Street *(see pages 71 and 79)*.

the Cape. From then on Table Mountain became an important landmark for mariners, a place where they could shelter their vessels, get fresh water and barter meat from the Khoi tribespeople.

Initially the Portuguese made no effort to establish a settlement in the area. Not only was the stormy Cape notorious among mariners, but

From 1610, the English used Robben Island as a penal colony and, in 1620, the Dutch threw mutineers overboard in Table Bay. The English briefly considered annexing the Cape at this time, but its reputation as a "Cape of Storms" discouraged them. Then, in 1647, the Dutch ship *Haarlem* ran aground in Table Bay, leaving some of the crew stranded for a year. The shipwrecked crew found the local Khoi friendly and helpful and they recommended permanent Dutch settlement to the VOC directors.

In 1652 the VOC, under the command of Jan van Riebeeck, occupied the Cape to set up a permanent refreshment stop for the fleets of the Dutch East India Company. This

a series of violent clashes with the Khoi seemed to reinforce European doubts about trade links with the indigenous people. In 1510, for example, a viceroy of the Portuguese Indies attacked the Khoi, whose retaliation forced the Portuguese back to the shore, where 50 sailors were killed. But English and Dutch ships regularly put into Table Bay to trade and get fresh water.

Dutch settlement

By 1590 the Dutch controlled the trade route to India, largely through the Dutch East India Company (Vereenigde Oost-Indische Compagnie or VOC).

event was later romanticised by Afrikaner nationalists, with re-enactments of the landing presented as pageants in 1938 and 1952, but it was a tentative attempt at colonisation and continued to be so for many years.

The directors in Amsterdam saw the Cape settlement as having a dual role: to establish a defensive fort that would protect Dutch interests against both the local Khoi and any antagonistic foreign power putting into the Cape, and to ensure a supply of fresh vegetables and meat for Dutch sailors.

But the soils of the peninsula are notoriously poor – one reason for the uniqueness of the Cape vegetation known as fynbos that thrives in such conditions – and until the Dutch began to explore beyond the bay, there was little in the way of food crops. And aside from the increasingly hostile Khoi, exploration was a hazardous affair. Lions roamed the bay and anyone wandering outside the fort was vulnerable to attack. In the early years the settlement was dependent on food supplies from Amsterdam and could produce very little fresh produce itself.

From 1657 freeholders were granted land along the Liesbeeck River on the southerly side of the mountain and colonisation began in earnest. These early burghers followed the practice of the Dutch in the East Indies and began to import slaves. Slavery was to be the key labour practice of the Cape for 200 years.

Khoi resistance

For centuries the Khoi pastoralists had followed transhumance grazing routes around the Cape mountains and valleys. They fiercely resented the intrusive settlement of the Dutch whom they had previously seen as simply passing through. Because the Dutch had seen no permanent settlement on arrival they had assumed that the Cape was largely unoccupied, which was not the case.

In 1659–60, open war broke out between the Dutch and the Khoi. Cape Town was settled by conquest and not negotiation, an ominous precedent for the future of South Africa, and Khoi leaders asked angrily: "Who should give way, the rightful owner or the foreign intruder?" Van Riebeeck marked out the settler territory with palisades and ditches, ordering that a hedge of bitter almonds be planted along the southern boundary. This hedge can still be seen today in Kirstenbosch.

The appearance of the Cape changed quickly as hedges and enclosures for sheep were erected and forested areas chopped down for shipbuilding timber.

Encouraged by the premiums paid by the Company, Dutch soldiers decimated the local lion and leopard populations, and killed seals for oil. Beyond the Cape lay the fabled lands of Monomatapa and Prester John, guarded by the Mountains of Africa (today's Hottentots-

Holland). Dutch expeditions were mounted in search of gold, but returned with the carcases of antelope and eland. Most activities though centred on the Cape settlement itself.

Slave labour

By 1648 more than half the recorded population of the settlement were chattel slaves, brought from Guinea, Angola, Mozambique and Madagascar. They worked as farm labourers and domestic servants, following the usage prevalent in Dutch Batavia. Many of these slaves fled across the Mountains of Africa under the illusion they could find their way back home to East and West Africa.

DEHUMANISING TREATMENT

Saartjie Baartman was born in 1789 into the Griqua tribe of the eastern Cape, a subgroup of the Khoisan. A local doctor examined her and was fascinated by her steatopygia – enlarged buttocks and unusually elongated labia – and persuaded her to go to London as a subject of anthropological research. At first, she was put under anatomical scrutiny by scientists, but in 1814, after spending four years being paraded around London, she was taken to Paris and handed to a "showman of wild animals" in a travelling circus. After her death her body was exhibited in the Musee de l'Homme. Eventually South African protests led to the return of her body for burial in 2002.

LEFT: an early view of Table Bay.
RIGHT: Saartjie Baartman, known popularly as the Hottentot Venus.

Newcomers

Gradually Cape Town came to resemble a pleasant Dutch colonial town, with low white-washed houses and market gardens set out on a strict grid of streets running down from the mountain to the bay; they were arranged to accommodate mountain streams channelled into watercourses from the Company Gardens down the Heerengracht.

Fears of a slave insurrection troubled the colonists almost as much as the Khoi incursions. Slaves were sorted into a crude hierarchy: the first were the mansoors born in the Slave Lodge *(see page 77)*, skilled and trusted with the distribution of food and clothing, then skilled artisans brought from Dutch East Indian colonies and finally the labourers cap-

As efforts were made by the free burghers to establish a cleaner, more respectable town the Cape began to acquire its less savoury reputation as the "tavern of the seas", with pubs (the *taphuis*), cheap lodging houses, gambling dens and brothels plying trade alongside the

tured on slave raids to Madagascar or Mozambique. But the slaves' resistance to their owners took many forms: running away, arson, poisoning, physical attacks and riots. Even after the legal emancipation of slaves in 1834, many farms across the Cape Colony continued to buy and sell slaves.

Slave resistance was organised to counter another form of oppression: the political exile of leading Muslim clerics such as Sufi scholar Sheik Yusuf, deported from the East to the distant Cape. The public practice of Islam was outlawed until the end of the 18th century and so developed a quality of resistance under such conditions.

premises of butchers, blacksmiths, tanners, shoemakers and bakers. Sailors boasted of the excellent food (spiced in the Malay tradition with curries and *bredies*) and cheap liquor.

Along with increased trade there came German mercenaries and French influences, a new European influx of deserters from the strife in the Low Countries and gold-diggers in search of new opportunities.

But in 1795 a British fleet of warships sailed into False Bay. Britain seized the Cape to prevent its use by France, which was then allied to Holland. The colony was returned to the Dutch in 1803 but was again occupied by the British in 1806. The 1814–15 Congress of

Vienna ceded the colony to the British on a permanent basis.

Prosperity came with the English as did intermarriage between "English officers and Dutch vrouws". Many of the Cape Dutch homesteads date from this period. World trade was expanding and wheat and wines from the Cape were much in demand. Demographics were changing too: the 1820 settlers arrived in the Eastern Cape and many would move to the Cape to avoid the violence of the skirmishes with the Xhosa on the eastern frontier.

Britain introduced a number of reforms. The Khoi were given the explicit protection of the law (including the right to own land) in 1828, and 1834 emancipated the colony's slaves, many of whom settled in the Bo-Kaap on the eastern slopes of Signal Hill. But although Britain was responsible for ridding the Cape of slavery, its new labour laws laid the basis for an exploitative system barely more liberal than the system it had abolished. Pass laws prevented thousands of dispossessed blacks from acquiring work in the colony. And the "multiracial" constituency of a parliament established in the Cape in 1854 excluded the vast majority of non-whites who could not meet the financial criteria of suffrage.

The descendants of the first settlers (known as Afrikaners or Boers) were dismayed by the liberalising tendencies and emancipation of slaves. In the 1830s the "trekkers", signalled their disapproval by leaving the Cape Colony and heading off to Natal and up north towards present-day Gauteng, a mass migration known as the Great Trek (1834–40).

A Victorian city

Cape Town now took on the characteristics of Victorian cities everywhere: churches were built (Anglican, Methodist, Presbyterian), as was Government House in the Company's Gardens; gentlemen's clubs and the Freemasons were established. There were trams, hansom cabs and railways reaching as far as the military camp at Wynberg. In the 1860s a South

LEFT: a view of St George's church, 1845.
RIGHT: Cecil John Rhodes, diamond magnate, arch-colonialist and national builder.

African museum of scientific, botanical and historical curiosities was created, the South African library was built, and the Observatory enlarged. The Dutch-style buildings of Adderley Street were replaced by Victorian shopfronts and hotels. Architects such as Sir Herbert Baker drew on the simple and beautiful Cape Dutch architecture and combined it with Arts

and Crafts influences in Grootes Schuur for the Cecil John Rhodes, prime minister of the Cape colony 1890–96. The Diamond Jubilee of Queen Victoria in 1897 was a glittering occasion in the city.

Capetonians were proud of their city and had little interest in the new cruder mining towns up north. but insularity was about to give way to the shadow of civil war. Colonial expansion under Rhodes was opening up the north in what is now Zimbabwe. *Uitlanders* (foreigners) streamed through Cape Town on their way to the goldfields and diamond mines of Johannesburg and Kimberley. A new century was about to begin. ❑

FROM APARTHEID TO DEMOCRACY

The Anglo-Boer War planted a militant Afrikaner nationalism in South Africa, ushering in an apartheid government whose draconian and divisive policies dominated the country for more than 40 years

The 20th century began inauspiciously with the Anglo-Boer War – sometimes referred to as the South African War – which would last from 1899 until 1902. It was not only a war waged by the British empire against the rebellious landlocked republics of the Transvaal and Orange Free State, but a civil war in which the Cape Colony was fiercely divided, with English-speakers and Afrikaners at loggerheads as to which side the Colony supported. Black civilians were summarily forced to support their employers' choices – many unarmed black men were killed playing a supportive role in combat. English troops poured into the Cape, from where they made their way north.

The Cape Colony's relative isolation, in part already altered by the late 19th-century scramble by foreigners for gold and diamond resources around Kimberley and the Transvaal, was ending as refugees and Boer prisoners arrived in the city. Prisoner-of-war camps and camps for women and children were established in crowded tents on Greenpoint Common and in Wynberg. It was a hard-fought war and it left a residual legacy of bitterness that would give impetus to a militant Afrikaner nationalism which would bring in an apartheid government after World War II.

But the immediate result of British victory in the Anglo-Boer War was to unite South Africa

politically and economically, so that in 1910, the Union of South Africa was created out of the Cape, Natal, Transvaal and Free State. It was essentially a white union in terms of political rights and powers.

Rail and road

Cape Town and the peninsula and Boland had long been separated from the interior by mountain ranges. The passes built by Thomas Bain, a geologist and roadbuilder known as "the man with theodolite eyes" were the only routes out. In addition to these mountain pass roads, which still stand as a testament to stonewalling techniques, the first railway from

LEFT: jubilant celebrations on hearing news of Nelson Mandela's release from prison in 1990.
RIGHT: the South African Light Horse regiment parades down Adderley Street in the Anglo-Boer War.

the Cape had reached the ramshackle mining town of Johannesburg in 1892. By 1894 there was a Cape road to Rhodesia (present-day Zimbabwe) via Mafeking. In 1897 crowds gathered in Pretoria to admire a small Benz Voiturette with wire-spoked wheels, the first motor vehicle to reach South Africa. With the discovery of the enormous Cullinan diamond – intact at 3,106 carats — on the Rand, the South African economy began to shift from agriculture towards industry.

The widespread hope of a prosperous unite d Union of South Africa was dampened by World War I. South African Prime Minister Louis Botha launched an attack on

THE COST OF THE BOER WAR

The Boer War was the bloodiest, longest and most expensive war Britain engaged in between 1815 and 1915. It cost more than £200 million and more than 22,000 British people were lost. The Boers lost over 34,000 people, mostly women and children. More than 15,000 black people were killed.

German-held South West Africa (now Namibia), a wildly unpopular move, especially amongst Afrikaners who remembered Germany's support for their Boer commandos in the Anglo-Boer War. English-speaking young South African men were gradually

BLACK INSPIRATION

Black protest found inspiration in a number of prominent black figures in the late 19th and early 20th centuries. These included the mission-educated writer Sol Plaatje, who as well as writing the first novel in Setswana, *Mhudi*, an account of black history not defined by white and Western understanding, was part of two delegations to Britain to protest against the Land Act of 1913. Also influential was Clements Kadalie, the first black trade unionist, who was born in Nyasaland in 1896. He formed the Industrial and Commercial Worker's Union in the Cape in 1919 ; for a brief period the ICU was the most powerful political force outside parliament.

drawn into the European conflict and more than 2,000 South African soldiers died in the Battle of Delville Wood alone. Far worse casualties were sustained when the Spanish influenza swept across continents in 1918 just after Armistice Day.

Early black protest

Invisible for so long, the history of black consciousness and liberation is now a matter of public record and no longer an afterthought to Western events and the ambitions of white South Africans. Along with the American civil rights struggles, many nascent black movements emerged out of independent churches, land movements and a growing urban discontent.

Black opposition was inevitable. Organised political activity among Africans started with the establishment of the South African National Congress (later to become the African National Congress or ANC), in 1912 in Bloemfontein in the Free State.

In 1921, the Communist Party came into being at a time of heightened militancy, not yet fully multiracial but connecting South African workers to international political struggles. Yet, in the face of a groundswell of opposition to racially defined government, the Natives Land Act was legislated in 1913.

UNGODLY DEFENCE

The powerful Dutch Reformed Church produced a biblical defence of apartheid and kept churches, schools and graveyards segregated.

alism, fuelled by job losses arising from worldwide recession, was on the march.

Conflict and depression

Almost without warning conflict broke out in 1922 with a miners' strike (predominantly white miners) on the Rand. It was violently suppressed by the government. Prime Minister Jan Smuts used martial law to brutally sup-

This defined the remnants of black ancestral lands for African occupation. The "homelands", as they were subsequently called, eventually comprised about 13 percent of South Africa's land. More discriminatory legislation – particularly relating to job reservation favouring whites and the disenfranchisement of coloured voters in the Cape – was enacted. Meanwhile, Afrikaner nation-

LEFT: memories of the perils and pioneering spirit of Great Trek of the 1830s inspired Afrikaner nationalism in the 20th century.
ABOVE: in 1919 Sol Plaatje (bottom right) led a duputation to England to protest against the Land Act of 1913.

press the strike and, in killing more than 200 miners, lost himself the next election. Afrikaner nationalism was growing, even in the more sedate Cape, fuelled by a determination that the brutal tactics of the Anglo-Boer war and the execution of pro-German sympathiser Jopie Fourie in World War I would not happen again. With the Depression and a disastrous drought of 1933, the Cape, together with the rest of South Africa, struggled with soup kitchens and relief programmes.

In 1937 Afrikaners re-enacted the Great Trek, an emotive and charged event, the significance of which was missed in the dramatic build-up to the outbreak of World War II. Here again, South African support for the Allies was ambivalent. Many Afrikaners joined a pro-German Fascist organisation named the Ossawa Brandwag. Black servicemen were conscripted to lend support or even to bear arms in the battle raging against Rommel in North Africa and in Italy.

The winds of change

After World War II colonialism was ending for the British Empire, but in 1948, ironically following on from a highly successful royal visit to the country during which Princess Elizabeth broadcast from a small stinkwood table in Government House on her 21st birthday, a new government came into power in South Africa, shocking the more liberal Cape. Field-marshal Jan Smuts, an internationally reputed peacemaker and statesman who had worked with the League of Nations as well as the Allies, lost the election to Dr D. F. Malan of the Nationalist Party, which was supported by the predominantly Afrikaner white population. The Nationalists stood for racial segregation and the creation of Afrikaner wealth to oppose the economic power of English businesses and the mining houses.

These experiences would lead many black soldiers from Kenya, West and East Africa to begin the struggle for independence from colo-

THE PAN AFRICANIST CONGRESS

The Pan Africanist Congress (PAC) was established in 1959 by ANC dissidents who opposed that group's multiracial orientation and advocated black liberation within an exclusively black nationalist context. The party was founded in the townships of Orlando and Soweto, outside Johannesburg, although support was also found in Cape townships. The government declared the PAC an unlawful organisation in 1960. Like the ANC, it was recognised by the United Nations (UN) and by the Organisation of African Unity (OAU) as an official South African liberation movement. It was legalised on 2 February 1990. The PAC's senior leaders included Robert Sobukwe.

nial powers. As Ghana, Zambia and Kenya moved towards independence, the situation in South Africa became more anomalous. In 1963, ending the Federation of Rhodesia and Nyasaland, the British Prime Minister Harold Macmillan would stand up in the Cape parliament to declare that "The winds of change are sweeping across Africa."

Apartheid rules

Malan's first speech to the House of Assembly was an ominous foretelling of what was to come. "The principle of apartheid," said Malan, "is that we have two separate spheres, not territorial spheres, but with separate rights." Despite the protests of many white Cape citizens belonging to multiracial organisations such as the Torch Commando, black and coloured people were systematically stripped of any political rights. Leaders emerged from the racially integrated District Six: Dr Abdurahman and his daughter Cissie Gool were to lead protests and civil disobedience campaigns for many years. The South African Communist Party moved from protecting the interests of white workers to a multiracial position, only to be banned as the Cold War intensified in the 1950s.

Peaceful protest achieved nothing as ever more degrading and dehumanising legisla-

Within weeks the shanties would rise again.

The Cape Coloureds could not be granted a homeland, so the western half of the Cape province was declared a "coloured preference area" in which no black person could be employed unless it could be proved that there was no suitable coloured person for the job.

"Petty apartheid" meant that black people could not travel on trains or buses in the same coaches with whites, could not enter shops or post offices, could not be born in the same hospital wards as whites, could not lie dead in the same morgues. Examples of the infamous "Non-Europeans only" and "Whites Only" signs dating back 40 years can be seen on dis-

tion was passed, making relationships across the colour bar illegal (the Mixed Marriages Act, 1949), demanding that all black people carry passes if they entered "white areas", enforcing the eviction of black and coloured people from land declared white-owned. Whenever illegal black shanty towns mushroomed on the sandy plains to the east of Cape Town, they would quickly be flattened by government bulldozers, their occupants dragged away and dumped in the homelands.

play in the District Six Museum *(see page73).*

The Defiance Campaign of the early 1950s carried mass mobilisation to new heights under the banner of non-violent resistance to the pass laws. In 1955, a Freedom Charter was drawn up at the Congress of the People in Soweto. The Charter enunciated the principles of the struggle, binding the movement to a culture of human rights and non-racialism.

Sharpeville and its aftermath

In 1960 an anti-pass march by the Pan Africanist Congress under the leadership of Robert Sobukwe in Sharpeville, near Vereeniging on the Rand, led to unprecedented state violence.

LEFT: Princess Elizabeth (right) in South Africa in 1947.
ABOVE: large numbers of black women worked as maids in white households.

Armoured cars, fighter jets and soldiers armed with sten guns killed 67 unarmed black marchers, including women and children. Riots took place the following day in Cape Town's Langa township and a 23-year-old university student and PAC member named Philip Kgosana led a crowd of 30,000 protesters from Langa up over De Waal Drive to Caledon Square Police Station. Thanks to the pre-science and diplomacy of a police colonel there, the marchers were persuaded to return home and no force ws used.

The inevitability of armed resistance to apartheid had moved a step closer. As international protest about the Sharpeville massacre

mounted, local arrests made it clear that the struggle against apartheid would be multi-racial: arrested along with Sobukwe, Nelson Mandela and Walter Sisulu was Helen Joseph, the president of the South African Federation of Women.

In 1961 South Africa became a Republic and thereafter began the social and political isolation that would characterise it as a pariah state for more than 30 years. In 1963 the Rivonia trials sent Nelson Mandela and seven other members of the African National Congress to prison on Robben Island. The armed struggle had begun.

The good life for some

Throughout the 1960s and '70s prosperous white Cape Town was largely oblivious of the impact of apartheid on black people living in townships and ghettos around the peninsula. (It was against the law for unauthorised whites to enter black locations or settlements.) The average white lifestyle resembled that of southern California, with household servants, gardeners, nannies and chauffeurs ensuring relative leisure and luxury.

But southern African politics were shifting. The unilateral declaration of independence by Ian Smith in Rhodesia was supported by South Africa: white Rhodesia, like South Africa, would "go it alone" against international sanctions and disapproval. South African prime Minister Hendrik Verwoerd, a leading architect of apartheid, was stabbed to death in the Cape parliament in 1966 by a parliamentary messenger. Demetri Tsafendas. This assassination was

CAPE TOWN'S DISTRICT SIX

District Six was so named in 1867 as it was the sixth municipal district of Cape Town. Originally established as a mixed community of freed slaves, merchants, artisans, labourers and immigrants, it took on a polyglot bohemian and tolerant character, vibrant and unconventional, with close links to the city and the port. By the beginning of the 20th century, however, the history of removals and marginalisation had begun. The first to be "resettled" were black (mostly Xhosa) South Africans, forcibly displaced from the District in 1901. As the more prosperous inhabitants, including German and European immigrants, moved away to the suburbs, the area became the neglected ward of Cape Town. In 1966, District Six was declared a white area under the Group Areas Act of 1950, and by 1982, the life of the community was over. Some 60 000 people were forcibly removed to barren outlying areas aptly known as the Cape Flats, and their houses in District Six were flattened by bulldozers.

Restitution attempts have only just begun for descendents of original Cape coloured families wishing to return. The District Six Museum, which opened at 25 Buitenkant Street in December 1994, documents the lives of the original inhabitants and the trauma of their resettlement. It is well worth a visit *(see page 73)*.

presented as the act of a madman and only much later did the extent of Tsafendas's political hatred of apartheid emerge.

The spirit of resistance was confined to universities – University of Cape Town students faced tear gas and baton charges in St George's cathedral in 1974 – and to clandestine organisations including the militant wing of the ANC, Umkhonto we Sizwe or "Spear of the Nation", which developed in the historically black universities such as the University of the Western Cape and the black communities.

Two episodes served as important catalysts to change, provoking black outrage and attracting international condemnation. In

(see panel below). The then Minister of Police Jimmy Kruger announced in public that Bilo's death "leaves me cold".

With the independence of Zimbabwe in 1980, South Africa became isolated from the rest of southern Africa. The final decade of apartheid was the most brutal, with South African forces leading incursions and bombing raids into Zambia and Lesotho as well as black townships. State of emergency legislation was passed to deal with anyone opposing the Pretoria government. Hundreds were detained in prison without trial, died after torture or were sentenced to death.

Church leaders led protests, with leaders

June 1976, the black township of Soweto, near Johannesburg, exploded into violence as black schoolchildren marching in protest at a new requirement for all lessons to be taught in Afrikaans, the language of the oppressor, were killed by police. Riots followed countrywide, but were suppressed. Media censorship was extensive

The following year, Black Consciousness leader Steve Biko, an activist from the Eastern Cape, was murdered in police detention

LEFT: Nelson Mandela in prison in Pretoria, before being moved to Robben Island.
ABOVE: the funeral of Steve Biko in 1977.

DEATH IN POLICE CUSTODY

Steve Biko, a co-founder of the Black Peoples Convention (BPC), which united some 70 black consciousness groups, was interrogated four times between August 1975 and September 1977 under apartheid anti-terrorism legislation. On 21 August 1977 he was detained by the Eastern Cape security police and taken to security police headquarters where, on 7 September, he sustained a head injury during interrogation. Biko was then taken to Pretoria – a 12-hour journey which he made lying naked in the back of a Land Rover. A few hours later, on 12 September, alone and still naked, on the floor of a cell in the Pretoria Central Prison, Biko died from brain damage.

such as Anglican archbishop Desmond Tutu calling apartheid a heresy. Police brutality was deplored internationally and economic sanctions and disinvestments led to many international companies withdrawing from South Africa. As organisations were banned (the

Buthelezi, which was seen as collaborating with the apartheid system, frequently clashed with the ANC during this period.

As media reports commented, it was evident that civil disobedience had become a way of life, that change was not only inevitable but unstoppable. In 1991, a multiracial forum led by de Klerk and Mandela, the Convention for a Democratic South Africa (CODESA), began working on a new constitution. In 1993, an interim constitution was passed, which dismantled apartheid and provided for a multiracial democracy with majority rule.

The peaceful transition of South Africa from one of the world's most repressive societies into

United Democratic Front had been formed in 1983), the Mass Democratic Movement emerged and organised several vast marches through Cape Town calling for political change.

From prisoner to president

Apartheid's grip on South Africa began to give way when F. W. de Klerk replaced P. W. Botha as president in 1989. De Klerk, who belonged to a new generation of Afrikaners, was elected on a platform of unspecified reform. He removed the ban on the ANC, and released its leader, Nelson Mandela, in 1990, after 27 years of imprisonment. The Inkatha Freedom Party, a black opposition group led by Mangosuthu

a democracy is one of the 20th century's most remarkable stories. Mandela and de Klerk were jointly awarded the Nobel peace prize in 1993.

The 1994 election, the country's first multiracial one, resulted in a massive victory for Mandela and the ANC. The new government included six ministers from the National Party and three from the Inkatha Freedom Party. A new constitution was adopted in May 1996.

In 1997 the Truth and Reconciliation Commission, chaired by Archbishop Desmond Tutu, began hearings regarding human rights violations between 1960 and 1993. The commission promised amnesty to those who confessed their crimes under the apartheid system. In 1998,

most far-sighted and gracious statesmen, retired in 1999. Thabo Mbeki, the pragmatic deputy president of South Africa and leader of the ANC, was elected president in a landslide victory. In his first term, Mbeki wrestled with a slumping economy, a rocketing crime rate, and the country's rising Aids epidemic. South Africa, which has the highest number of HIV-positive people in the world (nearly 5 million, about 12 percent of the population and mostly heterosexual), has been hampered in fighting the epidemic by its president's controversial views. Mbeki denied the link between HIV and Aids, claiming the West had exaggerated the epidemic in order to sell its drugs.

F. W. de Klerk, P.W. Botha, and leaders of the ANC appeared before the commission, and the nation continued to grapple with the enlightened but painful process of national recovery. Rightwing Afrikaner groups threatened to disrupt the peace process, but failed to do so.

Passing on the torch

Nelson Mandela, whose term as president cemented his reputation as one of the world's

LEFT: in 2004 a ceremony was held to mark the return of former residents to District Six.
ABOVE: President Thabo Mbeki in Cape Town for his annual State of the Nation address.

The international community as well as most South African leaders, including Nelson Mandela and Desmond Tutu, have condemned Mbeki's stance. Finally, in August 2003, after years of delay, Mbeki reversed his hands-off policy on Aids, but the government's ambivalence toward combating the epidemic persists.

As expected, on 15 April 2004, the African National Congress won South Africa's general election in a landslide, taking about 70 percent of the vote, and Thabo Mbeki was sworn in for a second term. The country is now prospering economically and Cape Town has now become one of the world's most popular destinations for travellers. ❏

Decisive Dates

30000BC San hunter-gatherers, probably descendants of a Late Stone Age people, live in South Africa area.

AD300 Emergence of Khoikhoi tribespeople, closely related to the San.

900 Iron-Age Bantu-speaking tribes, probably ancestors of the Xhosa, settled in the coastal grasslands in the far east of the Western Cape region.

1487 Portuguese explorer Bartolomeu Dias rounds the Cape, which is named the Cape of Good Hope.

1658 The first major group of slaves arrive from the Dutch East Indies.

1659 The first wine from Cape grapes is pressed.

1679 Simon van der Stel is appointed commander of the Cape settlement.

1688 Arrival of 200 French Huguenots.

1713 First smallpox epidemic hits the Khoisan community.

1755 Second smallpox epidemic all but wipes out the Khoisan.

1795–1803 British occupy Cape Town.

1779 Skirmishes between the settlers and Xhosas.

1803 The colony reverts to the Dutch.

1498 Vasco da Gama completes the route to India via the Cape.

1503 Antonio de Saldanha anchors at Table Bay and encounters the Khoisan inhabitants.

1580 Francis Drake reaches the Cape.

1647 The Dutch vessel *Haerlem* is wrecked in Table Bay. Survivors bring back glowing reports of the region.

1652 The Dutch East India Company sends Jan van Riebeeck to the Cape to establish a supply station.

1657 The station becomes a permanent settlement when company servants are granted their own farms.

1814–15 Cape Colony is formally ceded to the British by the Congress of Vienna.

1820 British settlers arrive in the Eastern Cape.

1834 Cape slaves are emancipated.

1834–1840 The Great Trek.

1854 The Cape establishes its own representative parliament.

1870 Diamonds are discovered in Griqualand West; Alfred Dock opens.

1880–1 The Transvaal declares itself a republic. The first Anglo-Boer War.

1886 Gold is discovered in the Transvaal and the mining town of Johannesburg is founded.

1890 Cecil John Rhodes becomes prime minister of the Cape Colony.

1895 Jameson Raid; Rhodes resigns.

1899–1902 The second Anglo-Boer War, in which the Boers are beaten and their settlements destroyed.

1910 Crown colonies unite as Union of South Africa with the Cape as the legislative capital.

1912 A black civil rights movement, the South African National Congress, is formed, known after 1923 as the African National Congress (ANC).

1913 The Native Land Act is passed, limiting land ownership for blacks.

1936 Black voters in the Cape are disenfranchised.

1939 World War II breaks out. South Africa joins the Allies.

1948 New National Party government launches policy of colour segregation.

1950–53 Apartheid is entrenched still further with the Group Areas Act, and the forced removal of communities.

1956 Cape Coloureds lose voting rights.

1960 ANC and PAC march against pass laws. Protestors killed at Langa and Nyanga townships. Warrants issued for arrest of ANC leaders.

1961 The Cape becomes a province of the Republic of South Africa.

1963 ANC leader Nelson Mandela is sentenced to life imprisonment.

1966 60,000 residents of Cape Town's District Six are forcibly removed. Prime minister Verwoerd is assassinated.

1976 Soweto schoolchildren protest against new measures to make Afrikaans the language of instruction in all black schools.

1983 New constitution gives coloureds and Asians limited rights. The anti-apartheid United Democratic Front is founded.

1984 Anglican Archbishop Desmond Tutu is awarded the Nobel Peace Prize. Various "petty apartheid" acts are abolished, including ban on mixed marriages.

LEFT: early view of Table Bay from the William Fehr collection in the Castle of Good Hope.

RIGHT: F. W. de Klerk and Nelson Mandela, joint winners of the Nobel Peace Prize in 1993.

1986 A state of emergency declared.

1989 F. W. de Klerk becomes president.

1990 Nelson Mandela is released after 27 years in prison.

1991 Apartheid is officially dissolved.

1993 Mandela and F. W. de Klerk jointly receive the Nobel Peace Price.

1994 The first democratic general election results in a landslide victory for the ANC. Nelson Mandela is elected president.

1995 South Africa hosts and wins rugby's World Cup. The Springboks team includes one black South African.

1996 Robben Island prison opens to the public as a museum.

1997 South Africa's new Constitution comes into effect.

1998 Truth and Reconciliation Commission hearings get underway as South Africa comes to terms with its past.

1999 Mandela retires. His deputy Thabo Mbeki becomes president following ANC general election victory. Robben Island is declared a UNESCO World Heritage Site.

2004 South Africa's third democratic election is held. Mbeki and the ANC win a 70 percent majority. South Africa wins the bid to host the 2010 World Cup.

2005 Mbeki sacks his deputy president, Jacob Zuma, over a corruption scandal. ❑

CAPE COMMUNITIES

For centuries a magnet for migrants, Cape Town has one of
South Africa's most diverse populations. And in spite of
their differences, the majority of its 3 million inhabitants
wouldn't want to live anywhere else on earth

At first sight, Cape Town seems very much a tale of two cities: one in which affluent whites enjoy a leisurely, luxurious lifestyle, with access to good healthcare and education, and another in which the overwhelming majority of blacks live on next to nothing in the shacks of the Cape Flats, so visible on any journey to and from the airport. The city centre itself seems to fall into two halves: the eastern side, around the Castle of Good Hope, run-down and black, the western side prosperous and white. The two halves meet in Adderley Street, one of the few streets to have a racially integrated look and feel.

But spend more time here, visit the different areas and start to understand the many strands in Cape Town's history through its museums and culture, and you will notice that it is not two cities, but many cities. There is perhaps no city that is more of a melting pot of different groups and communities. The historical background to this diversity is often tragic, one of imported slaves, refugees, economic migrants and displaced peoples through the centuries. As the so-called Mother City, from which settlers spread north, it has also become the Mother City of Africa, to which many groups from elsewhere on the continent come in search of a living. It is a vibrant, cosmopolitan city shaped by an amazing range of communities.

PRECEDING PAGES: making a song and dance.
LEFT: a reveller in a Long Street bar.
RIGHT: mother love in the Mother City.

Local politics

Historically Cape Town has had a liberal political tradition, shaped by its strong English-speaking community, who enjoy poking fun at the Afrikaners' gung-ho chauvinism. The seat of parliament, and packed with Victorian public buildings, the city still has an unmistakably European feel, which is somewhat scorned by Johannesburg but loved by visitors and home-grown liberals. But the Western Cape to which Cape Town belongs is strongly Afrikan and tied traditionally to the National Party.

As a legacy of slavery, the Cape also has a large Coloured population, either of Asian or mixed descent, who in the first democratic election of 1994 voted overwhelmingly for the National Party, fearful of losing their relative privileges under the ANC. It wasn't until the 2004 elections that the ANC won the Western Cape. Most English-speaking white Capetonians tend to vote for the Democratic Alliance or the Independent Democrats.

The affluent white community

Cape Town is widely perceived as a white, English-speaking city. It certainly isn't in terms of numbers *(see box, below)*, but it is easy for visitors to get this impression, exploring Kirstenbosch or Groot Schuur in the Southern Suburbs, soaking up the sun at

OBSERVATORY LIVING

A good place to go to see genuine racial integration is Observatory in the Southern Suburbs, a young and funky area close to the University where a liberal attitude prevails.

Camps Bay, hiking on Table Mountain or dining alfresco on the Waterfront. All these are traditional stamping grounds for English-speaking whites and represent an easy lifestyle that is easy to like and link into even if you're only visiting for a short while. What other major city offers up a virtually traffic jam-less daily journey to and from work and the possibility of being able to sit on the beach at five minutes past five on a Friday afternoon?

The Southern Suburbs, with it oak-lined roads of spacious family homes, excellent private schools such as Bishops and Rondebosch Boys', Anglican churches and sedate but upmarket shopping centres such as Dean Street Mall, are prosperous in an established, old-monied way. A little further out is Constantia, one of the wealthiest suburbs of Cape Town, with a mix of Edwardian and modern homes set in extensive leafy grounds behind big walls, maintained by gardeners, cooks and maids. Social cliques are based on snobbish clubs and old school ties.

Equally expensive, but brasher and more youthful, Camps Bay, with its restaurant-covered pavements and stunning mountain backdrop, contains some of the most expensive real estate in South Africa. Here the Capetonians' preoccupation with the body beautiful reaches new heights. The atmosphere is superficially relaxed and easy, and staff in the café-bars won't give a hoot if you are wearing a bathing costume, but you'll need to make sure it's a good one, that your shorts are the right length and your body's toned and trim. If you can't own up to one, or all, of these, you may not get a seat at all.

In general, English-speaking Capetonians prospered under Afrikaner-inspired apartheid. When the new South Africa dawned, many of those who could afford it dusted down their British passports and connections and left the country altogether. Those that remained are keen to retain their advantages but, having done so for the first decade of democracy, are

---

VITAL STATISTICS

The 2001 census revealed the following statistics concerning the racial composition of Cape Town:
Black Africans 31.68 percent
Coloureds 48.13 percent
Whites 18.75 percent
Indian/Asian 1.43 percent.
The average annual income of working adults was:
Black Africans $2,025
Coloureds $3,459
Indians/Asians $6,648
Whites $10,579.
Some 29.5 percent of people were officially unemployed.

also willing to invest in the country's future, if only by paying their taxes and parking fines in a responsible way.

Afrikaners in the Northern Suburbs

For Capetonians, the so-called "Boerewors Curtain" begins as you head out along the evocatively named Settlers Way or Voortrekker Road towards the Northern Suburbs with their predominantly white Afrikaner population. Many people here are descendants of farming families who moved to the cities after World War II. Suburbs such as Parow and Goodwood, where people are poorer and less educated, are perceived as right-wing, but even

> **FAMOUS CONVERT TO THE CAUSE**
>
> One of the highest-profile converts to the ANC and the New South Africa was Melanie Verwoerd, the grand-daughter of Hendrik Verwoerd, the architect of apartheid. Her grandfather was assassinated in 1966 by a parliamentary messenger.

The Northern Suburbs are widely regarded as the territory of the traditional Afrikaner, of *braais*, beer and rugby and right-wing politics, but "nuwe Afrikaners" or progressive free-thinkers are found everywhere from Durbanville to Stellenbosch University to the Boland. This reformation is rooted in a history

these are gradually accepting the change to the status quo and attitudes are softening.

More affluent suburbs such as Plattekloof, Tygervalley and Welgemoed, off the N1 freeway, are modern, suburban and bristling with new property developments, including upmarket shopping malls such as the Tygervalley Centre and Century City, set to rival the Waterfront as Cape Town's premier leisure complex, making it unnecessary for locals to venture into the centre of Cape Town at all.

LEFT: Cape Town is considered one of the world's most convivial cities for gays.
ABOVE: young and carefree in Camps Bay.

of dissident Afrikaans literature from the 1960s "Sestigers" movement, characterised by André Brink's *Kennis van die Aand* ("Knowledge of the Night"), a sensitive attempt to explore the colour bar and banned for many years.

Many younger white Afrikaners have engaged deeply and radically with the transition process and are highly committed to creating a strong and successful society for all. Desmond Tutu has remarked on how Afrikaners who were once bitterly opposed to the ANC have generally been more ready to embrace the new South Africa than English-speaking liberals. He puts this down to

Afrikaners having no liberal tradition and therefore no interest in a middle ground.

Township living

In spite of the ending of apartheid, most blacks in Cape Town continue to live in the townships in which they were confined by the Group Areas Act of 1950. This is largely due to economic necessity, but it is also because for the time being most township-dwellers prefer to stick to their own people, in spite of the inconveniences of township life. This is much less the case in Johannesburg, a much larger, more dynamic city, where a burgeoning black middle-class has

TOWNSHIP SUCCESS

The film *U-Carmen eKhayelitsha*, which was set in the sprawling township of Khayalitsha and based on Georges Bizet's *Carmen*, with a libretto translated into Xhosa, won the Golden Bear at the 2005 Berlin Film Festival.

left Soweto and moved to the city's prosperous northern suburbs. Cape Town's black middle class is smaller and less confident, often complaining of having no suitable place to go.

The biggest advantage of life in a township is the strong sense of community and the

THE HUGUENOTS OF FRANSCHHOEK

The Huguenots were French Protestants and members of the Reformed Church established in 1550 by John Calvin. Persecuted for their religious beliefs by Louis IX, many left France for England, America or Holland. Organised emigration of Huguenots to the Cape occurred in1688–1689, following the example of individual Huguenots who had already made the journey, such as François Villion (1671) and the brothers François and Guillaume du Toit (1686). By 1692 a total of 201 French Huguenots had arrived at the Cape. Most of them settled around the town of Franschhoek ("French Corner"), some 70 km (43 miles) outside Cape Town *(see page 177)*,

where many farms still bear their original French names (such as La Motte, Bien Donné, Grande Provence). The skills of the Huguenots contributed to the development of the local winemaking industry.

Simon van der Stel, the Dutch commander of the Cape at the time, insisted that the immigrants use Dutch rather than French for instruction and worship and so spoken French disappeared within a century. But many old Afrikaner families have French first names such as Etienne, Jean. André, Marie, Jacques, Pierre, Louis, and French surnames such as Du Toit, Le Roux, De Villiers, Labuschagne - *(pronounced La-boo-skag-nee)*, Marais.

vibrant outdoor life. Basic services and facilities have improved dramatically since 1994, with electricity, telephones and water supplies (at least in the form of a stand pipe) reaching more and more homes each year.

Unemployment, however, remains very high. Most township dwellers rely on the informal economy – selling merchandise on the pavement – to make a living, and with no state benefits to fall back on vast numbers of people are perpetually on the bread line. Initiatives to open up the townships to outsiders and create wealth include township tours for tourists and craft initiatives. But crime and violence are still rife. In some areas rival

Many elements of traditional African religion inform the AIC belief system. Healing and religion are closely interrelated and there is a strong belief in faith-healers. The biggest churches have several faith-healers, with constantly overcrowded consulting rooms, who sell their own range of herbal treatments.

The Cape Coloured community

"Coloured", originally pejorative but now used widely and no longer regarded as offensive, is the official term for South Africans of mixed descent. The Cape Coloureds population group is the third-largest population group in the country and today numbers just over three million.

gangs hold sway and rough justice is meted out by vigilante groups.

Perhaps because of this, religion has become an important focus in many people's lives. Popular are the (various) African Indigenous Churches (AIC), which broke away from the mainstream denominations in the 1880s and still operate independently from them today. Key features of their faith include a belief in prayer healing and baptism by total immersion, along with a general prohibition on tobacco, alcohol, medication and pork.

LEFT: school girls in Muslim Bo-Kaap.
ABOVE LEFT AND RIGHT: faces of Cape Town.

Coloureds (as they are usually called) live primarily in and around the Western Cape with subcultures existing within the broad grouping: Cape Coloureds, Griquas and Cape Malays.

The Coloured community has diverse origins. Dutch colonials in the Cape began importing slaves from as early as 1658. The slaves came from elsewhere in Africa (the coasts of East and West Africa) and from islands in the Indian and Atlantic oceans (Cape Verde, Guinea Bissau, Mauritius and Madagascar). Forebears were also local to the Cape: Khoi, San, Xhosa and white Europeans, especially Dutch, German and English along with Spanish and Portuguese sailors. The Cape Malay has Indian, Arab,

Malagasy, Chinese and Malay blood. The Griquas, who have a strong sense of identity, come from the Northern Cape. They are descended from Khoikhoi and white ancestors who lived about 200 years ago.

Coloured workers were traditionally fishermen, farm labourers and servants. Today, many are farm labourers working on farms across the Boland and Western Cape. Gradually more and more people from the coloured community are taking their rightful places in politics, commerce, industry, education and the arts. Coloured folklore and music has become an integral part of the cultural scene in South Africa.

After being forced out of District Six and older Cape Malay settlements in Newlands, Claremont and Simon's Town, coloured populations were relocated to the Cape Flats, Mitchells Plain, Bonteheuwel, Elsies River and Lavender Hill. Most coloured workers in Cape Town still live on the Cape Flats.

The living idiomatic heart of Afrikaans is coloured and not white, owing something to the work of Coloured writer Adam Small (*Kitaar my Kruis* and *Kanna Hy Ko Hystoe*) and District Sixer Richard Rive, whose 1986 novel *Buckingham Palace District Six* has been assigned as a set work in schools in the Western Cape.

Gay Cape Town

South Africa's constitution ensures the protection of gay civil rights and Cape Town is fast rivalling Sydney as a "pink" destination of choice, with a large number of gay-friendly clubs, restaurants and guest houses.

In the film *Proteus*, Cape Town film maker Jack Lewis and Canadian film maker John Greyson trace Cape Town's gay credentials to the start of the colonial era. They tell the story of an affair between a young Khoi man, Claas Blank, and Rijkhaart Jacobsz, a sailor from Amsterdam, who were imprisoned on Robben Island in 1735. The affair rocked the society of that time but passed into urban folklore.

For generations, cross-dressing and transgendered men from the Cape Coloured community have been known as "moffies", and the Cape boasts one of the most famous transseexuals of Victorian times, Dr James Barry, who reformed medical practice in the Cape, fought duels over a local beauty, and was discovered on his deathbed to be a woman. Known for its beautifully restored historical cottages, pretty tree-lined streets and vibrant village atmosphere, De Waterkant Village is the official gay village of Cape Town.

The Jewish community

The first significant immigration of Jews to the Cape, mostly from Lithuania, came with the diamond and gold boom of the late nineteenth century. Jews continued to arrive during the 20th century in spite of discrimination during the early years. Eastern European Jews formed the second-largest immigrant group after Western Europeans. Poor families settled in Woodstock, District Six or Salt River, moving later to Gardens, Tamboerskloof, Oranjezicht or Sea Point. They retained many of their cultural traditions, the strength of which was evident in the establishment of a Yiddish theatre, press and three Hebrew bookshops.

Many Jewish activists and lawyers participated in the struggle against apartheid, among them Progressive MP Helen Suzman, for many years the only dissenting voice in parliament, Albie Sachs, Arthur Chaskalson and Gill Marcus. ❏

LEFT: working together in a local store.
RIGHT: looking to a promising future.

SPORT MAD, SPORT CRAZY

South Africans are fanatical about sport, and none more so than Capetonians, whose agreeable climate makes it a year-round preoccupation

With two oceans to the fore and the Table Mountain National Park to the rear, and a year-round sunny climate, Cape Town is the perfect environment for sport and outdoor pursuits. The city is the focus for a host of national and international tournaments, rugby and cricket events in particular. But the competitive and body-conscious Capetonians don't just watch sport, they do it, whether it be adventurous sports such as rock-climbing, abseiling and surfing or more sedate forms such as golf.

Since the end of apartheid, during which South Africa was boycotted by many international teams and barred from the Olympics, the Springboks (as South Africa's national teams are known) have been welcomed back into the international sporting fold. In 1995 South Africa even hosted (and won) the Rugby World Cup, with a team that included the first-ever black Springbok. In 2010 it will become the first African country to host the football World Cup. This gives everyone something to look forward to, especially black South Africans who favour football over rugby or cricket, from which they were excluded in the past.

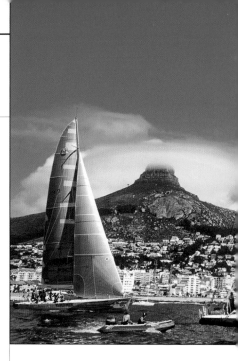

BELOW: two South African fans watch the visiting West Indies take on South Africa at the Newlands Cricket Ground. Sport can be a great unifier: the prospect of the 2010 football World Cup has given everyone something to look forward to.

LEFT: Springbok Bakkies Botha rises high during a Tri-Nations match between South Africa and Australia at Newlands Rugby Stadium. Rugby is also played at Boland Stadium in Paarl.

ABOVE: Cape Town hosts several big yachting events, including the Cape Town to Rio South Atlantic Race.

RIGHT: South African cricket captain Graeme Smith poised for action. Like every other country with an English colonial history, South Africa is passionate about cricket, and the national team is one of the best in the world. Many five-day internationals are held at Newlands Cricket Ground, one of the great Test venues in world cricket, picturesquely situated beneath Devil's Peak in the Southern Suburbs.

SPORTING CHANCES

If you like to get up and play a sport rather than just watch it, here are some of the participant sports and other outdoor activities on offer in Cape Town and the Cape Peninsula:

Canoeing and Rafting White-water enthusiasts can experience the turbulent rivers of the Western Cape such as the Breede, Berg, Dorings and Orange.

Golf The famous southeaster can play havoc with your aim, but the Cape has great designer golf courses. The best are Steenberg Estate, Milnerton, Rondebosch, Royal Cape and Clovelly Country Club overlooking False Bay. Erinvale Country Estate and Golf Club near Somerset West (Tel: 021 847 1160) is one of the most difficult courses in South Africa.

Mountain Climbing The Mountain Club of South Africa offers guides and group mountaineering experiences. To find out more contact www.mcsa.org.za.

Sand and Sea Surfers and windsurfers are all well served on the Peninsula. Big Bay in Blouberg is also good for power kites, on land and sea. Cape Town hosts numerous yachting competitions (Signal Hill is a good vantage point), including the Cape Town to Rio South Atlantic Race (www.southatlanticrace.co.za) in January and the pre-Christmas Governor's Cup (Cape Town to St Helena), held every two years (www.governorscup.com).

Two Oceans Marathon The Old Mutual Two Oceans Marathon, usually held in April, attracts international athletes as well as local enthusiasts. To join the competitors, apply six months in advance. Visit www.twooceansmarathon.org.za.

ABOVE: The annual Cape Argus Cycle Tour, usually held in March, is a 105-km (65-mile) cycle tour around the Cape Peninsula, beginning on Herzog Boulevard and ending at Green Point. For further information visit: www.cycletour.co.za.

COOKING UP A FEAST

A sophisticated food culture has emerged in South Africa, and Cape Town is leading the way. But its chefs aren't simply following international trends. They are rediscovering traditional regional cuisine and earning a place in the global kitchen

Foodie culture has developed exponentially in Cape Town in the last few years. The city is filled with interesting cafés and restaurants, and has many well-known chefs and caterers. Popular food and wine fairs such as the the Cape Gourmet Festival in May include tastings of all kinds of locally produced food and drink. Local lifestyle magazines feature recipes matching locally sourced food and wine.

Food shops and supermarkets have been quick to embrace this new trend and stock virtually anything you might need for a whole gamut of recipes, from Asian to North African, European to Japanese. And the variety of restaurants expands all the time; you're as likely to find good Chinese food as you are Cajun, Pacific Rim or Italian.

Global influences

World trends in food are as common in Cape Town as elsewhere. What you eat and drink in New York or Sydney you might well find in Cape Town's Southern Suburbs or in a trendy downtown eatery. That's great: the city has a window on the world and is proud of it. But what is also evident, as South Africans grow increasingly confident of their roots, is a renewed interest in their own unique cuisine. And chefs are not just dishing up old favourites. Instead, South African cuisine is being re-formed, re-tested and freshly presented in ways that acknowledge world trends

LEFT AND RIGHT: Africa Café on Shortmarket Street, is a good place to sample new-wave African cuisine.

and tastes without compromising unique characteristics. Old European favourites are also being rediscovered and presented in new and exciting ways.

Culinary traditions

But what is South African cuisine? In this "rainbow nation", with its rich cultural heritage and varied colonial past, there are plenty of culinary traditions to draw on. Diverse ingredients and flavours have enriched the cooking pot, from the first Dutch settlers and the slaves and artisans from Sri Lanka and Indonesia who arrived with the Dutch East India Company in the 17th century to the

French Hueguenot refugees of the 18th century, the German traders and missionaries and the colonising English, not to mention Indian indentured labourers brought to Natal in the 19th century.

African cuisine from rural peasant traditions has been slower to catch on. Although many city restaurants offer a few token dishes, some South African, others from across the continent, you have to visit a restaurant or shebeen in a township to taste the real thing: slow-cooked dishes, such as wild spinach or morog, tripe and pumpkins. Samp, for example, a mash of maize and beans, is best home-made.

Eastern flavours

But it's the cuisine of the Cape that is making an impact at an international level. Real Cape cooking is characterised by spiced, curried or sweetened dishes that originated as European meat, game, fish and dessert recipes, influenced by East Indian and Asian flavourings and preservatives. The most original dishes – and certainly those that all Capetonians know – are those that are either Dutch or Malay or a blend of both, like the *bredies*, *sosaties*, *boboties* and *breyanis*. *Bredies* are slow-cooked stews of meat, vegetables and spices. Most characteristic is *waterblommetjie bredie*, made from an indigenous pond plant layered with Karoo mutton. There are also potato, tomato, green-bean and spinach *bredies*. *Sosaties* are skewers of marinated chicken breast or cubed lamb, grilled and served with rice and spicy cooked fruit. But *bobotie* is best-known: ground meat, turmeric, cumin, pepper, fresh lemon leaves and a host of other spices are mixed together and baked, then topped with a savoury custard and served with yellow rice. Lastly, there are the ever-popular *samoosas*, deep-fried triangles of pastry filled with spicy meat or vegetables.

Country cooking

Much of the country cooking of the *boere*, the farmers, evolved in a climate of making do in a harsh living environment. *Potjiekos* (meat or fish stews cooked in a typical three-legged iron cooking pot), preserves and chutneys, and biltong (wind-dried strips of meat – beef, ostrich or game – cured with lashings of

EATING OUT IN CAPE TOWN

The biggest concentration of restaurants is in the city centre and along its edges in Kloof Street, the Waterfront, and in the Gardens and Green Point districts. These are Cape Town's older neighbourhoods, and some of their restaurants have a venerable vintage. There are first-class restaurants in most of the top hotels – the Mount Nelson, the Cape Grace and the Table Bay among them.

Capetonians of the older generation like to eat early, though this fashion is changing. However, eating at 8.30pm is considered very late, even by fashionable standards, and it's not unheard of for restaurant kitchens to close at 10pm. Some restaurants operate a first sitting at

7–7.30pm with a second sitting at 9pm. Don't forget to make a reservation; Capetonians love to eat out, and they often make bookings weeks in advance, particularly during the Christmas holidays.

Service has traditionally been poor, but it is improving, not least because waiting staff depend on their tips (expect to tip 10 percent on top of the bill). City venues have been criticised for refusing to serve tap water or for charging for it (it should be freely available). Smoking is illegal in restaurants, although some have dedicated smoking sections. Definitely check with the waiter before lighting up.

coriander seeds and pepper). Every South African keeps biltong in the store cupboard. Salted, spiced and hung up to dry, it is often the snack of choice during a busy working day. It evolved at a time when it was the only way to preserve meat, particularly when travelling the new lands on ox-wagon. You will also find *droewors* (dried sausage), which evolved in a similar manner.

Also popular are home-baked breads, *melk-terts* (milk tarts), cheesecakes and *koeksusters* (a very syrupy and moist plaited pastry), no doubt responsible for the large girth of many countryfolk. Afrikaans farmhouse cooking is enjoying a revival right now, perhaps due to

lope, warthog and even giraffe. South Africans love their meat – the rarer the better – and one thing you can be sure of is that any menu will almost certainly include a first-class steak. If you are a keen carnivore, try the Famous Butcher's Grill (Greenmarket Square or Cape Town Lodge Hotel on Buitengracht Street).

New twists

Nowadays, of course, you may well find various combinations of any of the above. Ginja, on Castle Street, for example, a trendy city restaurant famous for delectable combinations of African and Asian flavours and

the latest edition of *Leipoldt's Cape Cookery* by Louis Leipoldt. Doctor, writer and gourmet, in the 1930s and '40s Leipoldt collected traditional recipes, embellishing or editing them as he saw fit, producing in the process a foundation for a Cape style of cooking.

Great game

Many of Leipoldt's recipes centre on game and most of the best city restaurants will have a least one game dish on the menu. Venison in South Africa includes kudu, various ante-

---

LEFT: traditional country cooking is tasty but heavy.
ABOVE: hot work on the *braai* deserves an ice-cold beer.

ingredients, might serve Karoo lamb with a Thai green curry. One.waterfront, in the Cape Grace Hotel, has a great curried risotto. Other places, such as Biesmiellah, a wonderful Cape Malay eatery in a private house in the Malay Quarter of Bo-Kaap, remain unremittingly ethnic in their menu choices. Its speciality is tamarind lamb – *denningvleis* – and it doesn't need to be adapted: it's mouthwatering just as it is. Their crayfish *salomie* is a trademark.

Other restaurants present dishes not so much ethnic as simply locale-inspired. What about the handcrafted warthog sausages at Leinster Hall, the eland steak at Khaya-Nama

(Loop Street), or the ginger *soesie* with steamed salad at Emily's at the Clock Tower on the Waterfront? This is contemporary South African food and it's delicious.

Cape Town's chefs are leading this change. People such as Garth Stroebel, owner of the South African Chefs Academy,

a culinary school for aspiring chefs, is a leading light in this regard. His book, *Modern South African Cuisine*, highlights the new food-and-wine culture of South Africa and its integration with exotic new flavours and influences from abroad.

Barbecues are best

South Africans love their *braai* (barbecues) and al fresco eating is a way of life. Perhaps a legacy from the days when outdoor cooking was the only option out in the veld, cooking outdoors, like being able to throw off your shoes and walk around barefoot, is one of the luxuries of living in a hot, sunny climate.

Braai happen anytime, although late Sunday lunches are a favourite for which *boerewors* (a chunky spiced sausage) and lamb chops or snoek (a barracuda-like fish) basted with apricot jam are a favourite.

Other ingredients that cook beautifully over the hot coals are spatch-cocked chicken or lamb, and firm line-fish such as kingklip or red roman. Everyone gathers round, and there's much drinking of ice-cold local beers and chilled white wine.

Good ingredients

In addition to all this, South Africans are lucky to live in a fecund land where food production gets better and better. Mediterranean-style cuisines fit perfectly here. Olive oil from the Western Cape has won many international awards, while local cheese-making has gone from strength to strength. The annual cheese festival at Franschhoek is known for the varieties of local and unusual cheeses that the organisers have hunted down on remote country farms. Boerenkaas, "farmers' cheese" is a staple in many homes. Even the big supermarket chains such as Pick 'n' Pay, Woolworths, Spar and Checkers have exciting cheese counters where once they might have sold only a rubber-like orange cheddar.

And then there's the fruit, which is delectable. In season you can buy boxes of ripe grapes, melons, peaches, apricots and plums from roadside vendors – refreshing bounty that adds to the pleasure of motoring in the Western Cape.

Cape Town is also one of the best places in South Africa to eat fish and seafood. Indeed much of it is sent abroad and to Johannesburg. Fish to look out for are snoek, though it can be very bony, kabeljou (great grilled and served with lemon and garlic), galjoen (best baked), kingklip (a firm-fleshed fish that is delicious simply grilled), oysters, mussels and very occasionally perlemoen (local abalone), which is increasingly rare due to a variety of poaching catastrophes. There's also love sushi . For the best in town go to Willoughby's in Victoria Wharf on the Victoria and Alfred Waterfront or Wakame at Mouille Point). ❏

LEFT: fresh ingredients are key.

Cape Wine

The Cape Winelands are the centre of the South African wine industry, and in terms of wine production are virtually on a par with the better-known wine-producing regions of Australia and Portugal. Right at the heart of the city are the oldest vineyards, those of Constantia, their planting by Huguenot settlers in 1688 pre-dates even those near Bordeaux in France. Also close to the city centre is the Durbanville Wine Route.

Further afield are the country towns of Stellenbosch and Paarl (rich reds and crisp whites), Franschhoek (Semillon and Shiraz) and Wellington (whites). Some of the wine estates surrounding these towns, such as Meerlust, produce world-famous wines. There are literally hundreds of other vineyards out there: they sell their wine to the public, offer tastings, lunches and teas, and some of them make their own cheeses and olive oil as well. Many centre upon historic properties with 18th-century Cape Dutch farmsteads – Meerlust, Boschendal and Nederburg among them – some of them open to the public.

Until the 1970s, South Africa's winemaking tradition was strongly influenced by Germanic styles, despite Huguenot roots in the industry, and as a result South Africa was best known as a predominantly white wine-producing country. This is quickly changing however. Following the end of apartheid and the expansion of markets, South African wine-makers have been at pains to learn new skills and satisfy the international demand for reds. As a result, Chenin Blanc is slowly giving way to Cabernet Sauvignon.

On the red front, Shiraz is also gaining popularity, while the love-it-or-hate-it Pinotage is a unique South African cultivar, developed from a cross between Pinot Noir and Cinsaut. Sweet and simple or robust and regal, depending on its treatment, it accounts for a small percentage of what the country produces, but go and sample it: Paarl is a good source. It's a fruity, purple wine whose popularity increases year on year.

As for whites, Chenin and Chardonnay dominate the industry. The latter has evolved from the heavily wooded wines of the early 1990s to a more Burgundian elegance and complexity. Both are widely exported.

If you haven't time to get out to the Winelands, certain city restaurants offer very good wine cellar listings. Top-of-the-

range hotel wine lists are found at The Atlantic at the Table Bay, The Cape Colony at the Mount Nelson, and one.waterfront at the Cape Grace.

Alternatively, Belthazar, Baia, Emily's, Tides, Pigalle and the Famous Butcher's Grill are just some of the city restaurants with excellent all-round wine lists. Don't hesitate to ask for advice. ❑

Serious wine-lovers should buy a copy of John Platter's South African Wine Guide *which is updated annually. It's the definitive guide to cellars, vineyards and winemakers throughout South Africa.*

RIGHT: decanting a bottle of red.

CREATIVE CAPE TOWN

Cape Town has experienced an explosion in the arts scene in the past decade, in spite of cuts in funding. The city is buzzing with new ideas in all the media, from plays and literature to fine arts and jazz

The end of apartheid and the emergence of a democratic South Africa in 1994 created an entirely new social environment based on a constitution that guarantees freedom of speech and expression, with a clause in the Bill of Rights – the only one of its kind in the world – that specifically gives artistic expression greater latitude. Both practitioners and consumers of art are now multiracial, multilingual and cross-cultural.

The fundamental question for South African artists in the past decade was where to go once protest against apartheid was no longer the overriding imperative. It was actually with huge relief that performers and audiences alike, felt they could set aside ideological preoccupations and start to tell their own stories. Artists have eagerly taken to what is the natural province of the arts – a world where our preconceptions of the past, of good and evil, of true and false, are proven far from trustworthy.

The most dominant themes are social issues, such as the collapse of traditional values through urbanisation (often idealising rural life) and generational conflict. HIV and Aids, domestic violence and the position of women, unemployment, crime and alcoholism are the new arenas of artistic activism. Black artists have started to unlock themes previously taboo, such as homosexuality, black xenophobia, witches and violence against women in a deeply patriarchal society.

LEFT: jazz saxophonist Dewey Redman at the Cape Town Jazz Festival.
RIGHT: member of The Whole Drum Truth.

Influences from elsewhere in Africa, from which both black and white South Africans were previously shut out, are enriching local endeavours. The result is a renaissance in the arts with an extremely diverse cultural landscape both in form and content.

Art in the townships

Economic muscle lies with the whites, and European culture is still dominant. Most whites have embraced non-racial South Africa, though suspicion and fear remain, making Cape Town's whites not so different from all kinds of communities around the world. People agree strongly in principle – and

CULTURAL SENSITIVITIES

Among the many hangovers from apartheid is the enormous economic discrepancy between black and white. There is therefore great sensitivity about the dominance of English, the perceived precariousness of Afrikaans, and surrounding issues such as elitism and a Eurocentric hegemony.

take umbrage if they're accused of racism – but the fact is it's hard for most whites to appreciate what it is like to be black in the city. As a small example, white casting directors never consider how out-of-work black actors struggle to get to auditions in the city centre.

The lack of plays in African languages is also a sore point. Bars will screen Wimbledon tennis, rugby and international football, but you will be hard-pressed to find a watering-hole showing local football, the most popular black sport. Blacks resident in the city head to the township bars or party at home. At the same time, avenues to explore arts and culture in the townships are not geared up for white visitors.

Literature

Although literature does exist in all the 11 official languages, most is in English, with a very strong, especially poetic tradition in Afrikaans.

FUNDING THE ARTS

Even though South Africa has many desperate needs, the new democratic government is far more enlightened about art than the apartheid regime, and has grasped the important role that culture plays, not least in reconciliation. The ANC government abolished the monolithic provincial arts councils and created the National Arts Council to which all artists can now apply.

Although this is a far more progressive approach, its bureaucratic application has frequently been incompetent. Overall funding has decreased, though hopes of more investment have been recently raised as the treasury enjoys a surplus. The collegiate benefits of

repertory theatre companies have been lost, while orchestras, opera and ballet companies are no longer secure. Through its funding agencies, government is promoting work which celebrates diversity and highlights social ills, although this agenda is sometimes pursued to a fault by over-zealous functionaries and politically correct commentators.

An interesting legacy of apartheid is that there are still no effective trade unions for South African artists, and there is unhappiness surrounding remuneration and working conditions. Black women are especially under represented in theatre, film, fine art and publishing.

Many black writers, such as Zakes Mda, have returned from exile, and the luminary Wally Serote became adviser on heritage to the president. The Nobel Prize for Literature was awarded to J. M. Coetzee in 2004, who wrote most of his works in Cape Town, and to Nadine Gordimer in 1991, though internationally the most well-known Cape Town writer is probably the best-selling author Wilbur Smith.

The best-selling Afrikaans writer Andre Brink lives in Rosebank, and his work has been translated into every major language. Also living in Cape Town is Damon Galgut, whose critically acclaimed *The Good Doctor* was short-listed for the Man Booker Prize in 2004.

method of creation and returning to solid scripts such as John Kani's *Nothing but the Truth*.

Great works by black playwrights were denied platforms under apartheid. Many black writers (like Lesego Rampolokeng and Mbongeni Ngema) continue with overtly ideological themes, but the new protest theatre has moved on from simply blaming colonialism.

White English-language dramatists, including South Africa's most famous playwright internationally, Athol Fugard, have concentrated on reconciliation and the difficult reforging of relationships in the emergent "Rainbow Nation". Playwright Fiona Coyne challenges the hypocrisy of her white liberal contem-

Theatre

The sheer number of productions makes Cape Town the theatre capital of South Africa. It is also the seat of an emerging "Coloured" folk theatre, such as Oscar Petersen and David Isaacs's Joe Barber series, and the internationally acclaimed musicals of David Kramer.

Drama reached a low point in the mid-1990s, but traditional plays are making a comeback. Playwrights are abandoning the "workshop"

LEFT: a striking township mural.
ABOVE: J. M. Coetzee receiving the 2003 Nobel Prize for Literature, with Sonto Kudjoe, the South African ambassador to Sweden (left).

poraries and is one of the most articulate.

Although European formats – with proscenium arches and reticent audiences – still dominate, practitioners of community and educational theatre are eagerly importing African story-telling techniques, music and dance. Director Brett Bailey, resident at Spier, uses traditional healers and ceremonies, and has created a unique new form of theatre.

Theatre-maker extraordinaire Marthinus Basson cracked open the Pandora's box of Afrikaans theatre with his postmodern collaborations with poet Breyten Breytenbach in the 1990s. English plays by Afrikaners like Reza de Wet are well worth attending, and often concentrate on the reinterpretation of cultural symbols. The Boer War centenary was an important focus.

Post-apartheid satire has perhaps never been funnier, yet never scarcer, and its only real, current practitioner is the internationally acclaimed Pieter Dirk Uys, who has his own independent theatre in Darling.

Although the Cape Philharmonic Orchestra (formed in 1914) remains mostly white, unlike for instance the KwaZulu-Natal Philharmonic Orchestra in Durban, it runs outreach programmes, and is pursuing audience development. It's an orchestra with an enormous repertoire, playing its own symphony season and accompanying Cape Town City Ballet and the Cape Town Opera, which puts on grand full-scale operas by Verdi, Puccini and Bizet.

Cape Town Opera was for many years under the stewardship of Angelo Gobbato, and today is 85 percent black. More often than not the singing is world-class, with local

Commercial theatres, as everywhere in the world, favour fantasy and format over content, but a sense of social responsibility and pride in supporting the new South African culture, seems to be temporarily keeping this in check.

The classical arts

Cape Town takes pleasure in and feels uncomfortable about its reputation as a Eurocentric city. Popular with locals and tourists, that Eurocentricity finds its proud expression in a strong tradition of symphony concerts, operas and ballet galas, which have been around since the slave orchestras of the Dutch colonists in the 1600s.

leads performing alongside visiting international divas.

The Cape Town City Ballet pursues an increasingly varied repertoire. Evergreen favourites from Tchaikovsky are always on the programme, but new work by talented young choreographers such as Sean Bovim are attracting a younger following.

Modern dance

Out of all the performing arts in South Africa, dance has always enjoyed the greatest audiences, from packed theatres to public events. The blend of both a strong formal European choreographic tradition and a rich African heritage has created a new wave of exciting work that is gaining international recognition.

Jazzart's annual Danscape fund-raiser is a showcase of the best emerging work. The La Rosa Spanish Dance Theatre in Mowbray is making waves with its seamless blend of flamenco and such African styles as pantsula. RemixDance Project creates remarkable pieces using able-bodied and disabled – often wheelchair-bound – dancers. Jikeleza, based in Hout Bay, under the visionary guidance of Edmund Thwaites and Atholl Hay, takes children living on the streets, puts them in foster homes, sees that they get an education, and develops them as professional dances and tutors.

own creative language, both introspective and turning a critical eye on the world around them within and beyond the borders of South Africa. William Kentridge, with his powerful drawings and animated films, is world-famous.

Black artists were neglected by the establishment until recently. Exceptional painters such as Gerard Sekoto and George Pemba are now acclaimed. As most black artists were excluded from the benefits of formal education and the support of patrons and galleries, they developed a strong tradition in cheaper materials, such as lino and woodcuts. That situation has now changed, and the contemporary scene looks forward to a new burst of creative energy, fuelled

The fine arts

While Johannesburg is the powerhouse for South African fine art, Cape Town is home to the South African National Gallery, many resident artists and more commercial galleries than any other city in the country.

South African artists, though hardly registering at home, are making big waves internationally. No longer following trends from overseas and applying them to local subject matter, and no longer voicing tortured protests against State oppression, they are finding their

LEFT: dance class in Knyana, the Western Cape.
ABOVE: members of the Cape Town City Ballet.

FINE ART SHOWCASE

The best place to get the pulse of South African fine art is Michael Stevenson Contemporary, a custom designed white-cube space in Green Point. It has an active exhibition schedule and curates shows across the spectrum of media. Many of the brightest and best are represented by the gallery including Berni Searle, Wim Botha, Guy Tillim, David Goldblatt and Doreen Southwood. They also have a stock of select but pricey late-19th-century African art. All exhibitions come with published catalogues or books, a rarity in South Africa, back copies of which are available and make a valuable resource for anybody interested in South African art.

THE IRMA STERN MUSEUM

The eponymous Irma Stern Museum in the Southern Suburbs *(see page 119)* houses the work of one of Cape Town's greatest artists, and also has excellent contemporary shows in the gallery upstairs.

by such artists as Sipho Ndlovu, Mgcineni Pro Sobopha and Colbert Mashile. An important focus is Greatmore Studios in Woodstock, a base for artists such as Lindile Magunya, Boyce Magandela and Lonwabo Kilani.

The permanent collection of the South African National Gallery offers a good overview of South African art, and includes such

iconic works as Jane Alexander's *The Butcher Boys*. Several rooms are devoted to special exhibitions, often photography.

Crafts

Traditional crafts have finally been recognised for their artistic worth, and are now a vibrant part of the country's cultural life, with colourful markets everywhere. The government actively supports craft initiatives. seeing them as an opportunity for commercial stimulation and job-creation in the rural areas. The variety is overwhelming. A whole new aesthetic has emerged. using recyclables such as tins, plastic and metal bottle tops, wire, multicoloured tele-

phone flex and mass-produced beads. Craft markets and entrepreneurs abound, and the collective Streetwires in Shortmarket Street has engaged top designers from Europe to help generate ideas.

All that jazz

In the way the penny-whistle playing *kwela* defines Johannesburg internationally, so the unique strains of Cape Jazz are identified with Cape Town. Developed by musicians such as Basil Coetzee, Robbie Jansen and Hotep Idris Galeta, it's an infectious musical style brought to its apotheosis by the legendary Abdullah Ibrahim (formerly known as Dollar Brand), who created the unofficial anti-apartheid anthem *Manenberg,* and has recently founded a unique music school in the city – the M7 Music Academy. Cape Town abounds in good places to enjoy jazz, and big names like Hugh Masekela and Judith Sephuma regularly perform.

Gospel, choirs and church music have a strong African following. Imported and hybridised versions of reggae, hip-hop and rap are all present, though the major musical and cultural force since the 1990s is *kwaito*, the voice of the black youth who make up almost 50 percent of the population.

Film

A whole industry around film has sprung up in the past decade in Cape Town, and there is a continuous stream of visiting Hollywood stars. Locally made feature films are at last receiving recognition. In 2005 *U-Carmen eKhayelitsha* won the Golden Bear for Best Picture in Berlin and *Yesterday* received an Oscar nomination for the Academy's Best Foreign Film. Ironically, the first wave of internationally successful local films had their premieres abroad, and have hardly even been seen inside the country.

The industry's key annual event is the South African World Film Festival, known as Sithengi, a film market held in Cape Town in November. The well-organised Out in Africa: Gay and Lesbian Film Festival was for many years the biggest film festival of any kind in Africa. ❑

LEFT: the South African National Gallery is a good place to go for an overview of South African art.

Architecture

Devotees of world architecture would probably come to Cape Town to see three important things: the beautiful buildings of the Cape Dutch period (17th and 18th centuries); the work of the internationally famous architect Sir Herbert Baker; and a wide array of newly built contemporary houses.

There are some surviving buildings from the time of the first British Occupation in the 18th century, and masses of buildings both public and domestic from the second. The late Victorian era is particularly well represented, with streets and streets of villas, some in terraces, with ornate facades decorated with intricate wrought-iron fretwork.

There's plenty of art deco: houses and apartment blocks in Vredehoek and Sea Point, and commercial buildings in the city centre *(see page 76)*. The 1930s, '40s and '50s contributed mansions and bungalows to the suburbs, though it's not these that add to the city's resonance.

The so-called Cape Dutch style is characteristically gabled, low and whitewashed. It's a local adaptation of imported styles, in this case baroque and neoclassical, and unique to the Cape, shaped by the materials most readily to hand and the limited availability of inspired, well-trained craftsmen. All over Cape Town, the Winelands and further afield are wonderful examples of Cape Dutch buildings, from farmsteads, barns and outbuildings to churches and civic buildings.

In the 19th and early 20th centuries Sir Herbert Baker drew inspiration from this "indigenous" style of architecture. His interest began when Cecil Rhodes invited him to remodel his Cape Town mansion, Groote Schuur in Rosebank in the Cape Dutch style and tradition. This contributed to a widescale revival of interest in Cape Dutch. Apart from Groote Schuur, you can see his

RIGHT: high Victorian wrought-iron work on Long Street, where you will find a wide range of architectural styles.

work in ST George's Cathedral (his houses in the suburbs are unfortunately not open to the public).

Increasingly visible is the new wave of modern domestic architecture. This includes sleek homes by architects such as Stefan Antoni on the Atlantic Seaboard (in particular Camps Bay and Llandudno), and others by Van der Merwe Mysewski, who specialises in buildings that make the most of the city's extravagant views and panoramas (pass by the Tree House in Glen Crescent in the suburb of Higgovale) and the brilliant husband and wife duo Gwen and Gawie Fagan, with their preference for more

intimate scale, searching for styles that respond to changing light, topography and the vernacular of the surroundings. In that sense, they're as important to Cape Town and as unique as the traditional Cape Dutch style.

There are many architects today doing magnificent things in the city and elsewhere in South Africa. In this huge open country there's plenty of space to build and domestic architecture in particular has benefited. Easy, laidback lifestyles require a certain type of space in which to live. The evidence is all over the wealthier areas of Cape Town. ❏

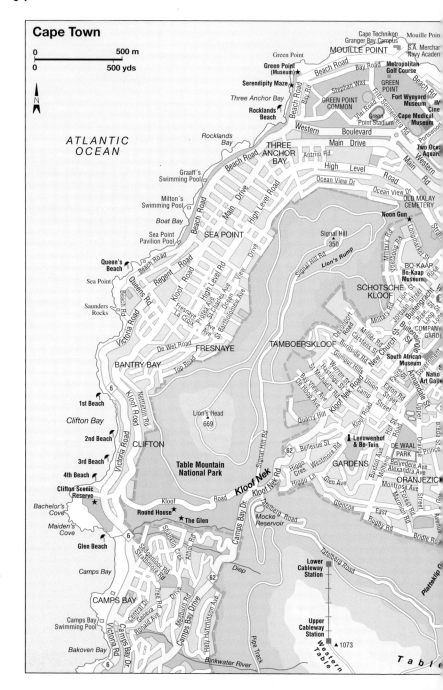

Cape Town

ATLANTIC OCEAN

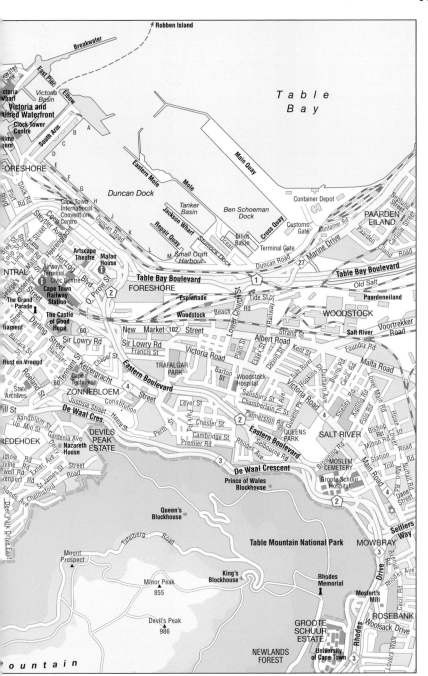

PLACES

A detailed guide to the entire city, with principal sites
clearly cross-referenced by number to the maps

L aid out on a grid system west of the Castle of Good Hope, central Cape Town is an easy city to navigate, with useful landmarks such as the ABSA tower block dominating the northern (ocean end) and Table Mountain the other. Running between these two are Adderley Street and Long Street, the former lined with grandiose Victorian civic buildings and bank headquarters, and the latter a wonderfully eclectic thoroughfare where junk shops, second-hand bookstores, backpacker hostels, bars and galleries rub shoulders with historic churches and mosques. A short walk away are the African craft stalls of Greenmarket Square.

Detached from the centre, on the other side of a multi-lane highway, is the V&A Waterfront, the thriving redeveloped harbour area with malls, luxury hotels and a host of entertainment options, from jazz bars to pleasure cruises. It is a great spot to come for a pleasant evening stroll followed by dinner on an outdoor terrace. Indeed some visitors to Cape Town hardly go anywhere else, though to do so would be to miss out on the rich life of the city.

Cape Town is as much about its suburbs as its centre or waterfront. The well-established Southern Suburbs sweep around the base of Table Mountain, enfolding great 19th-century estates such as Groot Constantia and Groot Schuur as well as Kirtenbosch, one of the world's great botanical gardens, left to the city by Cecil John Rhodes. And just a stone's throw away over Lion's Head is fashionable Clifton and Camps Bay, from where the Atlantic seaboard sweeps down to Cape Point via a string of stunning beaches and the little fishing town of Hout Bay.

South African cities, including Cape Town, have a reputation for crime. In order to change this, and as part of a general attempt to revitalise the CBD area, the Cape Town Partnership (formed by the tourism authority, local businesses and government) has made huge efforts to improve security in the city centre. Surveillance cameras have been installed in large numbers and mounted security guards are abundant, both day and night, particularly around the ATM machines of major banks. As a result, crime has been substantially reduced, but it is still not a good idea to wander around the area late at night.   ❑

PRECEDING PAGES: the V&A Waterfront with the CBD and Table Mountain to the rear; buildings on Long Street. **LEFT:** far-reaching views from the top of Table Mountain.

THE CITY CENTRE

Cape Town is boom town. What was until recently a
sleepy colonial hollow is turning into an exciting
city proud of its diverse heritage, with new
museums, a newly vibrant street life and
an abundance of good restaurants

Famously beautiful and set at the foot of one of the world's great natural features, Cape Town has an impressive reputation. But if this is your first visit to the city you will most likely be surprised – and then delighted – by how small and low-key the city centre is. You can stand at one end of Long Street, with your back to Table Mountain, and see the foreshore, with its tiny cluster of high-rises, at the other end.

If this is your second or a subsequent visit to Cape Town, and you were last here about five years ago, there's no doubt you'll find the city massively changed. Cape Town is a busier, livelier city. Once the dust had settled following the end of apartheid a property boom swept through South Africa, particularly Cape Town and its Peninsula. As a result, long-defunct city-centre areas suddenly became sought after, their central location, once discounted, lauded. Trees were planted and new roads laid out, busy, noisy thoroughfares were pedestrianised, and new hotels and shopping areas built. Many of the centre's handsome art deco buildings, which have stood empty and closed up for many years, have been earmarked for development as luxury apartments.

For visitors, not only are more of the city centre's monuments and attractions open to the public, but they're better staffed and their custodians display a new pride in them. There's a sense that the city's cultural patrimony at last belongs to everyone. Aspects of the city that were once ignored are being included, so that a visitor's interpretation of a monument or cultural artefact is balanced and unprejudiced.

Orientation

The heart of Cape Town, known as the City Bowl, is a very small area,

Map
on page
70

LEFT: City Hall
on Grand Parade.
BELOW:
Greenmarket Square.

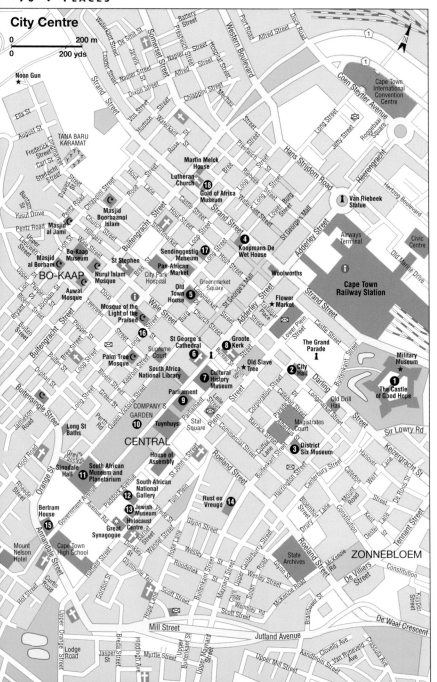

City Centre

0 _____ 200 m
0 _____ 200 yds

Noon Gun ★

TANA BARU KARAMAT

Ella St
August St
Frederick Street
Carl St
Stadzicht Street

Yusuf Road
Pentz Road

Masjid al Jami
Masjid al Borham
Bo-Kaap Museum
St Stephen
Nurul Islam Mosque

BO-KAAP

Auwal Mosque

Mosque of the Light of the Praised

Masjid Boorhaanol Islam

Palm Tree Mosque

Supreme Court

South Africa National Library

Parliament

COMPANY'S GARDEN

Long St Baths

Sinodale Hall

South African Museum and Planetarium

Bertram House

Mount Nelson Hotel

Cape Town High School

Martin Melck House
Lutheran Church
Gold of Africa Museum

Sendinggestig Museum
Pan-African Market

Old Town House

St George's Cathedral

Groote Kerk

Old Slave Tree

Cultural History Museum

Tuynhuys

Stal Square

House of Assembly

South African National Gallery

Jewish Museum

Holocaust Centre

Great Synagogue

Koopmans De Wet House

Van Riebeek Statue

Airways Terminal

Woolworths

Cape Town Railway Station

Flower Market

The Grand Parade

City Hall

The Castle of Good Hope

Military Museum

Old Drill Hall

Magistrates Court

District Six Museum

Rust en Vreugd

State Archives

ZONNEBLOEM

Civic Centre

Cape Town International Convention Centre

CENTRAL

Mill Street

Jutland Avenue

Lodge Road

originally laid out on a grid system, with streets running from south to north and west to east. This makes getting about straightforward and maps easy to read. Historically the city was bounded in the east by the Castle of Good Hope (which is where we start) and in the west by the lower reaches of Signal Hill (where Bo-Kaap is today), with the Company Gardens in the south and Table Mountain and the modern suburb of Oranjezicht behind, not forgetting the port at Table Bay. The street names of Buitengracht, Buitensingel and Buitenkant indicate the boundaries ("buiten" meaning outer) of the original town.

Castle of Good Hope

This tour begins with the oldest building in South Africa, the **Castle of Good Hope** ❶ (entrance on Buitenkant Street; open daily 9am–4pm; tel: 021 787 1249; admission charge; it is worth buying the fold-out plan available at the entrance). If you blink when you're driving past, you may well miss the castle, so dwarfed is it by the surrounding modern buildings, including the central railway station. Dating from 1666, this rather small, pentagonal fortress was built of brick (imported from Holland) and stone, with lime from Robben Island, and is typical of Dutch colonial settlements from America to Asia.

It has five bastions – named Buren, Leerdam, Oranje, Nassau and Katzenellenbogen after the titles of Prince William of Orange, the Dutch ruler at the time of the settlement – and replaced a simple square fortress built by the Cape's first governor, Jan van Riebeeck. Its design, by the engineer Simon Stevin of Bruges (1548–1620), perfects the idea of the simple, fortified bastions that first appeared in Italy during the 16th century. Surprisingly, the fort has never fired a shot in anger, and

no attack has ever been launched against it. That it has survived at all is due to the efforts of Mrs Marie Koopmans-De Wet, of the Koopmans-De Wet House *(see page 74)*, who fought its proposed demolition in the 19th century.

For the first 150 years of colonial rule the Castle of Good Hope was the centre of government. It housed the governor and the military, and had dungeons built below sea level. Although there is still a military presence at the castle, it is minimal (you may occasionally see a soldier crossing the yard), and the complex now functions mainly as a museum and as a venue for exhibitions and other cultural activities.

Visitors enter through a handsome gate, topped by a 17th-century bell tower, on the castle's northwest side. This replaced the original sea-facing entrance, which was vulnerable to high tides. As you enter, look up at the gateway to see the VOC monograms of the East India Company and the characteristic broken pediment containing a crowned lion. Commissioner Van Rheede van

TIP

All the sights in this chapter can be easily reached on foot. However, many of them are stops on the Cape Town Explorer, an open-top bus linking the essential sights of the Downtown area as well as the Waterfront, Sea Point and the lower cableway station for Table Mountain. *(For more details on the Cape Town Explorer, see Travel Tips, page 204.)*

BELOW: outside the Castle of Good Hope.

The terrace of the Castle's restaurant, which overlooks the Kat wall and the central courtyard, is a pleasant spot for morning coffee or afternoon tea.

BELOW: the Kat balcony at the Castle of Good Hope. **RIGHT:** exhibit in the castle's Military Museum.

Oudtshoorn was responsible for building the Kat, a 12-metre-high (40-ft) building slicing across the open courtyard. The lovely Kat balcony is almost certainly the work of Anton Anreith (1785–91), the Dutch East India Company's master sculptor. Most famously it houses the bulk of the **William Fehr Collection** (9.30am–4pm; no extra admission charge) of Africana – oil paintings, furniture, silverware, glass, carpets and porcelain relating to the Cape's earliest colonial period. Of particular interest are the oil paintings depicting life in the Cape between the 17th and mid-19th centuries.

Diagonally opposite the Kat wall, between the Catzenellenbogen and Burren towers, is the **Military Museum**, displaying regimental costumes, weaponry and military artefacts, and documenting colonial expansion. There is a particularly interesting section on the Boer War.

Grand Parade and City Hall

From the castle cross Buitenkant Street, turn left and then right into Darling Street for City Hall and the Grand Parade.

Completed in 1906, the massive **City Hall ❷** replaced the Old Town House *(see page 76)*, which by the end of the 19th century had become far too small. Built of sandstone in a grandiose style, it is typical of the town halls that populated the British Empire. It became known internationally when Nelson Mandela addressed a 70,000-strong crowd from its main balcony following his release from prison in 1990, the first time he had been seen in public for 27 years. As well as housing municipal offices and the public library, City Hall has a handsome concert hall that is home to the Cape Philharmonic Orchestra (concerts all year, Thurs and Sun; tel: 021 410 9809). The exterior was restored in the 1990s as part of a wider project to regenerate the eastern side of the city centre, and the interior is also set to receive a make-over.

The **Grand Parade** was once a military parade ground. Nowadays it is home to a large flea market and a daytime car park for office work-

ers in the neighbourhood. Vegetables, fruit and traditional medicines are for sale here too.

From the City Hall, head left back down Darling Street and turn right into Buitenkant Street. A few blocks along on the other side of the road is the District Six Museum.

District Six Museum

The **District Six Museum** ❸ (25A Buitenkant Street; open Mon 9am–3pm, Tues–Sat 9am–4pm; tel: 021 461 8745; admission charge; www.districtsix.co.za) should ideally be located in the district it commemorates, named as the sixth municipal district of Cape Town in 1867. In some respects, though, it is fitting that the museum is some distance removed.

Like Bo-Kaap *(see page 105)*, District Six was originally a lively, colourful neighbourhood populated by the descendants of freed slaves, artisans, tailors, merchants, labourers and immigrants. Its population grew dramatically in the 1780s and the beginning of the 19th century as a result of a general rise in the population of the city. It was a mainly poor area, but its inhabitants had lived there for many generations and kinship networks and other relationships were intricate and solid.

In 1966, under the Group Areas Act it was declared a White Group Area, and for the next 15 years a policy of systematic forced removal of the inhabitants and the destruction of their homes and workshops was pursued until there was virtually nothing left.

The museum commemorates the community and illustrates the resulting devastation of the lives and livelihoods of its inhabitants. There are maps, photographs and poignant reminders – street signs and so on – of the character of a neighbourhood sadly gone. A room in a typical home of the neighbourhood has been recreated, along with a school house, a barber's shop and other original settings, all enlivened with evocative recordings of District Six inhabitants relating their stories. The museum also has an interesting bookshop and a cosy café selling good coffee and home-made cakes.

Map on page 70

TIP

Noor Ebrahim, who runs the bookshop in the District Six Museum and acts as a guide to visiting groups, grew up in District Six. His book *Noor's Story, My Life in District Six* is an engaging account of his family and community.

BELOW:
District Six Museum.

TIP

Just around the corner from the Koopmans-De Wet House, on the corner of Burg and Castle streets, is the downtown Tourism Visitor Centre (closed Sat and Sun afternoons). As well as providing maps and leaflets, it's the starting point for several specialist walking tours.

BELOW:
Adderley Street.

On the hill where the the neighbourhood stood is an ugly, scarred landscape, but in time the land will be fully restored to it original owners and life there can restart.

From the museum, retrace your steps along Darling Street, continuing until its junction with Adderley Street. St George's Mall is one block further on, on the other side of Adderley Street.

Adderley Street

The city's main thoroughfare, **Adderley Street**, is named after Charles Adderley, a 19th-century British politician, but its original name, the Heerengracht (Gentlemen's Street), indicates its early refinement. It retained its elegant ambience well into the 1950s and '60s, but then began to decline and now it's nothing special. A block away, pedestrianised **St George's Mall**, filled with traders who lay out their goods on the pavement, musicians, benches and cafés, has also seen better days. However, both contain a variety of fine 19th- and 20th-century commercial buildings, including some superb examples of art deco architecture *(see page 76)*. In particular, look out for the splendid Standard Bank, distinguished by its dome topped by a statue of Britannia, and the First National Bank. The area is now undergoing something of an upturn in fortune, and buildings that once housed offices are being turned into lofts and apartments for downtown living. New cafés and restaurants, hotels and gyms are following, heralding the kind of transformation that has already revitalised parts of downtown Johannesburg.

Adding a splash of colour just off Adderley Street is **Trafalgar Place Flower Market**, where Bo-Kaap women sell their wares. Not far away is **Woolworths**, a popular department store (along the lines of Marks & Spencer in the UK), whose excellent food hall is a good place to assemble the ingredients for a picnic.

Koopmans-De Wet House

From St George's Mall turn north into **Strand Street**. On the left-hand side as you climb sloping Strand

Street, at No. 35, wedged between two modern tower blocks, is a small but beautiful two-storey 18th-century townhouse, the **Koopmans-De Wet House ❹** (open by appointment Mon; tel: 021 481 3935; admission charge), a relic of the time when downtown streets were lined with elegant homes. With its mullioned windows, pilasters, classical pediment and magnificent fanlight,, it's a perfect example of neo-classical Cape architecture. Inside, look out for the murals depicting architectural details – dados, door cases and plinths.

The house was acquired by the De Wet family in 1806, and at the beginning of the 20th century was inhabited by Mrs Marie Koopmans-De Wet (1834–1906) and her sister. When they died it became the property of the city. The core of the collection of antiques in the house is the Koopmans-De Wet family's inheritance, and it would have been furnished as a fashionable townhouse at the beginning of the 19th century. It has a first-class collection of early Cape furniture, arranged traditionally, Dutch Delft ceramics, fine porcelain, glass and silverware.

Leaving the Koopmans-De Wet House to the right, walk up Strand Street, take the first right into Burg Street and continue for a couple of short blocks to Greenmarket Square.

Greenmarket Square

At the heart of the city, between Long Street, St George's Mall and Burg Street, cobbled **Greenmarket Square** is another surviving relic of old Cape Town. Originally a vegetable market, it's now the site of a flea market (Tues–Sun 9am–6pm) selling books, T-shirts, bric-a-brac, jewellery, boho-style clothing, shoes and sarongs, as well as all kinds of African carvings, beadwork and fabrics. At the top of the square is the Famous Butcher's Grill restaurant, an offshoot of the original Butcher's Grill on Buitengracht Street.

Although most of the surroundings have changed since the days when it was a vegetable market, there is one surviving landmark linking it to colonial times – the old Burgher Watch House, also known as the **Old Town House ❺** (open

Map on page 70

The Old Town House, displaying the Michaelis Collection of oil paintings.

BELOW: raking through the stalls on Greenmarket Square.

St George's Cathedral became famous during the apartheid era when Desmond Tutu was the Anglican Archbishop of Cape Town from 1986–95. The Archbishop, who was branded a dangerous communist by the government, ran his anti-apartheid campaign from here. In order to operate in this downtown area, the Archbishop was required to carry a pass.

RIGHT: flower seller on Trafalgar Place, off Adderley Street.

Mon–Sat 10am–5pm; tel: 021 481 3933; free, but donations welcome).

In a city bereft of a great many of its historic buildings, this is a very fine survivor. It was built in 1761 on the site of a thatched building of about 1716, and is thought to have been one of the first two-storey buildings in Cape Town. It originally housed the Burgher Council, which over the years altered and aggrandised it, then, in the 19th century, it became the magistrate's court. In 1840, when Cape Town became a municipality, the building was chosen to become the Town Hall.

It was in 1917 that the Old Town House first became an art gallery, and at the same time its interior was remodelled to have the look of a 17th-century Dutch guildhall. The interior is extremely handsome, but it's quite unlike anything you would have found in the Cape at the time. It is, in fact, a rather good example of the English Arts and Crafts movement of the late 19th century. The Dutch appearance was subsequently considered to be an appropriate setting for the **Michaelis**

Collection, a large collection of 17th-century Dutch and Flemish paintings amassed and donated by Sir Max Michaelis in 1914. The works include still lifes, portraits and landscapes.

St George's Cathedral

From Greenmarket Square, continue down Burg Street until you reach Wale Street. Just to the left you'll see **St George's Cathedral ❻** (open Mon–Fri 8.30am–4.30pm; tel: 021 424 7360 for details of services; free) at the top of St George's Street. Built in 1901 and designed by Herbert Baker, it replaced a lovely Greek Revival building which until 1954 sat alongside it. King George V, while still the Duke of Cornwall and York, laid the foundation stone.

The cathedral contains some fine stained glass, including *Christ in Triumph over Darkness and Evil* in the Great West Window, commemorating Lord Louis Mountbatten, who spent a lot of time in Cape Town during the latter stages of his life. The building is not considered one of Herbert Baker's best works, and

Cape Town's Art Deco

Art deco was the favoured architectural style in Cape Town during the 1930s. It marked a distinctive break in the way South Africans viewed themselves. No longer looking towards Britain and the colonial tradition (Victorian or neo-classical styles), South Africa's first giant corporations built towering new office blocks inspired by America, and new functions, like cinema, demanded new styles. Construction boomed as the country emerged from the Great Depression, and the price of gold rose when the gold standard was abandoned in 1932. As elsewhere in the world, art deco adapted to suit local tastes.

A good place for visitors to start is **Greenmarket Square**, three-quarters of which is 1930s, and close by the **Waalburg** (28 Wale Street, 1932). On the sumptuous **Old Mutual Building** (Darling Street, 1939) you'll find the only deco proteas, baboon and elephant heads in the world, and a stone frieze depicting the history of South Africa. On Parliament Street there are massive stone figures representing African tribesmen. A map plotting Cape Town's art deco buildings can be obtained from the Tourism Visitor Centre on Burg Street.

is more interesting, perhaps, for its political role during the last years of apartheid when Anglican Archbishop Desmond Tutu *(see margin note, page 76)* preached anti-apartheid sermons from its pulpit.

The Old Slave Lodge

Close by, at 49 Adderley Street, on the junction with Wale Street, is the Old Slave Lodge, which now houses the **Cultural History Museum** ❼ (open Mon–Fri 10am–4.30pm, Sat 9am–1pm; tel: 021 460 8242; admission charge, free Sat; audio tours available). Built in 1679, after the Castle of Good Hope, this is the second-oldest colonial building in Cape Town. It began life as a shelter for slaves of the Dutch East India Company, brought to Cape Town from India, Madagascar, Ceylon, Malaya and Indonesia in answer to the labour shortage. Following the abolition of slavery in 1834 the building became the city's first post office, then the library and then the supreme court. Today it contains an eclectic collection, which includes important ancient Greek vases, toys, silver-

ware, textiles and exhibits covering early Cape history, particularly artefacts relating to Khoisan herders. Among the numerous curiosities are postal stones found at Table Bay. Homesick mariners would leave messages inscribed with the name of their ship under a large stone in the hope that fellow sailors, explorers, merchants or missionaries travelling in the other direction would deliver them home.

But it is the building's history as a slave lodge that is most interesting, and eventually it will become a permanent museum of slavery. In the meantime, to learn more about slavery on the Cape the audio tour available at the entrance to the museum is highly recommended. It explains the original purpose of each room and describes the horrifying lives endured by the slaves.

The lodge once held an average of 500 slaves, rising to 1,000 at its peak, and also housed the colony's mentally disturbed citizens. At one point during the 18th century there were more slaves than there were free citizens at the Cape.

Also worth seeing in connection with the slave trade is the Bo-Kapp area, still inhabited by the descendants of freed slaves (see page 105), *and the Old Slave Church at 40 Long Street* (see page 86), *established in 1804 to spread Christianity among the slaves.*

LEFT:
St George's Cathedral.

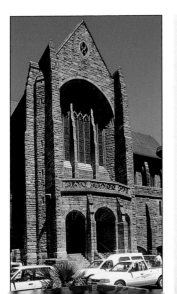

Life in the Slave Lodge

The slaves living at the Slave Lodge worked for the Dutch East India Company (VOC) in its farms, fisheries, quarries and Company Gardens. Some worked as bricklayers, bakers, blacksmiths, potters, carpenters and other trades. Mulatto slaves of part-European descent were generally given the better jobs, as well as better conditions.

Slaves could buy their freedom or were entitled to request their freedom after 30 years' good service (less in the case of mulattos), providing they were confirmed in the Dutch Reformed Church, spoke Dutch and had the means to support themselves outside the lodge. However, few attained the 30 years, as the death rate from disease and insanitary conditions was high (20–30 percent in some years). Others were too institutionalised to survive in the world outside.

Slaves who were born in the lodge were baptised and could not be sold to private individuals. They also received an education (in Dutch) up to the age of 12, something that few children living in the town received. They were taught by fellow slaves or freed slaves, who received a salary.

Detail on the magnificent baroque pulpit in the Groote Kerk.

BELOW: carrying a large load outside the Parliament building.

In 1803 Louis Michel Thibault, the Inspector of Public Buildings, described the insanitary, disease-ridden state of the lodge, which had no proper ventilation or provision for natural light. Seeing the building today, those conditions are hard to imagine – it has been beautifully restored, and is a pleasant lunch-hour retreat for nearby office workers. Nevertheless, this is an important site, since slavery had such a huge impact on the culture of South Africa and has directly affected its language, customs, cuisine, labour laws, religion and architecture. Today the Old Slave Lodge is an important leg on the International Slave Route Project established by UNESCO.

Just outside the building, in nearby Spin Street, a plaque marks the site of the Old Slave Tree where slaves were auctioned.

The Groote Kerk

At the top of Adderley Street, and just across Spin Street, is the **Groote Kerk ❽** (open Mon–Fri 10am–2pm; tel: 021 461 7044; free), the most important Dutch Reformed church in the country, and certainly the oldest in Cape Town. It was built in 1704, and is famous today for the magnificent baroque pulpit (1789) by master sculptor and wood-carver Anton Anreith and cabinet-maker Jan Graaf. Before the church was built, services were held in the castle, until Governor Willem Adriaan van der Stel decided that a new, permanent place of worship was needed.

The Anreith pulpit is still in use today, and is one of Cape Town's most treasured possessions. The lions supporting it symbolise the power of faith, the anchor is for hope and the urn on the canopy for mortality. Over the years the building was altered, and in 1841 was remodelled entirely. Now, only its steeple, which you can barely see, is original. The facades front and back are a strange mixture of Gothic and neo-classical style.

After visiting the Groote Kerk retrace your steps back up Adderley Street, past the Old Slave Lodge, to the Houses of Parliament and the Tuynhuys.

Cape Town as Legislative Capital

South Africa is unusual in having three capitals: Pretoria, the administrative capital and seat of government, Bloemfontein, the judicial capital, and Cape Town, the legislative capital. This arrangement dates from the foundation of the Union of South Africa in 1910 when agreement could not be reached on which of the four provinces, Cape, Natal, Transvaal or the Free State should contain the national capital.

Following independence in 1961, the government maintained the status quo that had prevailed previously, with non-whites excluded from national elections. Over the following years increased participation was given to coloured and Indian citizens, and in 1984 a three-chambered parliament was established consisting of one house for whites, one for coloureds and one for Indians, though whites were given greater power. Blacks were excluded from national politics until the country's first democratic elections in 1994, when Nelson Mandela and the ANC were swept to power. Today, the inconvenience of having three capitals sometimes leads to calls for power to be centralised in Pretoria, a move fiercely resisted by the Cape Province.

Parliament

At the top of Adderley Street, on the corner where it turns into Wale Street under the watchful eye of a statue of General Jans Smuts is the leafy entrance to the Avenue, the extension of the Heerengracht (now Adderley Street). To the left are the Houses of Parliament (enter from the Parliament Street side); to the right is a white stucco 19th-century building which houses the South African National Library, and beyond that the Company's Garden.

Parliament ❾, once the bastion of white supremacy, is now open to all (tours Mon–Fri 9am, 10am, 11am, booking essential and you will need to bring your passport; tel: 021 403 3683; free). The massive building of red brick and tall white pilasters was completed in 1864 using mostly imported materials. Presided over by a statue of Queen Victoria, it owes nothing to its African setting, but it's worth a visit to see how Parliament works. Ask to see the art collection and the interesting collection of early maps of the African continent.

Further up Government Avenue, just behind the Houses of Parliament, is the office of the State President, the **Tuynhuys**, once called Government House. At the Treaty of Amiens, which ratified the British occupation of the Cape, this mid-18th-century residence of the Governor of the Cape was Georgianised by Lord Charles Somerset. It was restored in the late 1960s by Gawie Fagan, who attempted to revive its earlier Dutch appearance, visible through the railings from the Avenue. Behind you now is the entrance to the Company's Garden.

Company's Garden

Right at the heart of the city, the **Company's Garden ❿** (gates opened daily at 8am and closed at 6pm) of about 6 hectares (15 acres) is all that survives of the original 18-hectare (44-acre) vegetable garden laid out by the Dutch East India Company and developed as a source of fresh fruit and vegetables for their ships as they passed by on their way between Europe and the East. Its origin dates back to 1648,

Map on page 70

The statue of Cecil John Rhodes is a focal point in the Company's Garden.

BELOW: walking through the delightful Company's Garden.

TIP

Company's Garden has a good little tearoom with a shady terrace, where you can get inexpensive hot and cold meals, cakes, cool beers and other refeshments, including daily specials.

BELOW: the skeleton of a whale in the South African Museum.

when the crew of the shipwrecked Dutch vessel *Haarlem (see page 18)* sowed vegetable seeds near a stream of fresh water coming down from Table Mountain. In 1652, the settlement's master gardener, Hendrik Boom, prepared the first beds.

Over time, as farming was established on the Cape, the Company's Garden became a botanical garden. Oaks were planted by Governor Simon van der Stel, whose master gardener laid out an elaborate system of canals that were fed by mountain springs. Pines were introduced, and so were roses, herbs and medicinal plants. In 1751 Jan Andries Auge became Superintendent of the Gardens, and was responsible for adding many indigenous species that he had collected on his trips around the Cape.

There are some very interesting specimens here, if only because of their great age. There's a Saffraan pear, which is thought to have come from Holland in the time of van Riebeeck, making it one of the first trees to have been cultivated in South Africa. There's also an Out-

eniqua yellowwood, thought to have been planted in the late 1700s, and a 17-metre (56-ft) tree aloe, believed to be the tallest in the country. There's also a black mulberry, said to have grown from a seedling from one of the original mulberry trees planted by van Riebeeck in an attempt to establish a silk industry in the Cape (the venture failed because van Riebeeck ordered the wrong kind of mulberry trees).

There are now more than 8,000 species of trees and plants here, plus a fernery, a palm grove, a herb garden, a fuchsia house and a conservatory. The abundant grey squirrels were introduced from America by Cecil John Rhodes.

Until 1803 the upper part of the Gardens was used as a zoo, and at the top of the Avenue is the so-called Lioness Gateway, with stucco animals by Anton Anreith *(see page 72)*, that once led into the Menagerie. On the left-hand side was the bird and antelope park, and to the right, the beast of prey park. The Lioness Gateway now leads

into the aviary. There are enough of these old structures left to give an idea of Louis Michel Thibault's plans to turn the area into a handsome public park (Thibault was Inspector of Public Building in the early 19th century).

The garden is hemmed in by Queen Victoria Street on the west side and the Avenue on the east. To the north it's overlooked by the National Library and to the south, beyond a more formal area of rose gardens, water gardens and fountains, is the South African Museum and the South African National Gallery.

The South African Museum

The **South African Museum** ⓫ (25 Queen Victoria Street; open daily 10am–5pm; admission charge) has permanent collections on both the natural and the human sciences. Oddly, San artefacts are exhibited alongside fossils (come here before you go fossil-hunting in the Karoo), rocks and minerals, and skeletons of animals and whales, and there's a magnificent collection of South African beadwork and other cultural items from the country's indigenous people. Among the highlights is the mysterious rock art of the San *(see below)*. This indigenous people, who were wiped off the map of South Africa but survive in the Kalahari in Namibia, are represented in life-size dioramas of their everyday life.

Also look out for the coelacanth, a prehistoric fish found in the 20th century still to be living off the coast at East London, and the Lydenburg Heads, seven ceremonial terracotta heads dating from 500 BC.

The South African sky at night is remarkable, and one of the best places to view it is the Karoo, in Sutherland, for instance. However, city-bound stargazers have the **Planetarium** (open Mon–Fri 8.30am–4.30pm, Sat and Sun 10am–4pm; tel: 021 481 3900; admission charge). Part of the South African Museum, it has a "theatre of the stars" projected onto the interior of a huge dome. The wide programme of events includes "star finder" astronomy courses, changing exhibitions (some designed for chil-

Map on page 70

Dioramas portray the lives of the San bushmen in the South African Museum.

LEFT: an example of San rock art.

The Rock Art of the San

The most interesting exhibits in the South African Museum relate to the rock art of the San, hunter-gatherer "bushmen" who lived in southern Africa until the end of the 19th century and still live in neighbouring Namibia. The examples here are perhaps no more than 200 years old, but they are of considerable interest. In particular, look out for the Linton panel, removed from a cave on a farm in the Eastern Cape in 1918. About 2 metres (6 ft), it depicts eland, a swift and powerful animal, and a supine human form with cloven hooves. It is thought that the painting represents a spiritual experience attained through trance, during which the shaman (medicine man) is at one with the animal and acquires supernatural powers to heal. The museum shows a short film of a trance dance performed by the San of today.

To learn more about the rock art read *The Mind in the Cave* by David Lewis-Williams, the leading anthropologist in this field. Lewis-Williams has found links between the rock art of the San and that of ancient Europe, such as the cave paintings at Lascaux in the Dordogne in France.

The inside of Cape Town's Great Synagogue, with its huge copper-clad dome.

dren) and field trips to the country to explore the night skies there.

Halfway along Paddock Avenue, situated amongst the old oak trees just a stone's throw from Parliament, is the **South African National Gallery** ⑫ (open Tues– Sun 10am–5pm; tel: 021 467 4660; admission charge, free Sun). One of the premier showcases of South African art, it also has an eclectic collection of European works, including British, French, Dutch and Flemish art. Ultimately, though, it's the local paintings, sculpture, ceramics, beadwork and textiles that people come here to see, and for changing exhibitions.

Cape Town's Jewish legacy

Facing the Avenue at 88 Hatfield Street is the **Jewish Museum** ⑬ (open Sun–Thur 10am–5pm, Fri 10am–2pm; tel: 021 465 1546; admission charge). As well as presenting an interesting and interactive account of the long history of the Jewish community in Cape Town, it stages some of the liveliest temporary exhibitions in town.

The museum incorporates the city's **Old Synagogue**, recognisable for its classical temple front, built in 1862. The complex also includes the Cape Town Holocaust Centre and the Jacob Gitlin Library. Next door is the **Great Synagogue**, built in 1904. There has long been a Jewish population at the Cape, but it wasn't until 1804 that freedom of worship was permitted. A large contingent of Jews arrived from Europe in the 1860s, drawn by the discovery of diamonds, and in the 1880s refugees from the pogroms in Russia coincided with the discovery of gold. South Africa has a large Jewish community to this day, and this is its oldest congregation.

The **Holocaust Centre** (same hours as the Jewish museum; tel: 021 462 5553; free) is the only one in Africa. With changing exhibits, archival documents and film footage, recreated environments and survivor testimonies, its aim is to create a place of remembrance and learning about the disastrous consequences of unchecked racial discrimination.

Rust en Vreugd

The old houses of Cape Town once had wonderful gardens. Sadly, few survive, but **Rust en Vreugd** ⑭ (78 Buitenkant Street; open Mon by appointment; tel: 021 465 3628; free), a fine Cape Dutch mansion built in 1777, has had its garden restored. It's slightly out on a limb but it is well worth coming to see, not only for the garden, but also for the William Fehr Collection of Africana – part of the bigger collection housed in the Castle of Good Hope *(see page 72)*. Drawings, etchings, watercolours and other works depict views and scenes of life in early Cape Town, historical events, and notable people and buildings.

Rust en Vreugd is a lovely and peaceful spot. Remember to look up at the facade of the building, with its lovely period fanlights and handsome architraves. The carved teak doors are almost certainly by Anton Anreith, and are the finest rococo ornament in the Cape.

Retrace your steps as far as the Company's Gardens, cross Queen Victoria Street on the west side, go over Keerom Street, and you'll come to Long Street, the liveliest as well as the longest street in central Cape Town.

Bertram House

Another old home worth visiting in this area of town is **Bertram House** ⑮ (open Mon by appointment; tel: 021 481 3940; admission charge), which belongs to the South African Cultural History Museum. It's a small, little-known museum housing the Winifred Ann Lidderdale Bequest – a collection of English porcelain, silver and 19th-century furniture. The late-Georgian, red-brick building stands at the top of the Avenue, shaded by the oaks on the university's Hidding Hall campus and facing the magnificent columned entrance to the sumptuous **Mount Nelson Hotel**, a landmark for discerning travellers since it opened in 1899. Past guests at the hotel have included Lord Kitchener, the young Winston Churchill and the Prince of Wales (later the Duke of Windsor), for whom the hotel's

Map on page 70

TIP

After visiting Bertram House you can take afternoon tea on the veranda of the Mount Nelson Hotel. This venerable establishment, which has hosted royalty and international statesmen, remains one of Cape Town's top hotels. Its buffet breakfast (before 11am) is good, too.

BELOW LEFT: the entrance to the Mount Nelson Hotel. **BELOW:** the facade of Rust en Vreugd.

Long Street is the place to come for vintage-clothing shops, second-hand bookshops and characterful cafés.

BELOW: there's an interesting variety of architecture along Long Street, from art deco to Cape Dutch.

grand entrance, the Prince of Wales Gate, was commissioned in 1925. From Mount Nelson Hotel, head back towards the centre of town along Kloof Road, which eventually leads into Long Street. Kloof Road is an interesting area for upmarket groceries and delis, with some good cafés along the way.

Diverse attractions

Long Street ⓰ is the most famous – some would say infamous – street in Cape Town. It links mountain and sea, and you can stand with your back towards the mountain at one end and see ships berthed in the dock at the other. Table Bay and the coast at Blouberg can be seen away in the distance.

For a long time it represented the heart and soul of this maritime city, and today it has many faces. Anything – and everything – happens here. There are delis, cafés, restaurants, all-day bars and nightclubs; churches and two mosques; vintage-clothing shops, bookshops, antiques and bric-a-brac shops, markets and pharmacies; banks, pawn shops and

porn shops; apartment blocks, hotels, backpackers' lodges and offices.

It's a street of seemingly endless possibilities. A man once bought some 18th-century English silver by Paul Storr in a junk shop on Long Street, and it's now in the Metropolitan Museum in New York. Less fortunate men have met beautiful women in dodgy bars here, then accompanied them home only to discover that they're not women at all, but a singular brand of South African cross-dresser commonly known as a "moffie".

It's safer by far to stick to the shopping – perhaps invest in a limited edition book with rare views of early Cape Town – or dine out on Asian or African food, or have an old-fashioned shave with a cut-throat razor, or lie around in a hot, steamy Turkish bath.

The tone of the street ranges from smart to seedy to downright sleazy, and this is the very essence of Long Street. Over the years there have been attempts to tidy it up, rid the pavement of the drunks, transvestites and the prostitutes (and the

street children), but somehow change has always been resisted.

Architectural melting pot

The buildings on Long Street are a textbook of the architectural styles that have come and gone in Cape Town. The buildings span every century, from the earliest days of the colony to the present. At No. 206 is Cape Town's most exuberant High Victorian building, awash with ornate metalwork, turrets and fancy gables. At No. 185 is the **Palm Tree Mosque** (not open to non-Muslims), converted from a house on the site early in the 19th century. The palm tree is still at the door in what was once the garden.

Long Street Baths (pool: daily 8am–7pm; Turkish Baths: women Thur, Sat, Mon and Tues am, men at all other times; tel: 021 400 3302), at the corner of Orange Street at the mountain end of Long Street, have been a city institution since they opened in 1908. The complex includes a heated swimming pool, steam and dry-heat rooms and a massage parlour.

But the most interesting sights on Long Street are generally the transient ones. Shops come and go, but there are some that are well established and worth looking out for. The **Pan-African Market** at No. 76 (open Mon–Fri 9am–5pm; tel: 021 426 4478), halfway along the street, is filled with artefacts and curios from all over Africa, including carvings, textiles, beadwork, ceramics, tableware, clothes, shoes, baskets, jewellery and music CDs and cassettes. Also on an African theme is the **African Music Store**, at 134 Long Street, selling a wide and wonderful range of music from all over the continent.

The Old Slave Church

Continue north, in the direction of the harbour. The **Sendinggestig Museum** ⓱ (open Mon–Fri 9am–4pm, Sat 9am–12 noon; tel: 021 423 6755; free) is at 40 Long Street, between Shortmarket and Strand. Also known as the Old Slave Church, this is the third-oldest church surviving in its original form in the country. It was built in 1799

Map on page 70

Enjoying the heated swimming pool at Long Street Baths.

BELOW: hanging out in one of Long Street's many bars.

Map on page 70

This item in the Gold of Africa Museum shows a chief holding an egg, symbolising the fragile nature of good governance.

BELOW: detail in the Lutheran Church.

for the Coloured congregation and was the Dutch Reformed Mission Church. Its handsome facade resembles that of the old Lutheran Church in Strand Street, with its fluted Corinthian pilasters and handsome gable. It is difficult to believe that in the 1970s the church was scheduled for demolition and for reconstruction in replica in a "Coloured township". Thankfully it received a last-minute reprieve, and today it houses a museum detailing the missions in the Cape.

Continue seaward to Strand Street, where you'll see the Gold of Africa Museum and the Lutheran Church next door.

Gold of Africa Museum

At 96 Strand Street, the **Gold of Africa Museum** ⑱ (open Mon–Sat 9.30am–5pm; tel: 021 405 1540; admission charge; audio guide available) is the city's newest museum and well worth a visit. Established by Anglo-Gold, the world's largest gold mining company, it is based on a collection originally displayed in the Barbier-

Mueller Museum in Geneva, it houses a stunning collection of gold jewellery and cultural artefacts from around the African continent. West Africa, particularly the Akan kingdoms, gets a good showing – there are examples from Mali, Senegal and Ghana – but there are items from Zimbabwe and South Africa as well, from ceremonial objects used by royalty to smaller amulets carried by traders and warriors. Pieces are beautifully displayed, with good background information on the cultural and symbolic importance of gold in African cultures.Early maps illustrate gold and other trade routes

The museum is housed in the 18th-century Martin Melck House, a fine original townhouse dating from 1788. There is a delightful courtyard café that serves coffee and cakes, an excellent selection of wine and light meals.

The Lutheran Church

Next door to the museum is the **Lutheran Church**. In 1780 the Lutheran congregation was still worshipping in an old barn in Strand Street, given to them by Martin Melck, a wealthy Lutheran merchant. In 1791 the congregation commissioned Anton Anreith to transform the barn into a church. The bulk of the facade is almost certainly his design, but in the 19th century the top half was altered and the bell tower built. It's the only known facade by Anreith.

The interior is filled with late 18th-century and early 19th-century decorative art. Like the Groote Kerk *(see page 78)* it has an Anreith-designed pulpit, rococo rather than baroque, and a lectern also by Anreith. The interior is finer than that of the Groote Kerk. With the flanking period houses – No. 96 (the Gold of Africa Museum) and No. 100 – it is part of a unique surviving 18th-century street frontage. ❏

RESTAURANTS & BARS

Restaurants

In addition to the CBD delineated by Buitengracht, Buitensingel and Buitenkant, it is worth trying the area known as De Waterkant on the north side of Buitengracht. Popular with the gay community, it is a lively source of bars, cafés and restaurants.

The Africa Café
108 Shortmarket Street. Tel: 021 422 0221. Open: D only daily, closed Sun in winter. $$$
Somewhat overpriced, Africa Café nonetheless offers pan-African cuisine, from South African to Moroccan, served by beautifully attired waitresses. Busy, central venue that fills up with tourists, so it is essential to book. Good wine list.

Anatoli Turkish Restaurant
24 Napier Street. Tel: 021 419 2501. Open: D only Tues–Sun. $$
The dining here is mostly about meze. Countless tasty morsels are brought to your table on vast trays, accompanied by chunks of hot bread for dunking into various Middle Eastern dips. The restaurant is built around a tiny internal courtyard.

Andiamo
Cape Quarter, Waterkant Street, De Waterkant. Tel: 021 421 3687. Open: B, L & D daily. $
A busy café attached to a deli and bar, Andiamo is great for Sunday brunch. For lunch there's good pasta and large, filled sandwiches bursting with interesting fillings. Good for people-watching and for nursing a cappuccino.

Beluga
The Foundry, Prestwich Street. Tel: 021 418 2948. Open: L & D Mon–Fri. D only Sat–Sun. $$
This is a busy, high-profile American-style venue for smart, young professionals. Menu varies from steaks, ostrich and game to freshly caught fish and big seasonal salads. The emphasis is on South African specialities.

Bukhara
33 Church Street. Tel: 021 424 0000. Open: L & D Mon–Sat. D only Sun. $$$
Possibly the best curry restaurant in town, Bukhara is noisy and busy, so be sure to make a reservation. The food is authentic and delicious – the butter chicken is the all-time favourite. Helpful and informative staff.

Cara Lazuli
11 Buiten Street. Tel: 021 426 2351. Open: D Mon–Sat. $
A Moroccan venue, Cara Lazuli is all about a "dining experience" rather than just a meal. Tagines and couscous are on the menu and the atmosphere is exotic. Stay afterwards and watch the belly dancer, inhale North African fragrances of cinnamon, *harissa* and crushed mint.

The Cape Colony
Mount Nelson Hotel, Orange Street, Gardens. Tel: 021 483 1850. Open: L & D daily. $$$
Smart dining at its finest, in Cape Town's favourite old colonial-style hotel, situated just outside the CBD. The global glitterati, if they're in town, will be here too, dining under a huge mural depicting the city 200 years ago. Dress up and enjoy chic Afro cuisine – like smoked crocodile with a wafer-thin *samoosa* (samosa).

Chef Pon's Asian Kitchen
12 Mill Street, Gardens. Tel: 021 465 5846. Open: D Mon–Sat. $
Everybody knows Chef

PRICE CATEGORIES

Prices for three-course dinner per person with a half-bottle of house wine:
$ = under R140
$$ = R140–200
$$$ = R200–300
$$$$ = more than R300

RIGHT: The Africa Café in Shortmarket Street is one of the best places to sample African cuisine.

Pon's Asian Kitchen. All the best-known Asian dishes are here, not least of which is the crispy duck and tom yung soup. It is busy and noisy, the wine is affordable and the Asian beers are a treat.

Chef Ristorante Italiano
3 Rose Street, De Waterkant. Tel: 021 419 6767. Open: L & D Mon–Sat. $$
An Italian classic where the pasta is home-made. The menu may be Italian but it acknowledges the African location. Smart, crowd; chic venue.

Col' Cacchio
Seeff House, 42 Hans Strydom Ave, Foreshore. Tel: 021 419 4848. Open: L & D Mon–Fri. D only Sat–Sun. This is just outside the CBD, at the junction of Hans Strydom Avenue and Loop Street. Proper pizzas are the order of the day, and the toppings are generous and varied. Big barn of a place with a rapid turnover. There are also pastas and salads. Popular at lunchtime with office workers.

Dutch
34 Napier Street, De Waterkant. Tel: 021 425 0157. Open: L & D Mon–Sat. $

PRICE CATEGORIES

Prices for three-course dinner per person with a half-bottle of house wine:
$ = under R140
$$ = R140–200
$$$ = R200–300
$$$$ = more than R300

A smallish café in trendy De Waterkant, it fills with people whiling away their time reading a newspaper-nibbling on a croquette. This is the place to meet a gorgeous stranger.

Famous Butcher's Grill
Cape Town Lodge, 101 Buitengracht Street. Tel: 021 422 0880. Open: L & D daily. $$
If you want a good, wholesome steak, cooked to perfection, then this is the place for you. It's a carnivore's delight. And they go a step further – they will match the wine to what you're eating. There is another branch on Greenmarket Square.

Five Flies
14–16 Keerom Street. Tel: 021 424 4442. Open: L & D Mon–Fri. D only Sat–Sun. $$
A historic building gives this smart, roomy restaurant huge appeal. Always busy, it attracts lawyers from the nearby courts at lunchtime and a mixed bag of regulars in the evenings. The somewhat complicated menu offers wonderful fish-and-sauce combinations, and there's a fine selection of wines.

Frieda's Café
15 Bree Street. Tel: 021 421 2404. Open: B & L Mon–Fri. B, L & D Sat. $
Come in for a quick snack or for a long lazy breakfast on a Saturday morning. Unfussy and kitted out in

retro kitchen equipment, it is popular with a youngish crowd who pop in here after trawling the vintage clothing stores on Long Street.

Ginja
121 Castle Street. Tel: 021 426 2368. Open: D daily, except Sun in winter. $$$
This is one of the city's best restaurants, serving fusion-style food with some good South African-inspired dishes. Try the Karoo lamb with green curry rub. The food is delicious, the wine list extensive and the venue has a boho-chic that attracts a sophisticated crowd who move upstairs after dinner to the venue's Shoga bar.

Khaya-Nyama
267 Long Street. Tel: 021 424 2917. Open: L & D Mon–Fri. D only Sat–Sun. $$
Africa on steroids is how some people might describe the look of this trendy city venue. A good place to sample game. You can order all sorts, from a kudu steak to marinated warthog ribs.

Madame Zingara
192 Loop Street. Tel: 021 426 2458. Open: D only Mon–Sat. $$
Laid-back bohemian dining room with noisy diners, loud music and excellent food – lots of it. It's swinging at weekends, so a good place to come with friends and let your hair down.

Mesopotamia
Cnr Long and Church streets. Tel: 021 424 4664. Open: D only daily. $$
This is the only Kurdish restaurant in South Africa. Recline on cushions on the floor to eat the authentic Kurdish food (the *iskender* – oven-roasted diced lamb with bread, garlic yoghurt and tomato sauce – and the *beyti* – minced-chicken kebab rolled in Nan bread with garlic yoghurt – are delicious). There's tons of atmosphere and hookahs to smoke, kelims on the floor and belly dancers to entertain. It's always busy, mostly with a young crowd.

Moja
98 Shortmarket Street, Heritage Square. Tel: 021 423 4989. Open: L & D Mon–Fri. D only Sat.
If you like fondues, then this is worth trying. It's pleasantly messy and a great place to come with friends. Chunks of meat or fish are cooked on lava rocks and then dipped in the fondue.

95 Keerom Street
95 Keerom Street. Tel: 021 422 0765. Open: L & D Mon–Fri. D only Sat. $$$
This is Milan come to Cape Town. It is smart, cool and fashionable, attracting high-profile editors, film stars, bankers and rich Italians. The food is swankily simple; fresh line-fish with mashed potato,

gorgonzola-walnut gnocchi and so on. It is owner-run, so the service is personal. After dinner move on to Rhodes House next door, the city's smartest club and part of the same property.

The Nose Wine Bar

Cape Quarter, Dixon Street, De Waterkant. Tel: 021 425 2200. Open: B, L & D daily. $$
Situated in the heart of this trendy area, The Nose is a good option for sitting with friends over a glass or three of goodwine (available by the glass). The food is nothing special – just the usual array of burgers, toasted sandwiches and pastas – but it's all about the wine and the location and the friendly, helpful staff.

La Petite Tarte

Shop A11 Cape Quarter, Dixon Street, De Waterkant. Tel: 021 425 9077. Open: B & L Mon–Sat. $
A sweet French-style patisserie with melt-in-the-mouth dishes to eat. Come here for breakfast to find the best croissants in Cape Town. It's also something of a teahouse – choose from a wide selection of teas.

Savoy Cabbage

101 Hout Street. Tel: 021 424 2626. Open: L & D Mon–Fri, D only Sat. $$$

The Savoy Cabbage is famous for serving offal in all its forms (how about tripe with chorizo?), although other tastes are well catered for. What about lamb and rice-stuffed cabbage leaves poached in broth? Contemporary-style venue in landmark setting.

Strega Ristorante

Heritage Square, 100 Shortmarket Street. Tel: 021 423 4889. Open: L & D Mon–Fri. D only Sat. $
If you want a rumbustious Friday night out with friends, come to Strega. Everybody seems to know everybody else here. Dine inside or out, in the courtyard, which is great in the summer. Expect good pasta, pizza or line-fish, amongst other things.

Tank, Cape Quarter

Dixon Street, De Waterkant. Tel: 021 419 0007. Open: D Mon. L & D Tues–Sun. $$$
Ultra-trendy venue where you come to drink blue cocktails at the bar. The restaurant is known for its Pacific Rim-style menu; but it's a very cosmopolitan place and also known for its great sushi. Portions are small and decorative. It has nightclub lighting which makes catching a clear glimpse of the food on your plate rather difficult, but it is great for people-watching.

RIGHT: testing the pizzas at Col' Cacchio.

Veranda

Metropole Hotel, 38 Long Street. Tel: 021 424 7247. Open B, L & D daily. $$
The Metropole is Cape Town's coolest hotel, popular with a funky, gay crowd who frequent the very popular M Bar *(see below)*. The food in Veranda is cosmopolitan with a South African twist. The signature dish is a delicious duck *bobotie*.

Bars

In many of the aforementioned "restaurants" food is optional, the dividing line between bar and restaurant being fairly inidstinct in many Cape Town establishments.

In addition, De Waterkant, Long Street and Kloof Road are full of all kinds of bars.

On Long Street, try

Kennedy's Cigar Bar at No. 251 for a mellow evening spent sipping cocktails (also good for a late-night malt whisky and a cigar), or try the **M Bar** on the first floor of the fashionable Metropole Hotel at No. 38, where you will find a sophisticated, laid-back atmosphere.

Older customers in search of a chic venue for pre-dinner cocktails should try the **Planet** champagne and cocktail bar at the Mount Nelson Hotel on the corner of Orange Street.

At the other end of the scale, **Raffiki's**, on Kloof Road, is a good place to come to hang out with a mixed bunch of locals as well as young foreigners. Its balcony bar is always heaving, and you can also play pool.

THE VICTORIA AND ALFRED WATERFRONT

The regeneration of Cape Town's historic harbour has been a huge success. Capetonians of all ages and races, as well as tourists, come here to socialise, shop and hang out

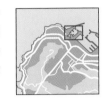

Map on page 94

Known locally simply as the Waterfront, the revitalised harbour of Cape Town, historically one of the world's busiest ports, is a model example of how to breathe life back into a dying area without losing its original function or sacrificing its character. It is still a working harbour with a thriving ship repair business, but it has a range of new uses, among which shopping, dining and entertainment are prominent.

The V&A Waterfront is home to hotels, restaurants and cafés, museums, an aquarium and craft workshops. It has a buzzing street life, and there are buskers, trees to sit under, benches overlooking the water, and covered shopping areas (the shops here remain open until about 8pm) selling everything from the latest Italian fashions to fresh fish. You could come here simply for an evening stroll along the quays. Alternatively you can test-drive the latest BMW, listen to music, meet your friends, watch movies, taste local wines, read the works of South Africa's new and upcoming authors, sail your yacht or catch a helicopter for a trip around the Cape Peninsula.

Amid all this, the V&A Waterfront retains its role as a harbour; passenger ships dock while you sip cappuc-cino on the quay, and it is still home to the city's colourful fishing fleet. This is also the place to come for all kinds of boat trips, including those to Robben Island. Serious yachts are berthed here, in the Marina Basin behind the Cape Grace Hotel, and every year some of the world's finest yachtsmen and women arrive in Cape Town to participate in various prestigious yachting events, such as the Volvo Ocean Race, the St Helena Bay Challenge and the BT Global Challenge.

BELOW:
the Waterfront is a great place to stop and stare.

History of the harbour

What began as a tiny staging post for ships putting in at the Cape to restock their supplies on the long and often gruelling journey between Europe and the East had, by the beginning of the 20th century, become an industrialised port serving the considerable demands of its imperial owners. The Anglo-Boer War had the most dramatic effect on its development. Between 1881 and 1899 shipping in Cape Town trebled and the docks could hardly cope. New jetties were constructed, cranes purchased and warehouses were built. The early buildings you see today date from this period. They centre on the two harbour basins commemorating Queen Victoria and her son Alfred, built between 1860 and 1920.

In 1980 Cape Town architect Gawie Fagan proposed regenerating the basins, which, too small for modern container vessels, had fallen into disrepair by the 1960s. In 1988 Fagan's brainchild became a reality, when the port authority was privatised and the Victoria and Alfred Waterfront Company came into being. The project had wide implications for the identity of the city as a whole, as old buildings were restored or adapted for new uses. The North Quay became a hotel and a small shopping mall, while Victoria Wharf was turned into a much larger mall with cinemas, restaurants and another hotel. Since then several other cities around the world have copied the Cape Town model and revived their own degenerating docklands.

The BMW Pavilion

There are two reasons for visiting the **BMW Pavilion** ❶ (Mon–Fri 9am–11pm, Sat and Sun 9am–11pm; tel: 021-419 5850; free). First, you can see the very latest BMW cars and motorbikes before they're available to the public, and browse among the BMW accessories at their Lifestyle Store; secondly, the pavilion houses the **IMAX Theatre** (tel: 021 419 7365; Mon–Sun 10am–10pm; admission charge). Showing 3-D films on a five-storey screen, with a mega surround-sound system, it allows viewers to get up close and personal

with places and creatures they might never otherwise see – or even know about. The films range from a safari in the South African bush (particularly good if you haven't had the opportunity to visit any of the country's game reserves) to expeditions into outer space or to the bottom of the deepest oceans.

Close by, in Portswood Road, are three hotels: Breakwater Lodge (originally the Breakwater Prison), The Commodore and The Portswood.

Consumer choice

One of the smartest shopping malls in the country, **Victoria Wharf ❷** (tel: 021-408 7600; daily 9am–9pm) is a magnet for locals and tourists alike. There's plenty of parking in a subterranean garage, and there are lifts and escalators to the main floors. If all you have is one day for shopping in Cape Town, then this is the best place to head. There are shops selling local fashion labels such as YDE, Juanita Pacheco, Sun Godd'ess, Marion & Lindie and Naartjie, as well as international ones such as Alfred

Dunhill, Dolce & Gabbana and the menswear shop and label Fabiani.

There are also plenty of places to go for home accessories and decor items (for example, @Home, Biggie Best, Carrol Boyes and Nocturnal Affair) as well as curios – African Image, Out of Africa and Out of the World are the best. People also pick up their weekly groceries here, at branches of the South African stalwarts Woolworths and Pick 'n' Pay, as well as fine wines and specialist deli items (Vaughan Johnson's Wine shop and Willoughby & Co.).

Exclusive Books, Wordsworth and CNA have a wide range of local and internationally published books, magazines and newspapers (Exclusive Books also has a great coffee shop where you can read while you sip.) There are plenty of restaurants for all purses, inexpensive fast-food joints, fish-and-chip takeaways and numerous busy cafés and bars. There are two cinema complexes, with one – the Cinema Nouveau – specialising in art house movies.

Map on page 94

The Table Bay Hotel, one of several luxurious places to stay on the Waterfront.

BELOW: Victoria Wharf offers late-night shopping and dining.

For individually designed crafts try Red Shed Workshop in Dock Road.

At the east end of the shopping mall is one of Cape Town's most luxurious places to stay, the **Table Bay Hotel**. The hotel also has direct links to Quay 6 and Jetty 2 where luxury cruise liners dock.

Creative crafts

In Dock Road, but more easily accessed from Victoria Wharf shopping Mall, the **Red Shed Craft Workshop ❸** (daily 9am–9pm; free) is a showcase for all kinds of crafts. There are fabric printers, furniture makers, jewellers and ceramicists, as well as people telling fortunes, offering tattoos or selling snacks. It's worth having a wander around, and you just might find something a bit more unusual than the pan-African goods on sale at the enormous African Trading Store on the Pierhead.

Linking Victoria Wharf with Alfred Mall, **Market Square ❹** is an open space for exhibitions and

fairs in season. To one side is the **Amphitheatre**, a venue for concerts, festival events *(see page 96)* and street theatre, and a popular meeting point.

Just below the Amphitheatre, along Quay 5, you can pick up one of a variety of boat trips (these are particularly magical around sunset) and also enquire about booking a helicopter ride over Cape Town and the Pensinula.

Alfred Mall

On North Quay and just to the west of Pierhead is **Alfred Mall**, at the quieter end of the V&A Waterfront. It has a variety of little shops, cafés and coffee shops and is directly linked to the **Victoria & Alfred Hotel**, fashioned from the historic 1904 North Quay Warehouse. Situated right in the heart of the docks, it is another great place to stay. From the hotel windows you can see, hear and smell the passing

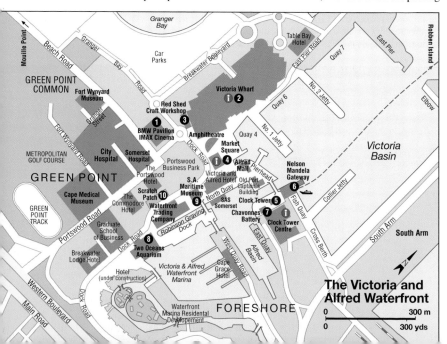

The Victoria and Alfred Waterfront

0   300 m

0   300 yds

boat traffic and watch the seals playing in the water, while all the amenities of the Waterfront are just a stone's throw away.

Clock Tower Centre

Follow the line of the quay to the Pier Head and the swing bridge (which regularly opens to admit the passage of large vessels between Victoria and Alfred basins) until you reach the distinctive **Clock Tower 5**, which may well have been your starting point for a tour of the Waterfront if you approached it on foot from the city centre. The Victorian tower is a famous city landmark. Built as the Port Captain's office in 1883, it overlooks Victoria Basin and marks the original entrance to the docks. With its pointed windows and little pinnacled belfry, it has a distinctly Gothic look. The tower now forms part of Emily's, an upmarket restaurant (the balcony makes a fine, if rather conspicuous, dining spot) , but even if you are not intending to eat here you are welcome to take a peek inside the tower to view its ornate interior.

There are benches in the sun, cafés and places to eat around the tower, and the **Clock Tower Centre** has a small number of boutiques for clothing, sunglasses and so on, as well as the **Tourism Centre** (tel: 021 405 4500). This centre is open later than the downtown branch, and is a good place to pick up information about tours and activities in and around Cape Town.

Boat trips to Robben Island

Close to the Clock Tower, adjacent to Fish Quay where the fishing boats dock, is the **Nelson Mandela Gateway 6** (tel: 021-413 4200; daily 7.30am–6pm), the point of departure (and the place to make bookings) for trips to Robben Island, Cape Town's 'Alcatraz'. Famous for holding Nelson Mandela for some 18 years of his 27-year imprisonment, it also held a host of other black and coloured anti-apartheid activists (whites were held elsewhere); the former maximum security prison *(see pages 102–3 for more details)* is now a UNESCO World Heritage Site of immense importance. A

Map on page 94

The Victorian Clock Tower is a useful landmark on the Waterfront.

BELOW: catching the catamaran to Robben Island.

What's Happening on the Waterfront?

There is always some kind of entertainment going on at the Waterfront, from buskers to fully-blown festivals and other annual events, many of them free. These are some of the highlights. For further information, tel: 021-408 7600.

JANUARY

Sounds of Summer (early Jan)
A series of music concerts including big bands and classics, held in the amphitheatre. Free.

Jazzathon (mid-Jan)
A four-day festival of jazz and other music promoting South African musicians. Venue: amphitheatre. Free.

FEBRUARY

Festival of Rhythm and Romance (mid-Feb)
Music throughout the Waterfront, from grand marches to Afro-jazz, rock and Cape sounds.

Aqua Opera
The Cape Philharmonic, a mass choir and the city's best new voices perform at North Wharf and the V&A Marina. Free.

APRIL

Club Crew World Championship Dragon Boating (mid-Apr)

One of the leading events on the International Dragon Boats calendar. Held at Jetty 2 and Victoria Basin.

Freedom Day Sing-a-thon
Presented by the Cape Town Opera and the V&A Waterfront, this is seven hours of popular opera, held at the amphitheatre. Free.

MAY

The Cape Times-V&A Waterfront Wine Festival (early May)
Meet the winemakers in Market Square and taste wine from over 90 of the Cape's top estates. Admission fee.

JULY

The V&A Waterfront Childrens' Festival
A festival for children and teenagers, held in Market Square.

AUGUST

Cape Times-V&A Waterfront-Vodacom Women of Worth Workshops (early Aug)
In the run-up to National Womens' Day, this event features inspirational female speakers.

National Womens' Day (9 Aug)
This tribute includes some of Cape Town's top female performers.

Winter Food Fair (mid-Aug)
Lots of exhibitors and demonstrations in the food theatre in Market Square.

V&A Waterfront Music Week Festival (last week of Aug)
South African music in the amphitheatre.

SEPTEMBER

Spring Flower Show. Displays of indigenous and exotic flora, landscaping, etc.

Blessing of the Fishing Fleet (mid–late Sept)
The Portuguese Welfare Association blesses fishing boats for a safe and plentiful season. Traditional folk dancing, music and food.

NOVEMBER

International Dragon Boat Festival
An exciting weekend of dragon boating, with lion dancers and dragon dancers thrown in.

DECEMBER

Festive Season Choir Festival (mid-Dec)
Held in the amphitheatre, this event features some of the city's best-known choirs.

Sunsetter Music Festival (last week of Dec)
A series of very popular sunset concerts at the amphitheatre. ❏

LEFT: entertaining the crowds.

penal colony from the earliest colonial days, it's celebrated now as a symbol of reconciliation.

The Robben Island catamarans (tel: 021-419 1300; vessels leave daily, 9am–3pm, on the hour; admission charge) will take you to the island on a 3½-hour round trip, which includes a coach tour of the island and a tour of the prison, guided by an ex-prisoner. It is highly advisable to book your trip in advance, as this is one of the most popular excursions in the city, and if you just turn up you may well be disappointed. There are set departure and return times so plan your schedule accordingly.

Chavonnes Battery

Underneath the new BoE/Nedcor building, on the south side of the Waterfront, are the 18th-century remains of **Chavonnes Battery ❼** (tel: 021-416 6230; Mon–Fri 9am–5pm, Sat–Sun 10am–5pm), a military installation built by the Dutch East India Company. It was discovered when the nearby Clock Tower Centre was under construction in

1999. An intrinsic part of the Cape's original fortifications, the Chavonnes Battery most probably remained in use under British rule during the 19th century.

Two Oceans Aquarium

Just to the west of Victoria Wharf, in Dock Road, is the **Two Oceans Aquarium ❽** (tel: 021-418 3823; daily 9.30am–6pm; admission charge), celebrating the meeting point of two very different oceans. The imaginatively designed three-level building contains more than 3,000 fish, invertebrates, mammals, birds, reptiles and plants, from sharks to seals, penguins to plankton, turtles to clown fish. Check out the Predators Tank for ragged-tooth sharks and stingrays; the mesmerising Kelp Forest, a habitat found off South Africa's west coast; and the Cape seals, whose ducking and diving can be viewed at basement level.

There are opportunities to don a wet suit and dive with the sharks (you must be an experienced diver), or you can feed the fish, touch a variety of sea creatures in shallow tanks, and,

Cape Town is rightly proud of its distinguished maritime past.

BELOW: shark overhead in the Two Oceans Aquarium.

All kinds of boat trips depart from the Waterfront, ranging from a 30-minute harbour cruise to a 1½-hour sunset cruise in Table Bay. The Waterfront is also the place to take a helicopter ride over the peninsula.

RIGHT: the lighthouse at Green Point.

with the help of the very friendly staff, study the tiniest form of aquatic life under a microscope. Children of all ages love the Aquarium, as will any adult with fond memories of delving in rock pools as a child.

SA Maritime Museum

Virtually next door to the Aquarium is the **SA Maritime Museum** ❾ (tel: 021 405 2880; daily 10am–4.45pm; admission charge; www.aquarium.co.za). Though rather traditional in its presentation, it is nonetheless an essential venue if you want to make sense of Cape Town the maritime city. It illuminates the long history of shipping in this part of the world. There's a large collection of model ships, a history of Table Bay Harbour and a display documenting the huge array of shipwrecks littering the Cape coastline, many of which can be seen on walks along the beaches and the coastal paths.

Look for the diorama explaining the purpose of the wartime **SAS Somerset**, moored close by (daily 10am–5pm; separate admission charge), the last of the boom defence vessels used to protect harbours from enemy submarines during World War II. Built on Tyneside, England in 1941, the ship was brought to South Africa in 1942, where it served in Saldanha Bay, a large industrial port northwest of Cape Town.

All that glistens

Just across Dock Road from the SA Maritime Museum is the aptly named **Scratch Patch** ❿ (tel: 021 419 9429; daily 9am–5.30pm; free, but you are required to spend a minimum of R10); the inspiration behind this place was the amazing variety of minerals in South Africa. You can have fun picking out your favourite stones from colourful heaps scattered about, have them weighed, then take them home and keep them in deep bowls on the coffee table. Or you might like to choose a more serious gem from **Mineral World** (admission free), including rare and unusual specimens, some of which have been turned into jewellery. Gleaned from

Rock Pool Riches

More than 2,000 marine invertebrate and vertebrate species have been identified along the southern African coastline from Namibia to Mozambique, and as many as 33 percent of them occur on the Cape Peninsula, which makes up only 3 percent of this coastline. All 24 species of fish that you find in the little rock pools of the Cape are endemic to southern Africa, and the large number of seaweed species found along the southern African coast reaches its highest density around the Cape.

The Cape's west coast is characterised by dense kelp beds, particularly sea bamboo and split-fan kelp, sheltering sea urchins, mussels, abalone (perlemoen) and rock lobster. And this is where you find rich troves of hake, pilchards and anchovy. The greater diversity of the east coast makes it even richer, with Indo-Pacific fish, including sharks, coming down even as far as False Bay.

Learn more about the marine life of the Cape at the Two Oceans Aquarium and explore it close up for yourself in the rock pools of the peninsula, the best of which are at Sea Point and St James near Muizenberg.

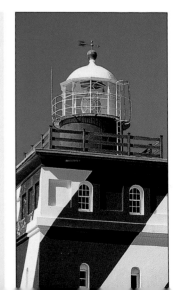

across Southern Africa, the stones here are an indication of the extraordinary wealth lying beneath the surface of this part of the world. Children also enjoy Scratch Patch, and another, bigger and better branch, can be found in Simon's Town (see page 158).

Mouille Point

The V&A Waterfront is a self-contained area, cut off from the rest of the city centre by major roads and the ocean, so most visitors do not venture further around the shoreline to **Mouille Point**, even though the Cape Town Explorer links the two and operates a regular bus service. Until recently this was the last stretch of undeveloped coastline in the heart of the city, but Mouille Point is now cloaked in new upmarket apartment blocks and other luxury developments, their sweeping sea views helping to push their prices sky-high.

The area gets its name from a mole (*moilje* in Dutch) that formed part of Cape Town's harbour in the 18th century. This is long gone, but if you

come up here on a stormy day you'll see the kind of tremendous waves that swept innumerable ships on to the rocks at this point. The remains of one such casualty can still be seen.

Green Point

To the southwest of Mouille Point is **Green Point**, only a small stretch of which fronts the sea. **Green Point Common**, a protected area with a stadium and golf course, was originally common pastureland for local farmers. The lighthouse here, constructed in 1824, still acts as a beacon for ships entering and leaving the harbour, but its handsome red and white striped bulk is today practically dwarfed by the new apartment blocks behind. On Sundays and public holidays a popular flea market sets up in the main carpark of Green Point Stadium.

Green Point stretches over the Common and up onto the flank of Signal Hill. It is a lovely neighbourhood characterised by 19th-century terraced houses and steep old streets. To the north of Green Point lies Sea Point (see page 150). ❏

Map on page 94

BELOW: the Sunday flea market at Green Point Stadium.

RESTAURANTS & BARS

Restaurants

The V&A Waterfront is an extremely popular place to come to eat, not just for tourists who, nervous of wandering around Cape Town's downtown area at night, like its safe environment, but for locals too, who like to come here after work. This listing also includes a few restaurants at Green Point and Mouille Point, a little further along Beach Road.

PRICE CATEGORIES

Prices for three-course dinner per person with a half-bottle of house wine:
$ = under R140
$$ = R140–200
$$$ = R200–300
$$$$ = more than R300

The V&A Waterfront
The Atlantic
The Table Bay Hotel, V&A Waterfront. Tel: 021 406 5688. Open: B & D daily. $$$.
The decor and ambience are rather overbearing in this smart hotel restaurant. The food, however, is worth coming for, particularly if it is a special occasion. It's fine dining with silver-service, but expect interesting twists on old favourites.

Baia
Upper Level, Victoria Wharf, V&A Waterfront. Tel: 021 421 0935. Open: L & D daily. $$$$
A tourist-crowded venue where the food and drink will cost you an arm and a leg. However,

the choice of seafood here is legendary, and most of it is caught locally. There's a wine list to match.

Balducci's
Lower Level, Victoria Wharf, V&A Waterfront. Tel: 021 421 6002. Open: B, L & D daily. $$
www.balduccis.co.za
Popular, high-visibility café-bar-restaurant well situated for people watching in the V&A Waterfront. The busy terrace is especially popular in the early evening. The full breakfast is a must, as are the Californian-type lunch salads and burgers, but there is a large and eclectic range of other possibilities, from South African game to Thai green currry or sushi. There's also great coffee and a popular wine list. Arrange to meet your friends here after shopping or simply meet for a glass of wine before a film.

Belthazar Restaurant & Wine Bar
153, V&A Waterfront. Tel: 021 421 3753. Open: L & D daily. $$$
www.belthazar.co.za
People primarily come here to drink wine by the glass (there are around

100 such wines to choose from), and it's very popular indeed. The food is simple but excellent: superb fillet and T-bone steaks and an extensive range of seafood. The attached shop sells chefs' knives, glassware and T-shirts as well as beef and sauces.

Den Anker Bar & Restaurant
Pierhead, V&A Waterfront. Tel: 021 419 0249. Open: L & D daily. $$$
Prominently situated on the Pierhead, Den Anker has great views of the passing scene, including the comings and goings of the fishing boats and yachts. It is a large, bustling place, serving Belgian food such as marrow on toast and bowls of mussels and fries.

Emily's
202 Clock Tower, V&A Waterfront. Tel: 021 421 1133. Open: L & D daily. D only Sun, Mar–Nov. $$
Occupying the famous Victorian Clock Tower near the Pierhead, this is a famous Cape Town establishment. It serves inventive South African dishes that impress and amaze in equal measure. Classics have been

LEFT: the V&A Waterfront has plenty of places to choose from, most with outside terraces.

updated and typical South African dishes have been borrowed from the kitchen table and smartened up.

one.waterfront

The Cape Grace Hotel, V&A Waterfront. Tel: 021 418 0520. Open: B, L & D daily. $$$.
www.capegrace.co.za.
This is one of the nicest hotel dining rooms in the city. The interior decoration picks up on an African theme which carries over into the food and wine. Exotic combinations of local specialities: what about milk-poached kingklip, or a curried risotto? The food is exceptional. After dinner visit Bascule, the convivial terrace bar (see Bars).

Willoughby's

Lower Level, Victoria Wharf, V&A Waterfront. Tel: 021 418 6116. Open: L & D daily. $$
It may be situated deep inside the V&A's main shopping centre, with no ocean views, but this venue serves the best fish in town and is always packed. Come here for a broad range of impeccably prepared dishes, from sushi to good old English-style fish and chips with a glass of champagne. You can't book, so just turn up and wait your turn. Also sells deli items and wet fish.

Green Point/ Mouille Point

Bravo

121 Beach Road, Mouille Point. Tel: 021 439 5260. Open: B, L & D daily. $
On the ground floor of the upmarket Splendido apartment block, Bravo is a stylish Italian-inspired restaurant with a relaxed terrace. A great spot to watch the sun set. Good anti pasti, pasta and main-course fare, as well as pizzas.

Mario's

89 Main Road, Green Point. Tel: 021 439 6644. Open: L & D daily except Tues and Sun. $$
A neighbourhood favourite that has an extensive menu of Italian country dishes such as osso bucco (stew made with knuckle of veal). It's comfort food of the very best kind, served in simple, unadorned surroundings by the family who own and run it.

Pigalle

57 Somerset Road, Green Point. Tel: 021 421 4848. Open: L & D Mon–Sat. $$
If you like the idea of a dinner-dance, then Pigalle is for you. There's a live band, lots of red plush on the walls, floor and banquettes, chandeliers and bling. It's the kind of place in which you could comfortably wear a cocktail dress. Come with a party of people, because all the tables are huge. Great steaks and fantastic prawns.

Sérénité Lifestyle Bistro

87–91 Beach Road, Mouille Point. Tel: 021 434 2950. Open: B, L & D daily. $
For the healthiest food in town. The food concept is linked to the adjoining spa; come for a make-over or massage, then slip round to the café in your robe for a "Nurturing Ritual" lunch. Or just come for a salad lunch which you'll wash down with freshly juiced carrot and beetroot.

Wakame

Cnr Beach Road and Surrey Place, Mouille Point. Tel: 021 433 2377. Open: L & D daily. $$.
Busy seaside restaurant and sushi bar with a fantastic terrace overlooking the ocean. Expect Pacific Rim food with Asian-style fish, meat and poultry dishes and a sprinkling of classic European and American fare. There's also excellent sushi. A fashionable crowd comes here, sometimes just for a drink.

Zero 932

79 Main Road, Green Point. Tel: 021 439 6306. Open: L & D daily. $
A Belgian venue renowned for its hefty pots of mussels with frites and mayonnaise. Alternatively, try the beef and Leffe-beer pie served with mash. Saturday lunchtime is great; sit out on the terrace and watch the world go by.

There are South African wines available, but you should really go for the Belgian beer which they serve in authentic beer glasses.

Bars

Many of the restaurants listed above also operate as bars, including **Balducci's** and **Wakame**, two fashionable but relaxed venues, the former on the Waterfront, the other at Mouille Point. One of the best bars on the Waterfront is the **Bascule**, the busy whisky bar and wine cellar overlooking the marina at the Cape Grace Hotel. It offers more than 400 whiskies, an extensive wine list and interesting nibbles and platters.

If you want to sample some of South Africa's best beers, pay a visit to **The Ferryman's Tavern** on East Pier Road, which has a beer garden, or **Mitchell's**, East Pier Road, which has its own brewery.

For a mellow evening of good jazz and good wine, try **Manenbergs** (tel: 021 421 5639) at the Clock Tower.

Mouille Point is a fine spot for enjoying a sundowner (providing it isn't windy). Further along the Atlantic Seaboard are Sea Point and Camps Bay (see pages 150–4), the latter packed with fashionable restaurants and cocktail bars.

ROBBEN ISLAND

Robben Island may seem like a formidable fortress island, but the political prisoners incarcerated here turned it into a university of the struggle

The most evocative symbol of the apartheid era is undoubtedly Robben Island, the maximum-security prison where Nelson Mandela spent 18 years of his 27-year imprisonment. Other important prisoners included Pan Africanist founder Robert Sobukwe, Walter Sisulu and Govan Mbeke, father of the current president. The island, which was awarded World Heritage Status in 1999, is now run as a museum by former political prisoners and their ex-guards, an example of the spirit of reconciliation that has generally prevailed since the end of apartheid.

To find out more about life in the prison, in particular the extraordinary resilience, resourcefulness and solidarity of the political prisoners, read Nelson Mandela's autobiography *Long Walk to Freedom*.

LEFT: the lookout tower. The only prisoner to escape from Robben Island was one of its first: Makana, imprisoned here after leading 10,000 Xhosa in the Battle of Grahamstown in 1819.

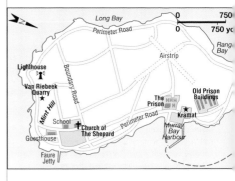

BELOW: Nelson Mandela's cell in Section B. The cells are about 1 metre (3 ft) wide. Each prisoner was given three blankets and a grass mat to sleep on. The cells were perpetually damp.

ABOVE: this image of Nelson Mandela and fellow prisoner Walter Sisulu was one of the few photographs Mandela allowed to be taken during his incarceration on Robben Island. It was taken by a British journalist working for London's *Daily Telegraph*. In general, activists felt it was demeaning to be photographed as a prisoner, and photographs could not be taken without their consent unless authorised by the Commissioner of Prisons.

BELOW: Robben Island ("Seal Island") is a ruggedly beautiful spot 11 km (7 miles) from Cape Town. Its south coast offers fine views over Table Bay, but few prisoners ever saw them. A visit to the island today includes a coach tour of the island.

THE MAIN POINTS OF INTEREST

A visit to Robben Island comprises a coach tour of the island to take in some of the more scattered features, followed by a guided tour of the main block, conducted by an ex-political prisoner.

Robert Sobukwe's Prison House It was here that the founder and leader of the Pan Africanist Congress was detained without charge for a full six years after his sentence ended. When Sobukwe was eventually released he was kept under house arrest.

The Lime Quarry Many of the political prisoners spent their days mining lime. But the quarry *(see below)* was also an important arena for communication and education concerning the struggle.

Section B This is the corridor on which Nelson Mandela's cell was situated. His cell can only be seen through the bars, but others can be accessed. You can listen to recordings of some former inmates.

The Exercise Yard As conditions on the island improved during the latter stages of apartheid, tennis was introduced to the exercise yard. Unknown to the guards, the political prisoners hid messages inside the balls which they then lobbed into the quarters of regular prisoners on the other side of the yard. The guards imagined that the prisoners were simply bad shots.

ABOVE: the lime quarry where Mandela and other prisoners spent their days labouring. The small cave was effectively used as a clandestine classroom, though the guards, who never bothered to check, imagined the prisoners used it as a lavatory.

BO-KAAP

On the slopes of Signal Hill, Bo-Kaap was traditionally populated by the descendants of Cape Town's slaves, brought here from Asia by the East India Company. Their legacy is apparent in the area's attractive architecture and tasty cuisine, known as Cape Malay

The old Bo-Kaap district of Cape Town is also sometimes known as Schotschekloof, taking that name from a pre-existing farm (the homestead survives much altered in Upper Dorp Street). It's a vibrant district on the slopes of Signal Hill, and, now that District Six has vanished, it is the place to find the real flavour of old Cape Town. Also sometimes known as the Old Malay Quarter, it is bounded by Wale, Rose and Waterkant streets and to the north by Signal Hill. "Bo-Kaap" means "above Cape Town".

Uniquely in Cape Town, you can walk the streets in this lovely neighbourhood and see people sitting on their high *stoeps*. They watch you pass by, neighbours chat over the wall, and children play ball on the cobbled streets. It's not a big district, but it is densely packed, and its flavour is not unlike what you might find in an Arabic city somewhere in the eastern Mediterranean or perhaps in the old quarter of a city in Sicily. Spicy cooking smells waft up from the kitchens, Muslim women cover their heads as you pass, and you can hear muted conversations and muffled radio sounds from deep within the labyrinth of buildings.

There are bakeries, shops selling spices, ad hoc cafés set up in people's houses, butchers, tailors, and artisans fixing cars and bikes. There are many mosques in the district; indeed, a characteristic sound of the area is the muezzin's daily calls to prayer.

Highlights of the area

Visitors come to Bo-Kaap to see its attractive early Cape Dutch and Cape Georgian houses, to visit the little Bo-Kaap Museum and to absorb the atmosphere of the neighbourhood streets. The area is credited with having been the birthplace

Map on page 106

LEFT:
one of Bo-Kaap's mosques.
BELOW
Wale Street.

TIP

To get the most out of a visit to Bo-Kaap, it is a good idea to take a guided tour. Tana-bara Tours specialises in walking tours of the area. Their tour (duration two hours) includes the Bo-Kaap Museum, notable mosques and architecture, shrines at the Tana Baru burial ground, and tea and traditional Malay cakes. Tel: 021 424 0719 or email: info@bokaap.co.za

of Islam in South Africa and also the location of the origin of the Afrikaans language.

Today Bo-Kaap has an insular feel, and you may feel as though you're intruding. But that's not true, particularly if you meet the residents on a guided walk of the district.

Architectural gems

Bo-Kaap was originally an area of *huurhuisies*, little houses for rent, put up by the landowner Jan de Waal on his property Walendorp in the 1780s. Wale Street, today a major city artery running from east to west and up the slopes of Signal Hill, was named after it. It was during this period that the architectural character of the district emerged: rows of flat-roofed houses with two rooms at the front facing the street and a narrow passage up the middle. Many have little roofless *stoeps* in front of them, and a courtyard at the back in which inhabitants can cool off in summer. Originally

roofs were made of a mixture of whale oil and molasses, and were hidden behind a curved parapet. The perfect example of this is the Bo-Kaap Museum building (*see page 108*), once a *huurhuisie*, dating from around 1763. Many homes have their original sash windows – and original glazing (rare in an inner-city district, but possibly only because people were too poor to alter it).

Bo-Kaap proper, and the adjacent streets, make up Cape Town's largest concentration of architecture predating 1850. Some are still lived in by descendants of the original owners. Many have been restored and are painted in distinctive bright colours.

The people of Bo-Kaap

Bo-Kaap was also a district of artisans brought in to assist with the development of a quickly growing town. As the town developed, the Europeans who lived here tended to move on to places like Woodstock

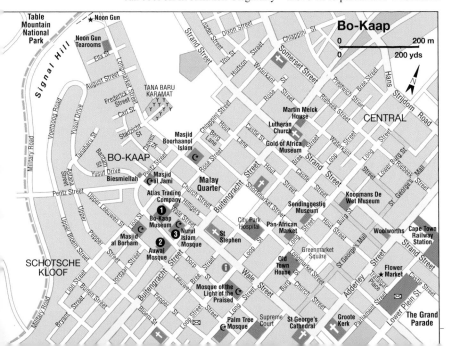

and Mowbray, and the Muslim population moved in, particularly after 1834, when slaves were liberated. They moved into the better houses of the district, including many of the places you see here today.

The area is mostly associated with the Muslims who arrived in the Cape from 1658 onwards, as convicts, slaves, political exiles and convicts from East Africa and South East Asia. The political exiles tended to be people of high rank and culture, and from the beginning they bonded through their religion. They were known as Cape Malays – an incorrect term since the majority of Bo-Kaap's residents are of non-Malaysian descent. Many of today's residents are the descendants of skilled craftsmen, silversmiths, shoemakers, tailors, fishermen and cooks.

Cape Town still has a reputation for good-quality cabinet-making, fine plastering and other building trades, and Cape Malay cuisine is uniquely South African, with its combination of Asian, Arab and European influences. Dishes such as *bobotie* (spiced patties of ground lamb) were created

when slave women and their masters' wives worked together in the kitchen. The hands of slave artisans are evident in the Cape Dutch architecture they built.

Today this is not a wealthy area by any means, and attempts to gentrify Bo-Kaap have met with fierce resistance. If you join an organised tour you'll hear passionate defence of the area, whose history reflects the political machinations of South Africa. Under the Group Areas Act it was declared a residential area strictly for Muslims, and if you didn't fit the bill you had to leave. At the time, Coloured Muslims in Cape Town were encouraged by the divide-and-rule government to see themselves as ethnically distinct from the rest of the non-White population.

Ironically, Bo-Kaap is one of the few working-class areas left in today's South Africa that is situated right on the edge of a city centre. All the others were cleared under the Slum Clearance Act. Today Bo-Kaap has a renewed lease of life as it enters a new phase in its unique development.

Map on page 106

A Muslim woman covers up in Bo-Kaap.

LEFT:
celebrating Tweede Nuwe Jaar, Bo-Kaap's principal festival.

New Year Celebration

If you're in Cape Town over New Year, fight your way through the traffic and pay Bo-Kaap a visit. The area, including many of the surrounding streets, throng with banjo-playing minstrels, dressed in flamboyant suits, dancing through the streets in commemoration of Tweede Nuwe Jaar (Second New Year). The festival, known as the Minstrels Festival or the Coon Festival, was traditionally confined to 2 January, the only day in the calendar when slaves were allowed to down tools and enjoy a holiday.

Traditional Malay choirs are an important element of the festival. Only men and boys take part, singing a mixture of *ghommaliedjies* (folk songs), hymns, funeral dirges and the gypsy violinist's wistful songs of homelessness. The different troupes of singers are in fierce competition with each other. The celebrations culminate at Green Point *(see page 99)*, with the announcement of the winning troupe.

With its long history, Tweede Nuwe Jaar is a hugely important annual holiday, and the Coloured population, including Muslims, take it very seriously.

TIP

If you admire the African beadwork on sale in many gift shops in Cape Town, visit Monkeybiz at 43 Rose Street, Bo-Kaap (tel: 021 426 0145; www.monkeybiz. co.za). It sells a gorgeous array of beaded dolls, animals and bags made by women living in the townships. Monkeybiz has proved an astounding success and you will find its products in cities all over the world.

BELOW: the Asian-style grocery store opposite the Bo-Kaap Museum.

The Bo-Kaap Museum

Situated at 71 Wale Street (on the left-hand side as you ascend the street from Buitengracht), the **Bo-Kaap Museum ❶** (open Mon–Sat 9am–4pm; tel: 021 424 3846; admission charge) is where any visit to the district should begin. It has a "wavy" parapet above the facade which is a unique survival of a type of building common to the city in the third quarter of the 18th century. All the early woodwork survives, including the original teak windows, teak shutters, the doors and the lovely fanlight above the front door.

Inside, it's been restored to resemble the home of a Muslim household of the 19th century. Most of the furniture is either English or Dutch, and of a type found in such a house at the time. The kitchen is more 18th- than 19th-century, with a floor of original Robben Island slate.

The museum contains photographs and pictures depicting the lifestyle of the community as well as interesting relics of daily life such as a fish-seller's horn, once typical of the door-to-door fish hawkers who frequented the city's streets. There is also memorabilia of the 19th-century religious leader Abubakr Effendi, who came to the Cape from Turkey in 1862, brought by the British, who needed him to mediate between the city's feuding Muslims.

Upstairs the museum tells the story of the local community in its socio-political and cultural contexts, with an extensive picture gallery. In particular, it portrays the devastating effects that apartheid and the Group Areas Act had on the community.

There is a courtyard café downstairs. If it is closed (it tends to open only for group visits), pop over to the grocery shop opposite the museum.

Auwal Mosque

Bo-Kaap still has some of its mosques, burial grounds and shrines, known as *kramats* (there are three in Bo-Kaap and two more on Signal Hill behind the district). The **Auwal Mosque ❷** in Dorp Street, one block south of the museum, is the oldest mosque in South Africa. Founded in 1798 during the first British Occupation of the Cape, it is a Shafee mosque (conforming to the doctrines of Muslims of Indonesian origin), and was founded by Tuan Guru, Imam Abdullah Kadi Abdus Salaam. The mosque was the main Muslim religious institution in the in the first half of the 19th century.

Tuan Guru was its first imam. A prince from Tidore in the Ternate Islands, he was brought to the Cape by the Dutch government as a prisoner. He was incarcerated on Robben Island, and while there wrote a treatise on Islamic law and wrote down the Holy Qur'an from memory. His handwritten works became the main reference for Cape Muslims, and over the years had a tremendous influence on Islam here. He established the first organised school where the Qur'an was taught to slaves and free black children – in

fact his name, Tuan Guru, means "teacher". It is thought that Afrikaans first emerged at the Auwal Mosque.

Tuan Guru is buried in the Tana Baru Karamat. This can be seen at the top of Longmarket Street, high on the slopes of Signal Hill. This important burial ground also contains the graves of other holy men banished to the Cape from the East, Abubakr Effendi and Tuan Sayed Alawie among them. The latter came from the Yemen, and at the time was known for his work among the slaves kept in the Slave Lodge. He served a prison sentence of 11 years and, after his release became the first official imam of the Cape Muslims.

Nurul Islam Mosque

There are other mosques in Bo-Kaap. The **Nurul Islam Mosque** ❸ is in a lane off Buitengracht Street. The city's third-oldest (the second-oldest is the Palm Tree Mosque in Long Street – *see page 85*), it was founded by Imam Abdul Rauf, the youngest of Tuan Guru's sons, in 1844. At 62 Chiappini Street is the **Masjid al Jami**, and further on the

Masjid al Borhan which had the first minaret in Cape Town. The **Masjid Boorhaanol Islam**, in Longmarket Street is fairly large and has remained unaltered since it was built in 1886. There are others, all of them still in use.

Cape Malay cuisine

A fitting end to a tour of Bo-Kaap should be a meal at Biesmiellah or at the Noon Gun Tearoom *(see below)*, set in the sunroom extension to a Bo-Kaap home on Longmarket Street. In both you'll be served Cape Malay food from a limited menu.

The **Noon Gun** is located at the top of vertiginous Longmarket Street (for direct access follow the signpost up Military Street from Buitengrachtc). Following a long tradition in the city, a cannon shot is fired every day at noon. Though it is loaded by hand, it is fired automatically after receiving an electronic signal from Cape Town Observatory *(see page 118)*. There is not that much to see, but it is worth walking up for the magnificent views of the ocean and Table Mountain. ❑

Map on page 106

Call in at Atlas Trading Company at 94 Wale Street, opposite the museum, and buy some of the herbs or spices used in Cape Malay food. The owners will happily share recipes and cooking tips with you.

BELOW:
Cape Malay cuisine.

RESTAURANTS

Biesmiellah
Cnr Wale and Pentz Street. Tel: 021 423 0850. Open: L & D Mon–Sat. $.
This restaurant is a must. In fact it's a private house, and you come here to eat well-prepared and authentic Cape Malay cooking. No alcohol.

Noon Gun Tearoom
273 Long Market Street. Tel: 021 424 0529. Open: all day Mon–Sat. $
Also specialising in Cape Malay cooking, the Noon Gun Tearoom at the top of Longmarket Street serves set lunches and dinners and teas. No alcohol.

● ● ● ● ● ● ● ● ● ● ● ● ● ● ● ● ● ● ●
Price includes dinner per person, excluding tip.
$ = under R140.

THE TOWNSHIPS

No trip to Cape Town is complete unless you've paid a visit to the townships. Once you've seen the beaches, climbed Table Mountain and sampled the good life of the Cape, it's time to visit South Africa's monuments to social engineering, the flip side of the coin

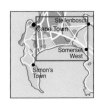

M ost visitors get their first glimpse of the city's townships on their drive from the airport. The worst of them butt up to the busy N2 highway as it sweeps into the city from the southern Cape, crossing the infamous Cape Flats, the windy, dusty flatlands prone to flooding that lie between the wealthy Southern Suburbs and and the Hottentots Holland Mountains. This is where the majority of Cape Town's population live.

The townships include Langa ("Sun"), Gugulethu ("Our Pride"), Nyanga ("Moon"), Khayelitsha ("New Place"), Crossroads, Bonteheuwel, Hanover Park (named after District Six's main street) and Bishop Lavis Town. They are the areas in which non-whites were forced to live during apartheid. Blacks, Coloureds and Indians were separated into their own areas.

Several of the black townships have evolved from what were essentially labour camps, where male-only hostels for migrant workers from the Transkei and elsewhere were set up to meet the needs of the nearby city. If a man lost his job or grew too old or ill to work, he lost his right to live in proximity to the city and was required to return to his designated tribal homeland.

The townships today

In spite of the ending of apartheid, mostly for economic reasons the status quo generally survives, and people continue to live in the townships in which they were born. But the inhabitants also stay for social reasons. Extensive communities of families and friends have evolved, many of whom have lived together for nearly half a century. These networks are difficult to leave. In Johannesburg some prosperous residents have chosen to invest in magnificent new

Map on page 112

LEFT: mosaic work at the Guga S'Thebe cultural centre in Langa.
BELOW: informal housing on the edge of Khayelitsha.

homes in the townships rather than move to former white areas.

That said, some affluent black, and more particularly Coloured and Indian Capetonians have started moving into white suburbs. It is virtually unknown, however, for poor whites to move into the townships.

Since the ending of apartheid facilities in the townships have improved dramatically. The provision of basic services such as electricity and water was a priority of the new government in 1994, initially under Joe Slovo, Nelson Mandela's first Minister of Housing. But massive and continuing migration from the former homelands outstrips provision.

Visiting a township

During apartheid, crime and violence escalated in the townships, and the legacy of this, perpetuated by the extreme poverty, is still evident today. It is therefore highly inadvisable for strangers to enter a township

independently. Roads are badly signposted and maintained, and it is easy suddenly to find yourself in an unsafe area. The only safe way to visit a township is to join an organised tour with people who know the locals and know precisely where to go.

A trip to a township won't reveal any sights per se, but it will offer the chance to experience a living culture – to meet the locals in township taverns, jazz clubs and restaurants, browse among roadside stalls where you can buy anything from a sheep's head to hair oil, have your car repaired or your hair cut.

In the face of often grinding poverty, visitors are encouraged to support local artists and community projects, and buy the produce and merchandise on sale. They can even spend a night in a township. Conditions will be simple, and almost certainly mean sharing a bathroom with a stranger, but this is about looking at the way township people do

TIP

If you want to immerse yourself in genuine, modern-day African culture, consider an overnight stay in a township B&B. Chances are it will be one of the highlights of your visit to Cape Town. *(For recommendations, see page 206 of Travel Tips.)*

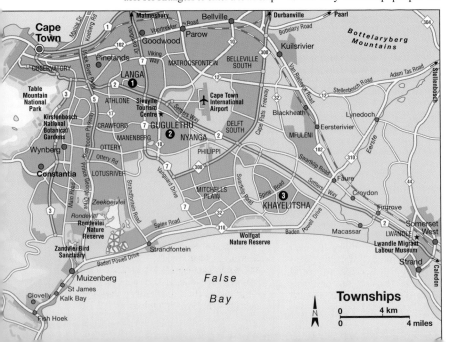

Townships

0   4 km
0   4 miles

things and, more importantly, it's about joining them. It is a relevant cultural exchange with people who rarely, if ever, get the chance to meet foreigners. This way the locals and visitors are exposed to other viewpoints, other languages and cultures. Strangely, it's something white Capetonians rarely do.

The economic advantages of the tours, too, are enormous. They help residents earn a living in a place where only about 30 percent of them are formally employed. People are taught to be guides, to wait at table, cook or pour the wine in township restaurants. There are opportunities to sell visitors home-made goods such as rugs, baskets and all kinds of decorative items from beaded dolls to papier-mâché bowls. If someone has a skill, he or she can use it to put food on the table. And there are more direct benefits to be had: whole containers have arrived from foreign parts filled with books, bicycles, even school furniture, sent by interested visitors.

The three most visited townships in the Cape Town area are Langa, Gugulethu and Khayelitsha.

Langa

Cape Town's oldest township, dating from 1927, **Langa ❶**, a few kilometres east of Mowbray, is currently being transformed into a modern suburb complete with schools, clinics and sports facilities. Perhaps it was here that township life as we now know it came into existence. The enforced intimacy of the residents, living in cramped conditions, meant that neighbours ate together, socialised and helped one another more than usual. The Church was, and remains, an important institution which helped keep society together. Langa today is at the opposite end of the scale from Khayelitsha; the former is more organised and suburban with homes of bricks and mortar, the latter is utterly impoverished, made up of little more than shacks.

Plenty of operators *(see box below)* will take you on a walking tour of Langa, visiting the vibrant **Guga S'Thebe Cultural Centre**, a hub of many and varied activities, from dance classes to arts-and-crafts workshops, a *shebeen* (tavern), and

Map on page 112

Christianity is an important influence in the lives of many black South Africans. For decades missionary schools were the only means by which black children could receive an education beyond primary level. Today, a huge number of pentecostal Christian sects are active in the townships.

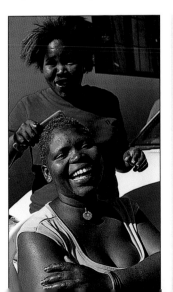

LEFT: much of everyday life in a township takes place out of doors.

Township Tours

It is estimated that 5–10 percent of all visitors to Cape Town take a township tour. Recommended operators include:

Around the Cape Tours, tel: 021 788 2739; www.aroundthe cape.co.za.

Cape Capers, tel: 021 448 3117; www.tourcapers.co.za. Varied programme, including a Trail of Two Cities on the Cape Care Route.

Cape Town Calling, tel 083 404 4433; www.capetowncalling.com.

e.zizwe Travel & Tours, tel: 021 697 0068; www.touringcapetown.com. Offers informative and diverse tours run by the ebullient Thabang Titoti.

Hylton Ross Exclusive Touring, tel: 021 511 1784; www.hyltonross.co.za. Includes Bonteheuwel, Nyanga and Crossroads in addition to the more usual townships.

Roots Africa Tours; tel: 021 987 8330; www.rootsafrica.co.za.

Thuthuka Tours, tel: 021 433 2449 or 082 979 5831. Offers diverse township tours, including the Xhosa Folklore tour, the Gospel Tour, on which you can listen to various gospel choirs, and the much-lauded Evening Jazz Tour.

TIP

One of the most interesting tourism initiatives in recent years is the Cape Care Route, focusing on self-help projects both in the townships and elsewhere that have community or ecological benefits. Cape Capers and Thuthuka Tours *(see page 113)* are among the tour operators offering the option in their programme.

BELOW: township dwellers are adept at putting old products to new uses, such as this freight container turned hair salon.

an informal settlement of adjoining shacks, often home to three generations of a single family. Langa's citizens grow their own food at **Tsoga Environmental Centre**, where they are also educated about the environment, an outcome of which is a successful community-run waste-recycling centre.

A tour may also include a visit to the men's hostels, where migrant workers lived for years without their families, and a traditional healer, who in spite of improved medical facilities in the townships still holds an important position in society. You may also visit the site where some 50,000 people, led by the Pan Africanist leader Philip Kgosana, protested against the pass laws in 1960, resulting in police opening fire on the crowd.

Variations on the tours may include lunch in a private house or in a neighbourhood restaurant.

Gugulethu

A tour of **Gugulethu ❷**, 20 km (12 miles) southeast of Cape Town, is likely to include visits to several struggle sites, where important and often tragic events during the fight against apartheid are commemorated. They will include sites associated with the Gugulethu Seven, seven young men who were shot in the head after driving into a police trap in 1986, and Any Biehl, a 26-year-old American Fulbright scholar stoned and stabbed to death in 1993. A white anti-apartheid activist, she had been giving friends a lift home when she was seized by young Pan Africanist Congress supporters responding to the call "one settler, one bullet".

Also on the itinerary will be the **Sivuyile Tourism Centre,** an offshoot of Cape Town Tourism, based at Sivuyile Technical College, a centre for about 80 artists, making pottery, painting fabrics and so on.

Khayelitsha

The second-largest township in South Africa (after Soweto near Johannesburg), **Khayelitsha ❸** features in all the programmes offered by the township tour operators. Covering an area of about 28 sq. km (11 sq. miles) 35 km (22 miles) east of Cape

Town along the N2 to Somerset West, it comprises a mix of formal and informal dwellings, the latter constantly growing as more and more people flow in from the countryside.

A visit to Khayelitsha normally begins with an overview of the township from **Lookout Hill**. It will also include the **Khayelitsha Craft Market**, set up in 1997 as a self-help organisation. There are all sorts of good-quality crafts on sale, some of them made for export to the US and Europe. You may also visit the **Abalimi Bezekhaya Peace Park and Community Garden**, set up as a means of bringing peace to communities in conflict and now operating as a successful market garden.

Another success story is Golden Nongawuza, a Khayelitsha man who makes flowers out of cut-up tin cans. Formerly destitute, Nongawuza was reputedly inspired to start his business by a recurring dream. You can join him painting his spectacular tin blooms.

One of the best ways of experiencing Khayelitsha is to attend a cultural event at **Oliver Tambo Hall** (the big white sports hall by the Mew Way turn-off from the N2). Khayelitsha Tourism Board (tel: 021 364 9660) sometimes operates tours that include such events. Look out for details in the local press.

Migrant Labour Museum

Further along the N2 from Khayelitsha, towards Strand on the False Bay Coast, is the **Lwandle Migrant Labour Museum** (open Mon–Fri 9.30am–4pm; tel: 021 845 6119; admission charge). Housed in a former hostel, it preserves life as it was for the migrant labourers and documents the rules by which they lived. The hostels were notorious institutions, designed for men only (who were fined if their wives stayed over), but towards the end of apartheid inhabited by whole families, each member allotted a single bed.

While the other hostels in Lwandle have now been converted into decent family homes, with innovative solar heating, Hostel 33 is a poignant reminder of how life was in Lwandle and many other townships just a few years ago. ❏

Map on page 112

Tribal traditions of rural South Africa live on in the townships. This boy in Khayelitsha is daubed with white clay, used to ward off evil, especially in circumcision rituals.

BELOW: visiting a township home.

THE SOUTHERN SUBURBS

Follow De Waal Drive around the base of Devil's Peak and you will enter the Southern Suburbs, a salubrious residential area containing several grand estates from the colonial era, including Groote Schuur and Groot Constantia

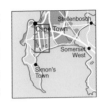

To the east of Devil's Peak, and directly behind the Twelve Apostles that tower over Camps Bay on the southeastern flank of Table Mountain, lie the Southern Suburbs. This is the collective name for a string of old villages that grew up as the road to Muizenberg developed, and after the railway line to Simon's Town opened in the 1860s. Traditionally these were the wealthiest parts of the city, although today the residents of Clifton and Camps Bay on the Atlantic seaboard would beg to differ.

At their distant edges, where their outlying reaches merge with the fringes of the Cape Flats, are the townships and dormitory suburbs to which the victims of the Group Areas Act were banished in the 1960s and 1970s. The Southern Suburbs are the oldest part of the urban sprawl that now pretty well covers the landscape all the way to the False Bay coast. There are some exceptional monuments out here, but it's more a cultural landscape and a place of great natural beauty, dotted with wine farms, restaurants and viewing points.

The landscape

In contrast to the Peninsula's hard and rocky coastal landscape, that of the Southern Suburbs is lush and green, particularly along the upper fringes of Newlands in the Newlands Forest, and Bishopscourt, where Kirstenbosch links it with Constantia. There's every chance it might be raining here when the sun is shining over the Atlantic coast; not for nothing was this area developed as gardens soon after the colony was settled. It was practically guaranteed that the land would yield sufficient produce to supply the ships passing by on their way to and from Europe and the East.

Map on page 118

LEFT: *Kniphofia uvaria,* commonly known as red-hot pokers, at Kirstenbosch Botanical Garden.
BELOW: George Frederick Watts's statue *Energy* at the Rhodes Memorial.

Woodstock and Observatory

This chapter roughly follows the M3 out of the city centre, accessible from the mountain end of Long Street. Between the city and the Southern Suburbs is the district of **Woodstock**, the earliest of Cape Town's suburbs, which was developed at the beginning of the 19th century, and is today one of the city's poorer areas. Its old houses are ramshackle and its streets are ghetto-like. But it has lots of character, with little squares and streets of Victorian terraces. If you want to get an idea of how District Six

Every day at noon an electronic signal is sent from the Royal Observatory to fire the Noon Gun on Signal Hill above Bo-Kaap (see page 109).

would have looked *(see page 73),* have a stroll around Woodstock. However, things are changing here as people looking for inexpensive housing cash in on the district's proximity to the city centre.

Next to Woodstock is **Salt River**, built near marshy ground surrounding the old Salt River lagoon, and today a busy, dirty industrial area of factories and workshops. In spite of this, like Woodstock, it also has plenty of character and is worth a closer inspection. In Victoria, Main and Albert roads there are down-at-heel bric-a-brac shops and factory

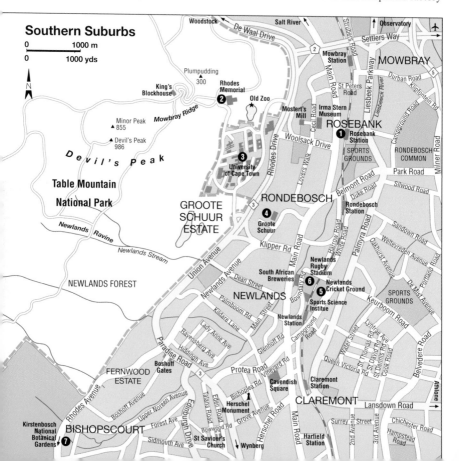

Southern Suburbs

Map on page 118

outlets selling seconds from the many clothing manufacturers that populate the district.

Next to Salt River is **Observatory**, which derives its name from the Royal Observatory established here in 1821, and then **Mowbray**, named after the English town of Melton Mowbray. Mowbray developed around a crossroads where in 1724 a notorious murder took place in the Driekoppen tavern, owned by a certain Johannes Zacharias Beck. The murderers were caught and cruelly executed, their severed heads displayed on stakes.

Observatory is the most popular of these older neighbourhoods, and has a reputation as a bohemian quarter. Commonly known as Obz, it is filled with bars, cafés and cheap restaurants that are busy until the early hours. Its Victorian terraced houses are characterised by their ornate "broekie-lace" decoration, elaborate cast-iron balconies and old gardens. Once a prosperous, middle-class area, it is now a popular area for students and those taking a first step onto the property ladder.

Beyond Observatory lie the Southern Suburbs proper – Rosebank, Rondebosch, Newlands, Claremont, Bishopscourt, Kenilworth, Wynberg, Plumstead and Constantia. You hit them once you've turned the corner and passed beyond Devil's Peak. Each one has its own character and style.

Rosebank

Rosebank ❶ is known as the "learned quarter" due to its proximity to the University of Cape Town and the large proportion of academics who live here. Substantial Victorian and Edwardian villas and palm trees characterise its old streets.

The easiest way to get to Rosebank from the city centre is to take the Eastern Boulevard or the parallel M3 De Waal Drive higher up the side of Devil's Peak. They join just above Groote Schuur Hospital, and together sweep around to the south. To the right is **Mostert's Mill**, a working windmill dating from 1796 (by appointment; tel: 021 762 5127; admission charge). Of a type that was common in the Cape, it has been restored, complete with a thatch cap that rotates to catch the wind.

Just below Mostert's Mill is the **Irma Stern Museum** (Cecil Road; open Tues–Sat 10am–5pm; tel: 021 685 5686; admission charge), once the studio and home of the great South African painter Irma Stern (1894–1966), who lived here for 40 years. Set in a tranquil garden, the 19th-century building is now a museum to her life. Stern, of German-Jewish descent, painted in the German Expressionist style mainly scenes from her travels around Africa, Asia, the Mediterranean, Europe and South America. Her subjects included exotic figures, portraits, lush landscapes and still lifes, conveyed in a variety of media that ranged from oils and watercolours to gouache and charcoal.

BELOW:
Mostert's Mill, dating from the 18th century.

The rooms are filled with artefacts that she picked up on her travels. Most notable amongst these is a Buli Stool from the eastern region of the Democratic Republic of Congo, a pair of carved Zanzibar doors, and several fine examples of 17th-century Spanish furniture. The studio, with the artist's easel, palettes, paint and brushes left intact, is the focal point of the house.

Stern's home-decorating style is manifested in the paintwork of doors and cupboards throughout the house, not unlike the painted surfaces and panels of Charleston in Sussex, England, the country retreat of the Bloomsbury group. Stern's works are highly collectable today, and their prices are on the rise.

The Rhodes Memorial

Way above Rosebank, on the other side of the M3 highway, just next to the campus of the University of Cape Town, is the **Rhodes Memorial** ❷ (open daily 9am–6pm), Herbert Baker's classical monument to Cecil John Rhodes, who bequeathed all the land along the lower slopes of the mountain to the city of Cape Town. One of the most magnificently sited monuments in the world, it was built in 1905, and is an impressive U-shaped building fronted by Doric columns and a massive flight of steps flanked by sleeping lions. Its design is based on that of the Greek temple at Segesta in Sicily.

It is said that the monument occupies one of Rhodes's favourite spots, where he would sit for hours and admire a view he believed was "unsurpassed anywhere in the world". At the base is a bronze horse and rider called *Energy*, by the Victorian artist and sculptor George Frederick Watts. Another version of it stands in London's Hyde Park.

The monument is enclosed by tall Stone pines and surrounded by vast open grasslands filled with zebra, wildebeest and a variety of deer – an area favoured for fashion shoots by magazines and advertising agencies because it looks like the grasslands of the Highveld in the north. A little café to one side of the monument occupies a small cottage also built by Herbert Baker.

TIP

If you are interested in acquiring a work by Stern, watch the sales catalogues of South Africa's premier auction house, Stefan Welz in association with Sotheby's.

RIGHT: a bust of Rhodes surveys the parkland setting of his memorial.

Cecil John Rhodes

Cape and southern African history was shaped by the third son of an English parson, an Oxford graduate in poor health who would die before the age of 50. He was a consummate politician with a sharp eye for colonial real estate. In 1890, nine years after entering the House of Assembly in Cape Town, he was elected Prime Minister of the Cape Colony. He controlled De Beers Consolidated, a vast conglomerate of diamond mines, the Consolidated Goldfields of South Africa Company and the British South Africa Chartered Company, which would bring Bechuanaland (Botswana), Matabeleland and Mashonaland (most of Zimbabwe) under British protection.

Rhodes came to exemplify all that was wildly romantic and ruthless about colonial expansion. By the time of his death in 1902 he had added 2 million sq. km (772,200 sq. miles) to British possessions in Africa, established educational trusts (Rhodes scholarships) and farming grants, left a Groote Schuur redesigned by Herbert Baker as the home of future South African heads of state and created a new nation, the ill-fated Rhodesia (now Zimbabwe).

This is a lovely place to walk. Park beside the monument and take a picnic up into the woods. From every vantage point there's a view out over northern Cape Town and the Cape Flats and to the jagged Hottentots Holland to the east.

Once Khoikhoi pastoralists used these slopes (they were recorded there in the 1600s), but in 1667 the Dutch East India Company (VOC) colonised them as a farming area and built a huge barn called Groote Schuur – today commemorated by the nearby hospital of the same name. The VOC planted the Stone pines in the 1700s.

When Rhodes arrived late in the 19th century, he cleared most of the indigenous landscape, leaving the pines, to create a parkland setting for his house (also called Groote Schuur) and grazing for animals. Between 1891 and 1899 Rhodes purchased most of the properties on the eastern slopes of Table Mountain, creating the Groote Schuur Estate, which was incorporated into the Cape Peninsula National Park in 1999.

Just below Rhodes Memorial is the old zoo, built in 1897 to house lions. Rhodes had a particular fondness for the lion as "king of beasts", because to him it symbolised the aspirations of the British Empire. The lions' descendants remained here until 1975 when the zoo closed. Until then donkeys were kept in a field behind the zoo – as lion fodder.

Today the estate serves as a gateway to Table Mountain National Park. As well as access to the mountain, there are walks to Kirstenbosch, to the Cecilia Plantation and to the Newlands Forest. Paths and jeep tracks ascend the lower slopes of the mountain, and you can walk to the King's Blockhouse. If Rhodes's aim was to secure this landscape against encroachment, then he was successful. Today it is one of Cape Town's most important assets.

University

Built on former Groote Schuur Estate land, the **University of Cape Town** ❸ (tours by appointment; tel: 021 650 3748) is worth a look. It occupies a magnificent site, straddling

Map on page 118

Cecil John Rhodes died in Rhodes cottage in Muizenberg on the False Bay coast in 1902. The last words of the archetypal colonialist were "So much to do, so little done". His grave lies at World's View in the Matopos Mountains of Zimbabwe.

BELOW: the Rhodes Memorial, nestling on the slopes of Table Mountain National Park.

In Mowbray you may want to pay a visit to the small museum at Groot Schuur Hospital where, in 1967, Dr Christiaan Barnard made medical history by performing the world's very first heart transplant. The museum (open Mon–Fri am only; admission charge) is signposted off the main road.

the eastern foothills of Devil's Peak and facing out to the distant Hottentots Holland Mountain, Blouberg to the left and False Bay to the right. The first university in the country, it was founded in 1829, but didn't occupy its present site until 1911, after Rhodes had bequeathed the land to Cape Town.

UCT is a distinguished institution; its architecture and medical faculties are world-renowned, and it distinguished itself during the struggle against apartheid. Today it attracts national and international students.

Rondebosch and Groote Schuur

In the late 19th century Rondebosch was one of the city's smartest areas, popular with the English, who were keen to demonstrate their status in what had become a kind of rural suburbia. Houses with turrets and porte cochères and names chosen to remind their occupants of home – Ringmore, Silwood, Mayfield, for example – are the order of the day.

The name Rondebosch name refers to a round thornbush found on the banks of the Liesbeeck River, and it grew up around a garden established by the early Dutch colonists because it was discovered to be virtually wind-free. It's thought that at the time the thornbushes were cleared from the land and made into a protective hedge around the garden, preventing wild animals and Khoikhoi from entering. Today Rondebosch is famous for its schools.

Below the highway, and accessible from Klipper Road in the higher reaches of Rondebosch, is **Groote Schuur ❹** (by appointment only; tel: 021 686 9100; admission charge; you will need to show your passport in order to visit), the house remodelled for Rhodes in 1893 by Herbert Baker in a Cape Dutch Revival style. It's well worth a visit if you have the time. A tour takes in the public rooms and Rhodes's own bedroom, a small, spartan chamber more in keeping with a boys' boarding school than the sanctuary of the man who named a country after himself and who dreamed of linking Cape Town with Cairo. The public

BELOW:
Groot Schuur Hospital.

rooms house the remains of Rhodes's magnificent collections of Cape Dutch and Batavian furniture, porcelain, silver and glassware, as well as carpets, tapestries and paintings. Rhodes's library is still here, as is one of the famous stone Great Zimbabwe birds, thought to have been removed from the ruins of ancient Great Zimbabwe.

Groote Schuur is a cross between a Victorian country house and a gentleman's club. For a long time it was the Cape Town residence of the prime minister and then of the state president. It's located in a secure complex of other important houses, including Genadendal (formerly Westbrooke), now the state president's Cape Town residence.

Newlands

After Rondebosch come Newlands, Claremont, Bishopscourt, then high above Bishopscourt, where the Liesbeeck River begins, is Kirstenbosch.

The upper reaches of Rondebosch and Newlands are possibly the leafiest part of the city. In the early 1700s Willem Adriaan van der Stel created a new garden for the colony here. He also established oak plantations in the vicinity, the last vestiges of which you see throughout Newlands, particularly along Newlands Avenue, which was once the old wagon road to the south. The district is sprinkled with old farms, some with original houses and barns surviving in what is now dense suburbia. On the left as you drive down Paradise Road (now the M3), are the 19th-century Boshoff Gates, leading into leafy Boshoff Avenue for a short cut to Kirstenbosch. The air is cooler here; in the summer you can feel the change in temperature as you round the mountain beneath Devil's Peak.

These days Newlands is associated with cricket and rugby. In Campground Road is the famous **Newlands Cricket Ground** ❺ (tours Mon–Fri; tel: 021 657 2003; admission charge), where the 2003 Cricket World Cup was held. Cricket was popularised by the British military in the 1850s, and in the 1860s there were organised matches pitching "the Army and

Map on page 118

TIP

To book tours online for Newlands Cricket Ground or Newlands Rugby Stadium (or the Super Tour, combining both) contact www. newlandstours. co.za

BELOW: UCT, the distinguished University of Cape Town.

TIP

In contrast to the slick surroundings and international brands at Cavendish Square is the Montebello Design Centre in Newlands (31 Newlands Avenue), where a cluster of farm outbuildings have been converted into studios and workshops for high-quality pottery, jewellery and other crafts.

BELOW: Newlands Cricket Ground.

Navy against South Africa", and between "Mother Country and Colonial Born". In 1871, during an international tour to the Cape, the England team suffered an innings defeat by the locals.

In Boundary Road is the equally renowned **Newlands Rugby Stadium** ⑥ (tours Mon–Fri; tel: 021 659 4600; admission charge). The rugby field was first used in 1890, and is one of the oldest venues for the sport in the world. Its smart new stadium seats 51,000 spectators, and national and international matches are frequently held here.

Also in Boundary Road is the **Sports Science Institut**e (tours Mon–Fri; tel: 021 659 5600; admission charge), where professional sportsmen and women go to train, receive dietary and nutritional advice, and see their coaches. The **Rugby Museum** (open Mon–Fri 8.30am–5pm; tel: 021 686 2151; free) here is dedicated to the history of Newlands and the South African game, with rugby memorabilia, news clippings and so on. This is also home to the University of Cape

Town's Exercise Sports and Medicine Faculty.

Near by is **South African Breweries**, the second-largest brewery in the world. Newlands was chosen as the site of Cape Town's breweries because of the freshness of its mountain water. While the early breweries were higher up the slopes, closer to Newlands Avenue, the South African Breweries (SAB) are in Boundary Road. An old malt house and the old Ohlsson brewery on the site have been restored and can be visited (open Tues, Thur and Fri 10am–2pm; tel: 021 658 7511; free). Visitors to SAB will see how it works and learn what makes South African beer so special.

Commercial Claremont

Beyond Newlands is **Claremont**, one of the commercial hubs of the Southern Suburbs. **Cavendish Square** (open Mon–Thur 9am– 6pm, Fri and Sat 9am–9pm, Sun 10am–4pm; tel: 021 671 8042) is a huge, exclusive shopping centre with a superb range of top-end fashion boutiques, smart interior-design businesses, book-

shops, restaurants, coffee shops and two cinema complexes.

There's not much else to do in Claremont, although if you're passing along Bishoplea Road or Feldhausen Road behind Cavendish Square, have a look at the **Herschel Monument**, an obelisk in the grounds of Grove Primary School. It marks the site of the house where the astronomer Sir John Herschel (1792–1871) roamed the skies with his telescope. The telescope was a version of the one constructed by his father, William Herschel, of Bath, England, who discovered the planet Uranus. It was considered the finest telescope of its time, and enabled William to re-survey the whole of the northern sky. Son John's version was used to survey the sky in the southern hemisphere. At the time John Herschel, who had no peer in his knowledge of the southern skies, was widely revered, and when he died he was buried near Sir Isaac Newton in Westminster Abbey, London. His house, Feldhausen, stood on this site.

Not far away, in Bowwood Road, is **St Saviour's Church**, designed by Sophie Gray and consecrated by her husband Bishop Gray in 1853. Both are buried in the churchyard. The little stone-built church was enlarged on two occasions as Claremont grew, the first time by William Butterfield (1880), the High-Church Gothic Revivalist responsible for Keble College in Oxford, England, and then again in 1903 by Herbert Baker.

Imposing Bishopscourt

Claremont runs into Bishopscourt, an old suburb with enormous 20th-century mansions and massive gardens filled with shrubs and trees. The district is named after the seat of the Archbishop of Cape Town, which itself occupies a farm first granted to Jan van Riebeeck in

1658. Van Riebeeck never moved in and it was burned down soon after, but there's been a substantial house on the property ever since. Bishopscourt was renovated by Herbert Baker and made famous by Archbishop Desmond Tutu, who took up residence here in 1986. Even more famous is the graffiti once scrawled, in disaffection at the Archbishop's anti-apartheid activism, on a wall of a house in Edinburgh Drive near to Tutu's home. It said: 'I was an Anglican until I put Tu and Tu together'.

Kirstenbosch

The **Kirstenbosch National Botanical Gardens** ❼ (open Apr–Aug daily 8am–6pm, Oct–March 8am–7pm; tel: 021 799 8800; admission charge; www.nbi.ac.za) cover 528 hectares (1,320 acres), with 36 hectares (89 acres) under cultivation on the slopes of the mountain to the southeast of the Table Mountain range. They lie 13 km (8 miles) from Cape Town city centre. To get there direct from the city, take De Waal Drive (M3) in the direction of

Maps on pages 118/127

TIP

It is easy to spend the whole day in Kirstenbosch. If you don't have your own transport, you can get a bus to the gardens from the Golden Acre bus station near Cape Town railway station. Be sure to check on the times of the buses there and back as they are infrequent. A taxi one way will cost around R100.

BELOW:
Kirstenbosch National Botanical Gardens.

TIP

On Sundays from December to March, sunset musical concerts are held on the lawns of Kirstenbosch. Bring a picnic, a bottle of chilled wine and a rug, laze on the lawn and enjoy the music.

BELOW: among the aloes at Kirstenbosch.

Muizenberg, at the first traffic-light junction turn right (southwards) into Rhodes Drive (M63) and follow the signs to Kirstenbosch.

The gardens grow only plants indigenous to South Africa, and support a diverse fynbos flora and natural forest. In fact, it was established in 1913 to preserve and propagate rare indigenous plant species, and today it is one of the national treasures of this country and one of the most important botanical collections in the world.

The site had been occupied for centuries before the settlers arrived in the 17th century. Large stone implements and round perforated stones used to weight pointed digging sticks are the only record of the existence of any earlier inhabitants. In 1660 a hedge of wild almond *(Brabejum stellatifolium)* and brambles was planted to form the boundary of the colony, to keep livestock in and Khoikhoi locals out. It's known as van Riebeeck's Hedge, and you can still see the remaining sections of it.

The origin of the name of Kirstenbosch isn't clear, although there was a Kirsten family in the area; Kirstenbosch means Kirsten's Forest. Only in 1811, under the British Occupation, did the landscape up here begin to change. Two large land grants were made, and a Colonel Bird built a house at the foot of Window Gorge, planted chestnuts and probably built the lovely old 'bath' in the Dell, which still exists today. In 1823, the Ecksteen family acquired both properties, and they then passed to the Cloetes, who farmed here, planting oaks, fruit trees and vines. The old Ecksteen home stood on the site of the present Lecture Hall.

In 1895 Cecil Rhodes purchased the entire property from the Cloete family, and gradually it was allowed to grow wild again, though this time not without a large pig population that fed on the acorns and wallowed in big muddy pools. At this time the Camphor Avenue was planted (1898) – it still survives behind the restaurant buildings. In 1902 Rhodes died, bequeathing Kirstenbosch to the people as part of his great Groote Schuur Estate. Only then was a garden born here.

Professor Pearson, who came to South Africa in 1903 to fill the newly established Chair of Botany at the South African College, visited Kirstenbosch in 1911 and came to the conclusion that this wild, over-grown estate would be a suitable site for a botanical garden. On 1 July 1913 Kirstenbosch was set aside by the Government with a grant of £1,000 per annum to keep it going. Pearson became director and Kirstenbosch has never looked back, although at that time they had to supplement the income of the Gardens by selling firewood and acorns.

The Dell was the first location to be established, and cycads were planted there. In 1916 Pearson died of pneumonia – probably because the cottage in which he lived on the estate was so damp. He is buried in the garden and his tombstone reads: "If ye seek his monument, look around."

Indigenous plants

Come here to learn about South Africa's extraordinary floral heritage, in particular that of the Cape. Situated against the slopes of Table Mountain, the Kirstenbosch is especially significant as the Western Cape is home to one of the world's six floral kingdoms, the fynbos. It forms part of Cape Floristic Region, in which more plants can be found per square metre than anywhere else on earth.

The fynbos – a term first used by Dutch settlers to refer to the finely leafed plants they found growing here – is home to more than 7,300 species of plants. It represents about 45 percent of the flora of southern Africa, squeezed into about 4 percent of its surface area. It's the predominant vegetation of the mountains and coastal lowlands of the Western Cape and parts of the Eastern Cape.

But the garden also has cycads, a herb garden, a fascinating medicinal

BELOW: Kirstenbosch spreads up the slopes of Table Mountain and several good walks can be accessed from the gardens. One of the most popular is Skeleton Gorge, which was a favourite walk of General Jan Smuts, who walked it until he was well into his seventies.

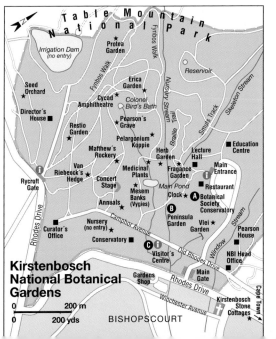

Kirstenbosch is one of the best places to spot birds. In particular look out for the glorious orange-breasted Cape Sugarbird.

RIGHT: bring a rug and a picnic and spend the day at Kirstenbosch.

garden with plants traditionally used by South Africa's indigenous people, and a fragrance garden.

The **Botanical Society Conservatory** Ⓐ displays indigenous plants that cannot be grown in the outdoor gardens. Here are plants from typical South African habitats – from high mountain peaks, shady forests and hot, dry deserts. The main house, dominated by a large baobab tree, features succulents from the arid regions of southern Africa. Special collections of bulbs, ferns and alpines are displayed in corner houses.

There is also a Restio garden, focusing on the incredible variety of texture and form found in the reed family (*Restionaceae*), a "waterwise garden", designed to survive drought (a severe problem in South Africa in recent years), and the **Peninsula Garden** Ⓑ, displaying some of the 2,500 plant species found on the Cape Peninsula. The Protea Garden is most magnificent in winter and spring, when the proteas, conebushes and serrurias are in flower. Pincushions provide a colourful display in early summer.

Kirstenbosch's **Visitor's Centre** Ⓒ includes an information point as well as various retail outlets and a coffee shop. The Centre for Home Gardening sells plants, seeds, gifts and books. There's also an ecellent café-restaurant called Fynbos for breakfast and lunch, and the Silver Tree for lunch and dinner.

Wynberg and Constantia

Continuing southwest along the M3, you come to **Wynberg**. Although it has no particular monument or museum, it is well worth making a stop. It grew up as a garrison village around a late-18th-century military camp. Today its charming little streets are lined with Regency-style cottages, many of them interior-design shops and art galleries.

The next stop after Kenilworth and Plumstead is Constantia, dominated by the back of Table Mountain and the Constantiaberg. It contains some of the city's best hotels, guesthouses and restaurants.

The **Constantia Valley** is, like Kirstenbosch, one of the country's most important national treasures.

Tours of Kirstenbosch

There are many wonderful walking trails in Kirstenbosch, some of them reaching far up into the surrounding kloofs and peaks of the Table Mountain National Park. Others are simple meanders through beds of indigenous plants and along avenues – such as the great Camphor Avenue. There are also numerous guided "theme" walks and tours, nature walks for children, educational walks for those keen to learn more about the local fynbos, and there's a Braille Trail in which a guide rope leads visually impaired visitors along a route through a wooded area alive with scented, textured plants. Many of these are self-guided (you can pick up an audioguide at the entrance), but interesting guided walks led by volunteers (no charge) normally take place at 10am. To find out more visit the website www.nbi.ac.za or tel: 021 799 8783. Group tours and special-interest tours can also be arranged for a fee.

For those unable to walk very far, golf carts for a maximum of five people are available from 9am–3pm (booking is advisable and a fee is payable – call the number above).

The cultural landscape here derives from the earliest days of the colony, when the original land grants were handed out and farms were established to supply vegetables and fruit to the Dutch East India Company.

It is also the cradle of the South African wine industry. Vines were first planted here in the 17th century by Simon van der Stel, who founded **Groot Constantia ❽** (open daily 10am-5pm; tel: 021-795 5140; admission charge). The magnificent Cape Dutch home he occupied from 1699 until his death in 1712 is the most famous property of all, but not because of Van der Stel. After he died it was bought and restored by Hendrik Cloete, who also built a wine cellar. On the pediment is a 1791 sculpture of Ganymede by Anton Anreith – a magnificent work that alone is worth a trip here.

This is the place to see how a colonial gentleman-farmer would have lived in the 17th and 18th centuries. Plenty of famous travellers have visited over the years, including the English naturalist William Burchell, Charles Baudelaire, Anthony Trollope and the Prince of Wales, before he became, briefly, King Edward VIII.

The building is approached along an avenue aligned with a magnificent peak in the distance. Its main gable is thought to be by Louis Thibault, with a niche high above its window in which Anreith placed the figure of Abundance. Towering over the main entrance, it faces down a long elegant avenue lined on one side with outbuildings and the *jonkershuis* (where the son and heir would have lived), and on the other by vineyards sloping gently down into the Constantia Valley. There are magnificent views from here out over False Bay in the far distance.

The Cloetes sold the estate to the government in 1925, soon after which

Map below

TIP

Book in advance for wine-production and cellar tours at Groot Constantia (daily 10am–4pm, on the hour; admission charge). For further information about Groot Constantia Estate, visit www.grootconstantia.co.za.

BELOW: Groot Constantia.

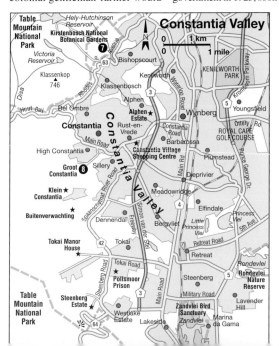

TIP

For information on Constantia's wine industry contact Constantia Valley Publicity & Tourism Association, tel: 082 953 7067, www. constantiavalley.com.

BELOW: Groot Constantia contains a fine collection of Dutch furniture.

it was gutted by a terrible fire. It was restored, and in 1927 became a museum. It contains a superb collection of Dutch furniture in stinkwood, ebony and yellowwood, priceless paintings, textiles, silver and ceramics, many of them donated by shipowner Alfred de Pass. There are copper pots and pans in the kitchen, and underneath the house are vaulted cellars and workshops. The old wine cellar that Cloete built behind the homestead has been turned into a Wine Museum (tel: 021 795 5140) with an interesting display of drinking and storage vessels and winemaking equipment.

In the grounds is an old oval swimming pool with a gabled end and niche containing a wooden statue of Triton, thought to be a ship's figurehead. The old coach house has a display of carriages, and it's worth popping into the orientation centre to learn about the development of the estate since 1685.

There are two restaurants – the Jonkershuis, with waiters dressed up in corny period clothing, and the superb Simon's at Groot Constantia *(see page 133)* – and a shop for wine sales and tastings (fee), books and curios. The Gouveneurs Reserve, Gouveneurs Merlot and Gouveneurs Shiraz are very highly rated wines.

Other wine estates

The other old estates in the Constantia Valley are inaccessible unless, in the case of Steenberg and Alphen, which are now hotels, you happen to be a guest. If you pop into **Steenberg**, take a walk down to the old homestead, now a private suite, and have a look at the charmingly simple facade. The estate was first settled by Catharina Ustings in 1682, a formidable settler who, by the time she died, had had five husbands. It was named after the surrounding rocky mountains – *steen* meaning stone.

When Catharina arrived here there were wild animals including lions, leopards and elephants in the valley, and one of her husbands was murdered by the Khoikhoi, who objected to the colonisation of their lands. Steenberg is now at the centre of a large golf estate directly

opposite **Pollsmoor Prison**. Nelson Mandela was moved here from Robben Island in 1982. His conditions in Pollsmoor were considerably better than at Robben Island, and his move here represented a turning point in relations between the government and the ANC. He was later moved to Victor Verster prison near Paarl (*see page 179*).

The homestead at Steenberg is not the original one but a later building dating from about 1740. After Catharina sold the farm in 1695, it became the property of the Russouws, and stayed in the family until quite recently. Come for the wine tastings and winery tours (open Mon–Fri 9am–4.30pm, Sat 9.30–1.30pm; winery tours Mon–Fri 10am and 3pm, Sat 10am by appointment; tel: 021 713 2211; admission charge). There's a good range of wines, here but the Sauvignon Blanc is particularly noteworthy.

Not far away, and quite different from Steenberg, **Alphen** is one of the finest houses in the Cape. Its estate came into existence in 1712 following the death of Simon van der Stel, who once owned all the land from Groot Constantia to Wynberg Hill. Built in the middle of the 18th century, the architecture of Alphen is quite different from any other building of this period. It's a two-storey property with massive pediments front and back rather than the more usual Cape Dutch gable. It passed through many hands over the years, ending up in the possession of the Cloetes, who also owned Groot Constantia.

Like Steenberg, it is now a hotel (tel: 021 794 5011), and is filled with the furniture and antiques of the Cloete family, who still own it. Even though its magnificent grounds are being encroached upon by the spreading suburbia of Constantia all around it, it isn't hard to imagine the building at the heart of a massive wine estate – the vineyards are still there, up the road behind the house.

Not far from Alphen is Constantia Village shopping complex, and there's a huge gym in Constantia Main Road, the Constantia Virgin Active (tel: 021 794 5010). ❏

Map on page 129

The wines of the Constantia Valley are among the finest in South Africa.

BELOW:
working on the Groot Constantia estate.

RESTAURANTS & BARS

Restaurants

Old and established, the leafy Southern Suburbs have numerous fine-dining options, including several good hotel restaurants. Constantia is particularly well endowed in this regard. But there are also many less exclusive options, especially in bustling and youthful Observatory.

PRICE CATEGORIES

Prices for three-course dinner per person with a half-bottle of house wine:
$ = under R140
$$ = R140–200
$$$ = R200–300
$$$$ = more than R300

Claremont

Famous Butcher's Grill
Corner of Protea and Dreyer streets, Claremont. Tel: 021 683 5103. Open: L & D daily. $$
www.butchersgrill.com
Like its popular sisters in the city centre (Greenmarket Square and Cape Town Lodge Hotel, Buitengracht street), this is primarily for meat-lovers. Top-quality steak and game are prepared by the resident butcher and expertly cooked. Line-fish, chicken and salmon are available for non-carnivores.

Newlands

Au Jardin
Vineyard Hotel, 60 Colinton Road, Newlands. Tel: 021 657 4545. Open: D daily,
closed Sun and Mon out of season. L on request. $$
This is a hotel restaurant, but an exceptional one. Housed in an early Cape farmhouse, it serves swanky French food and has one of the best wine lists in the city. Come here for a bit of old Cape history. You can also just enjoy a drink in the gardens facing the eastern flank of Table Mountain.

Barristers Grill Café and Fish Market
Cnr Kildare and Main streets, Newlands. Tel: 021 674 1792. Open: B, L & D daily. D only Sun. $$
Barristers has been around for a long time, and it's revered for its large and succulent steaks. If you prefer something lighter, it has a fish restaurant attached. Offers relaxed eating at its best.

Melissa's
Cnr Kildare and Main streets, Newlands. Tel: 021 683 6949. Open: 8.30am–8pm daily. $
A casual deli which sells the very best open sandwiches, salads and chicken pie. Serves healthy breakfasts, croissants and coffee to start the day, as well as lunch and teas. Eat as much as you like and pay by weight. A popular
meeting place for discerning locals.

Wijnhuis
Cnr Kildare and Main streets, Newlands. Tel: 021 671 9705. Open: B, L & D 8am–late Mon–Sat. Closed Sun. $$
As you would expect of somewhere called Wijnhuis (wine house), it offers an extensive list of wines to go with good, modern Italian food. Relaxed setting with comfy sofas for post-prandial lounging.

Constantia

Buitenverwachting
Klein Constantia Road, Constantia. Tel: 021 794 5190. Open: L Tues–Fri, D Tues–Sat. Closed July–mid-Aug. $$$.
www.buitenverwachting.co.za
The food at Buitenverwachting is classic (foie gras, lobster, rack of lamb, etc.) with contemporary influences and some local twists. It's pricey, and the place is a little stiff, but it's situated in a typical Cape Dutch homestead, with lovely views of the vineyards. In summer Café Petit, serving light, less pricey meals, operates in the courtyard.

Catherina's Restaurant Steenberg Hotel
10802 Steenberg Estate, Tokai Road, Constantia.

LEFT: the perfect light lunch.

Tel: 021 713 2222. Open: B, L & D daily. $$$
Come here only if you want to have a close-up view of Steenberg, the oldest farm in the Constantia Valley. The food is Cape colonial. Enjoy a drink under the old oaks out at the front before dinner.

La Colombe
Uitsig Farm, Spaanschemat River Road, Constantia. Tel: 021 794 2390. Open: L & D daily. Closed Sun nights low season. Closed Aug. $$$
This is Constantia's other great restaurant – and it's next door to Constantia Uitsig. Chef Franck Dangereux's menu tends towards French country cooking – only better. The decor, like that at Constantia Uitsig, is unpretentious and simple.

Green House Restaurant
The Cellars-Hohenort Hotel 93 Brommersvlei Road, Constantia. Tel: 021 794 2139. Open: B, L & D daily. $$.
www.cellars-hohenort.com
One of the grandest hotels in the Southern Suburbs, occupying an old private mansion set in a magnificent garden in the heart of Constantia. The Green House faces rolling lawns and serves Continental-style food. An extensive wine list.

Jonkerhuis
Groot Constantia Estate, Groot Constantia Road, Constantia. Tel: 021 794 6255. Open: B & L, D Tues–Sat. The olde-worlde ambi-

ence, gnarled beams and waiting staff dressed up in period costume are all a bit touristy, but the Cape Malay food is good and accompanied by fine wines.

Simon's at Groot Constantia
Groot Constantia Estate, Groot Constantia Road, Constantia. Tel: 021 794 1143. Open: L & D daily. Also offers breakfast and tea on Sun. Bar 12 noon–late. $
This is a relaxed venue serving big salads, fresh fish, Karoo lamb and game such as venison. It also has a good wine list. Take a table under the trees on the terrace.

Wasabi
Shop 17, Old Village, Constantia Village. Tel: 021 794 6546. Open: L & D daily. $
www.wasabi.co.za
This is the sister restaurant of the excellent Wakame at Mouille Point. It's a trendy venue with an open-plan kitchen displaying lots of flamboyant action. Serves a wide range of Japanese staples with interesting twists.

Spaanschemat River Café
Constantia Uitsig Farm, Spaanschemat River Road, Constantia. Tel: 021 794 3010. Open: B & L 8.30am–5pm daily. $
A relaxed, laid-back and informal sort of place, with rooms opening on a courtyard and a garden.

Try the Eggs Benedict for breakfast, or have a glass of Constantia Uitsig wine for lunch. Salads, pasta, sausages – good café food characterises this popular venue.

Uitsig Restaurant
Spaanschemat River Road, Constantia. Tel: 021 794 4480. Open: L & D daily. $$$
One of the most expensive restaurants in Cape Town and the best place to eat in Constantia. It is essential to book in advance. Frank Swainston's Italian-inspired cuisine and extensive wine list bring people back time and time again. Set right in the vineyards.

Observatory

Diva Caffè Ristorante
88 Lower Main Road, Observatory. Tel: 021 448 0282. Open: L & D daily. $
A good and inexpensive option for generously topped pizzas and pastas.

Woodstocck

Don Pedro
113 Roodebloem Road, Woodstock. Tel: 021 447 4493. Open: B, L & D daily. Big, bustling and inexpensive, with pizza, pasta and some South African specialities on the menu.

Sushi Zone
34 Lower Main Road, Observatory. Tel: 021 447 0884. Open: L & D daily. $
Well-priced sushi in an informal setting. Chinese and Korean food.also feature. There is a good-

value buffet lunch on Saturday.

Bars

The Southern Suburbs is awash with late-night drinking spots and clubs. Observatory is the place to go for all-night revelry, **Café Carte Blanche** in particular. Drinking here is like drinking at your grandmother's house, only she's gone out. It's noisy and frenetic. Another recommendation is **Obz Café** on Lower Main Road, a buzzing bistro-bar, with a chalked-up menu and wooden furniture, where you can also enjoy live jazz.

In Newlands head for **Billy the Bums**, where a sporty, boisterous set let their hair down. It's owned by ex-Springbok rugby player Bobby Skinstad. Still in Newlands, **Forrester's Arms** is about as like a pub in the English shires as you'll get in Cape Town. It has comfortable sofas and the scuffed appearance of an old and favourite haunt that simply won't die.

Not far away in Claremont, **Match** attracts a hip, young and sporty crowd from the wealthier parts of the Southern Suburbs, while **Peddler's on the Bend** in Constantia is similar in style, attracting the same kind of crowd only older. Good pub-grub, plus a more involved menu in the attached restaurant.

TABLE MOUNTAIN NATIONAL PARK

The undoubted highlight of Cape Town's characterful
topography is the flat-topped, often cloud-covered
Table Mountain. Wherever you are in Cape Town
it is a watchful presence, and at some point in
your stay you will want to get to the summit

able Mountain and its accompaniments, Devil's Peak, Lion's Head and Signal Hill, were known as the "mountains in the sea" – Hoerikwaggo – to the earliest inhabitants of the area, the indigenous Khoikhoi. The ensemble forms one of the most recognisable silhouettes in the world. To early mariners it was an important signpost on the shipping route to the east. A beacon of hope, it meant fresh water was close at hand.

But these famous landmarks form only part of the **Table Mountain National Park**, which since 1998 has been massively extended to include about 73 percent of the entire Cape Peninsula, the narrow strip of land jutting 60 km (36 miles) south of Cape Town as the crow flies. Everywhere you look are vast panoramas with beautiful valleys and kloofs, rugged cliffs, wetlands and wooded hills, many offering magnificent vantage points for views across False Bay and the Cape Flats to the Hottentots Holland Mountains in the east, and to Blouberg and the beginning of the West Coast in the north.

Some areas of the National Park are featured in other chapters of this book. For example, Kirstenbosch National Botanical Garden and Groote Schuur Estate are included in the Southern Suburbs (see pages 122

and 125) where they are most easily accessed. The beaches and towns are covered in the circular tour of the coastline outlined in the chapter on the Cape Peninsula (see page 149).

Dramatic topography

The Cape Peninsula comprises three types of rock – Malmesbury shale deposited here up to 540 million years ago (you can see it along the Sea Point shoreline and on Signal Hill), Cape granite (which forms a solid foundation for most of the

PRECEDING PAGES:
view over Table
Mountain
National Park.
LEFT: the easy way to
climb Table Mountain.
BELOW: the hard
way to the top.

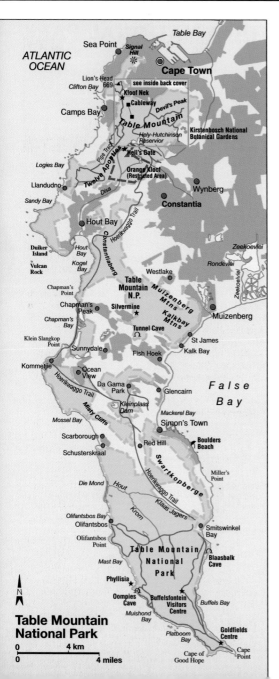

ATLANTIC OCEAN

Sea Point
Table Bay
Signal Hill
Cape Town
Lion's Head 669
Clifton Bay
Kloof Nek
see inside back cover
Cableway
Devil's Peak
Camps Bay
Table Mountain
Hely-Hutchinson Reservoir
Kirstenbosch National Botanical Gardens
Pipe Track
Logies Bay
Hell's Gate
Orange Kloof (Restricted Area)
Twelve Apostles
Wynberg
Llandudno
Disa
Constantia
Sandy Bay
Hout Bay
Hoerikwaggo Trail
Duiker Island
Hout Bay
Zeekoevlei
Vulcan Rock
Kogel Bay
Rondevlei
Constantiaberg
Westlake
Zeekoevlei
Chapman's Point
Table Mountain N.P.
Muizenberg Mtns
Chapman's Peak
Silvermine
Kalkbay Mtns
Muizenberg
Chapman's Bay
Tunnel Cave
Klein Slangkop Point
Sunnydale
St James
Kalk Bay
Kommetjie
Ocean View
Fish Hoek
Hoerikwaggo Trail
Da Gama Park
Glencairn
False Bay
Misty Cliffs
Kleinplaas Dam
Mackerel Bay
Mossel Bay
Simon's Town
Scarborough
Red Hill
Boulders Beach
Schusterskraal
Miller's Point
Swartkopberge
Die Mond
Hout
Hoerikwaggo Trail
Klaas Jagers
Olifantsbos Bay
Olifantsbos
Krom
Smitswinkel Bay
Olifantsbos Point
Table Mountain National Park
Blaasbalk Cave
Mast Bay
Phyllisia
N
Oompies Cave
Buffelsfontein Visitors Centre
Buffels Bay
Muishond Bay
Table Mountain National Park
Platboom Bay
Goldfields Centre
0   4 km
Cape of Good Hope
Cape Point
0   4 miles

Table Mountain chain) and Table Mountain sandstone, an incredibly hard sandstone that was laid down in successive layers over many millions of years.

When the supercontinent Gondwana broke up about 130 million years ago, the Peninsula was "block-faulted" into several giant blocks – hence Table Mountain's flat shape. Over the millennia, as the Table Mountain sandstone eroded, it produced sandy, shallow and nutrient-poor soils – not the best for vegetal growth. These are harsh conditions, and the plant species which have evolved in this spot, such as the indigenous fynbos, adapted to it. As a result, there are a great many endemic plant species in the park, and fynbos is so well adapted that, rather perversely, it reaches its greatest species diversity in places where the soil is at its poorest.

Table Mountain

Although it isn't known precisely when the first humans arrived at this dramatic spot under Table Mountain, it is thought that the first Khoikhoi pastoralists were here with their domestic animals about 2,000 years ago. Constant fresh water must have attracted them, just as it drew mariners on their way to the east.

Jan van Riebeeck was attracted by the sweet, fresh water flowing in an almost continuous stream from the steep Platteklip Gorge halfway along the face of Table Mountain. This became the first water supply for the settlement, and early stone-built reservoirs can be seen from Tafelberg Road, the scenic drive running past the cableway station. During winter this cold mountain stream becomes a torrent.

Cape Town was supplied with water from this and other springs and streams on the north face of the mountain until about 1880. However, in 1887 work began on a plan to tap the Disa Stream in the Disa Gorge on Table Mountain's back table and take it through a tunnel (the Woodhead Tunnel) in the Twelve Apostles, bringing it to the Camps Bay side of the mountain from which it would be fed by gravity to Kloof Nek and then down to the city. The tunnel and the water's route has been altered and upgraded over the years, but it's still in use today, and can be seen if you go walking on the Pipe Track. During the late 1800s and early 1900s five storage dams were built on the mountain to augment the water supply to the suburbs developing along the eastern and western slopes of the mountain.

The tablecloth phenomenon

One of the most famous images of Table Mountain is of its famous white "tablecloth". For hours on end at certain times of the year, this sits on top of the mountain, falling over the edge and down the face, always threatening to cover it but never quite doing so. It is formed when warm, moisture-laden air is pushed in from the sea and driven over the mountain, where it cools and condenses into cloud.

Exploring the mountain

The quickest way to climb the mountain is to take the **cableway** *(see below)*. Most people take this straight to the top, where they visit the restaurant or bar, have a quick walk around, then take the cable-car down. But it is worth making a half-day or day of it. There are plenty of picnic spots, viewing platforms and a variety of walks, some of which continue down the Peninsula. Whatever you decide, take some warm clothing; it may be sunny and hot down below but is likely to be quite cold on top.

Climbers and hikers have opened over 350 separate routes to the summit of Table Mountain, ranging from easy to very difficult. One of the most popular walks is the **Pipe Track**, which starts at Kloof Nek, where there's parking, and continues on to Corridor Ravine. It's about 6 km (4 miles) one way and the return trip takes about five hours. It's mostly (but not

Map on page 138

TIP

If you don't have your own transport, it is worth noting that the lower cableway station is a stop on the Cape Town Explorer open-top bus. A taxi to the cableway from the city centre will cost about 80R. Your taxi driver may offer to wait for your return (no charge made for waiting time).

LEFT: the cable-cars revolve to optimise the panoramic views.

The Cableway

The cableway is completely dependent on the weather, and if you are in Cape Town out of season you are advised to make your trip to Table Mountain on the first clear day of your stay, in case you don't get another chance. Even on a clear day the cableway doesn't operate if it is very windy. It is best to call before you set out. Operating times vary according to the time of year (Dec–end Jan 8am–9pm, last car down 10pm, Feb–Apr 8.30am–7.30pm, last car down 8.30pm, May–Nov 8.30am–5pm, last car down 6pm; tel: 021 424 8181 or www.tablemountain.net).

The cableway opened in 1929, and by the end of the 20th century had carried some 13.5 million people up to the summit. In 1997 it was closed for nine months for a major upgrade. When it reopened, the new cars were capable of carrying 64 passengers (opposed to 28 previously). The cars rotate through 360° so that passengers get the most remarkable views of the rock face and out over the city and coastline way below. It takes between three and nine minutes to get to the top, depending on the wind resistance.

Conserving the Table Mountain National Park

What you see today when you drive around the Table Mountain National Park is a sophisticated, coordinated attempt to conserve this unique natural heritage in a busy modern environment. But it hasn't always been like this. When the idea for a protected park was first suggested in 1929 by the South African Wildlife Society, it was complicated by the huge problem of who owned what. Much of the land had been devastated by alien vegetation introduced long ago by colonial settlers, and inappropriate farming had been allowed in sensitive areas. The first formal conservation of any part of this enormous area came about in 1939, when the Cape of Good Hope Nature Reserve was proclaimed at the southern tip of the Peninsula.

After the Table Mountain itself (all the land above the 152-metre/500-ft contour line) became a National Monument in 1958, several local authorities established nature reserves under their own jurisdictions. The City of Cape Town proclaimed the Table Mountain Nature Reserve in 1963 and the Silvermine Nature Reserve in 1965, con-

serving much of the mountain north of Fish Hoek. But that wasn't nearly enough. The problem was that these areas were owned and managed by 14 different public bodies, while over 200 private landowners controlled considerable chunks of the Peninsula and did virtually what they wanted with it. After numerous attempts over many years to consolidate land ownership under one conservation management authority, the first portions of the Cape Peninsula National Park were proclaimed in May 1998, and placed under a single management authority, the South African National Parks. In 2004 it was renamed the Table Mountain National Park.

The spin-off from all of this, is tourism. Once apartheid had ended Cape Town's exceptional scenery and climate had to be put to good use to attract visitors and make a meaningful contribution to the socio-economic development of citizens living on and around the park's borders.

The outcome has been very successful indeed – some 4.2 million people visit the Table Mountain National Park each year. But increased tourism brings its own problems, and the park is still threatened by a number of factors, many of them the result of its proximity to a dense urban area. They include the spread of invasive alien plants, wildfires, encroaching urban development and informal settlements, increasing recreational use and the illegal exploitation of the area.

The Table Mountain National Park is very much a work in progress, and as time goes by it is establishing partnerships with the many previously disadvantaged neighbouring communities, creating employment and educating people about caring for the environment, all the while looking at the paucity of water resources, conservation strategies where development cannot be avoided, and management of the landscape in the face of income-generating tourist use of the Park's precious resources. It all goes to show that one of South Africa's most attractive treasures has, in effect, been under-utilised and under-regarded for many years. ❑

LEFT: magnificent Lion's Head.

always) flat, running along the contours of the mountain, and the views down over the coast of the Atlantic Seaboard to Camps Bay and its surroundings are magical.

Another walk, popular with locals early in the morning before they go to work, is to the top of **Lion's Head**. At 669 metres (2,194 ft), the summit takes an hour or so to reach if you're fit, and offers a breathtaking bird's-eye view of the city on all sides. It's a favourite at sunset as well, and during a full moon (bring a bottle of champagne). Quite steep at the beginning, it then pans out, before ladders and chains embedded in the rock aid the final stretch to the top. There is an alternative route using the contour path. It's a safe walk and well worth the effort.

The climb up **Platteklip Gorge** is another very popular (perhaps too popular) route. The track zigzags to the top of the mountain from Tafelberg Road. It is about 3 km (1½ miles), and takes fit walkers about an hour to complete. If you want to take the cable-car down, turn right at the top (Fountain Peak) and follow the path to Upper Cableway Station.

Skeleton Gorge is another popular Table Mountain climb. You can pick it up at the back of Kirstenbosch *(see page 125)* or along the Contour Path from Rhodes Memorial *(see page 120)* or from the Newlands Forest. The gorge, which is very steep, was a favourite walk of the South African statesman General Jan Christiaan Smuts, who walked it regularly until he was well into his seventies. It leads through dense, lush forest (deliciously cool in summer), then climbs over steep rocky sections to Maclear's Beacon, at 1,086 metres (3,560 ft). Erected in 1843 by the astronomer Sir Thomas Maclear, the beacon was part of an experiment to measure the circumference of the earth more accurately.

Up here you'll see the Hely-Hutchinson Dam (look for the red disas in late summer) and the aqueduct leading to it.

Serious hikes

The walks listed above can easily be done in a day. There are others which can take up to a week. The

Map on page 138

To the Xhosa, the earth goddess Djobela placed giants in the four corners of the earth and turned them into mountains to guard the world. The greatest of these was Umlindi Welingizunu, Table Mountain, Watcher of the South.

BELOW: the tablecloth phenomenon.

Numerous hiking trails take in a wide range of scenery, from rugged terrain to sylvan slopes.

BELOW: Table
Mountain is one of the
best places to watch
the dawn or sunset.

first overnight trail to be established was the **Cape of Good Hope Hiking Trail**, which takes two days and covers about 33 km (20 miles) in all (call the Buffelsfontein Visitor Centre, tel: 021 780 9204 for more information and to book). The first day, which covers about 10.5 km (6 miles) of rugged terrain, leads past lonely, windswept beaches on the Atlantic coastline, passes the wreck of the *Phyllisia*, and then follows the eastern boundary of the reserve to overnight huts near Cape Point. Herds of bontebok, eland and other antelope are usually seen grazing along this stretch. The second day, covering 19 km (12 miles), concentrates on the Cape of Good Hope and Cape Point.

The overnight huts (ex-World War II observation points of the Coastal Defence Corps) are equipped with toilets, hot showers, bunks and mattresses, gas stoves and *braais*.

A new hiking trail, **Hoerikwaggo**, after the Khoikhoi name for Table Mountain, runs the full length of the peninsula. The trail is a five-day, six-night hiking trail starting from Deer

Park, above Vredehoek. Overnight stops are made on the Back Table, then at Silvermine, Red Hill, above Smitswinkel Bay, and finally at the Goldfields Centre near Cape Point. Accommodation is in huts or tents.

Access to the **Orange Kloof Protected Area** – encircled by Constantia Corner Ridge and Bel Ombre, the Back Table and the Twelve Apostles – is strictly by permit only (contact the Table Mountain National Park office, tel: 021 701 8692). Groups of up to 12 people can organise a free permit and a guide to take them through this magnificent wilderness area. Highlights include the indigenous forest, including yellowwoods, milkwoods, red alder and Cape beech, and beautiful kloofs adorned with ferns.

Other guided hikes take visitors to remote and beautiful spots such as **Hell's Gate** with its tumbling waterfalls and pools, and **Disa Gorge**, up which one can ascend to the Back Table. Contact the Table Mountain National Park for information and permits.

Fabulous flora

The vegetation types in the Table Mountain National Park constitute a flora so rich in species that it is not only the most diverse section of the Cape Floral Kingdom *(see pages 78–9)*, but also, from a botanical point of view, the richest area, for its size, anywhere on the planet, surpassing even the tropical rainforests in its diversity.

The most common vegetation type is fynbos, including heaths *(Ericaceae)*, noted for its lovely colours ranging from butter yellow to red and purple. Fynbos also includes reeds *(Restionaceae)* and proteas *(Proteaceae)*. Some of the most conspicuous fynbos species on the mountain are from the protea family, and include the King protea *Protea cynaroides*, South Africa's national emblem. Of the 112 protea plants in the world, 69 occur in fynbos. Apart from the King Protea, there's the sugarbush, yellow pincushions, tree pincushions, golden cone bushes and silver trees which grow on the flank of Lion's Head.

Among the shrubs below these larger species is evidence of the extraordinary species diversity for which fynbos is famous. This is particularly so with the geophytes, such as members of the disa, gladiolus, moraea, watsonia, babiana and iris genera. Many geophytes are well known for their spectacular displays when flowering en masse, particularly in the wake of fire. Strangely, fynbos needs fire to survive and flourish. It stimulates it to germinate and flower. Even smoke has the same effect.

While fynbos dominates, there are at least three other significant vegetation types in the park. The first of these is renosterbos ("rhinoceros bush"), which is also rich in geophytes. Found principally on Signal Hill and on the lower slopes of Devil's Peak, it takes its name from the drab, grey shrub *Elytropappus rhinocerotis* that is common here. Also characteristic of renosterbos is the presence of grasses, which in this veld type take the place of restios, and the virtual absence of proteas.

Another vegetation type is afromontane forest and thicket. This

Map on page 138

TIP

If you go hiking, it is important to be security conscious. Always stick to the paths and trails, and if the mist comes down stay where you are rather than try to make your way back down, which can be perilous. It is essential to let someone know where you are going before you set off and also to take a cell phone.

BELOW: far-reaching views from the top of Table Mountain.

Dassies are common inhabitants of the Cape Mountain National Park. Along with sea cows, they are an unlikely relative of the elephant. All three share some physiological similarities in teeth and in leg and foot bones.

BELOW: abseiling is one exhilarating way of enjoying Table Mountain.

covers only around three percent of the Cape Peninsula, and is mainly established along the cooler, well-watered ravines on the eastern slopes of Table Mountain – above Constantia and Newlands, and in Orange Kloof.

From dassies to bontebok

Once upon a time you would have climbed Table Mountain at your peril. Lion, leopard and hyena lived here. Early callers at the Cape commented on the abundance of large animals they encountered here.

The large predators were shot or driven away in the early years of European settlement (the last lion, for example, was killed in 1802), but many of the smaller animals found here historically still survive, which is remarkable when you consider that Cape Town has experienced over 350 years of urban, agricultural and industrial development. The park still supports viable populations of bontebok, grysbok, caracal, mongoose, dassies, otter and Chacma baboons.

Baboons have been part of the

fynbos ecosystem on the Cape Peninsula for about a million years, but are now critically endangered. With the arrival of the settlers and the subsequent development of the Cape Flats, cutting off the Cape Peninsula from the rest of the Western Cape, Peninsula baboons were effectively stranded. Increasingly they compete for space with humans. Although not threatened as a species, there are only about 360 baboons left in the park, living in 10 troops mostly in the southern Peninsula *(see page 158)*. You will almost certainly see them as you drive around Scarborough to Cape Point, and if you do, slow down. They like to sit on the tarmac because it is warm, and they won't necessarily get out of your way. They live off fynbos plants, including sour fig, and forage on the shore for mussels and limpets. If you are caught feeding them you will be fined.

You will also almost certainly also chance upon the ubiquitous dassie (rock hyrax), whose closest living relative is, strangely, the African elephant. Dassies thrive in

areas of nutrient-poor unpalatable plant species. Look down from the cable-car as it's travelling to and from the cable station and you'll see them sunning themselves on the rocks. They're diurnal – that is, they come out when the sun's up and retire when it goes in again.

Of the reptiles you could encounter, Cape cobra, puff adder, rinkhals and boomslang snakes are the most deadly. On the footpaths of Table Mountain in the summer Cape cobras and puff adders are a definite possibility. You should wear stout shoes or hiking boots when out walking or hiking.

Best birds

A large variety of birds also call the park home, but not in the numbers often found in other parts of South Africa. The problem is the fynbos vegetation. However, some are endemic, and have evolved specifically for this habitat. One is the beautiful Cape sugarbird, another the orange-breasted sunbird. The former is found wherever you see proteas or pincushions in flower. There are also plenty of raptors to be seen, including hawk, eagle, buzzard, kite, kestrel and falcon. Some, like the peregrine falcon, rare in the rest of Africa, are quite common in the park, especially in the more rugged areas. The African fish eagle can be seen in both central and southern sections of the Cape Peninsula.

The best places for birdwatching are Kirstenbosch (*see page 128*, particularly if you want to see the Cape sugarbird; Silvermine for other fynbos birds), and Cape Point for seabirds *(see page 158)*. On the summit of Table Mountain, where the vegetation is quite sparse, expect to see the orange-breasted sunbird, ground woodpecker, Cape rock-thrush, Cape brassbird, African black swift and Alpine swift.

Sports and activities

Lastly, Table Mountain National Park is a playground for adventure sports, from abseiling and rock climbing to mountain biking and hang-glinding. *For information on how to access such activities see pages 226 of Travel Tips.* ❑

Map on page 138

Look out for the orange-breasted sunbird. For more information on birding in the Cape log on to www.cape birdingroute.org.

BELOW: rest and refreshment at the top of the cableway.

RESTAURANT & BAR

On a warm day the best option is to bring a picnic and enjoy the views. Failing that, there is a self-service restaurant and a cocktail bar *(see below)*. Alternatively, you could stop at one of the restaurants in Clifton or Camps Bay.

Self-service Restaurant

Hot and cold meals and snacks. Locals recommend coming here for breakfast before setting out on a day's hike.

The Cableway Cocktail Bar

Situated above the top cableway station, with panoramic views. The terrace, if you can find a free table, is nicer than the inside.

THE CAPE IN BLOOM

In spring the Cape bursts into flamboyant colour, but other seasons offer horticultural highlights, such as the winter-blooming Crane flower

The characteristic vegetation of the Cape Floral Kingdom is a low heath-like evergreen ground cover known as fynbos (fine bush). It can appear rather drab at first glance, especially during the dry summer months. On closer inspection, however, the apparent monotony of the summer fynbos landscape is transformed into a rich sprinkling of subtle pastel hues – and the entire region explodes into colour during the spring wild-flower season. Most conspicuous in spring, especially along the Garden Route, are the brightly coloured blooms of various ursinia, senecio and cotula species of the daisy family *(see picture page 190)*.

Perhaps the best-known floral feature of the region, however, is its profusion of proteas, notably the spectacular King protea, with its conical 30-cm (12-inch) red flowers, and other members of the genera protea and mimetes. These proteas are at their most spectacular in winter.

LEFT: to see cycads, visit the Cycad Amphitheatre at Kirstenbosch Botanical Gardens.

ABOVE: you will find the spectacular Crane flower, also known as Bird of paradise *(Strelitzia reginae)* in many Cape Town gardens, including Company's Garden. It blooms in winter.

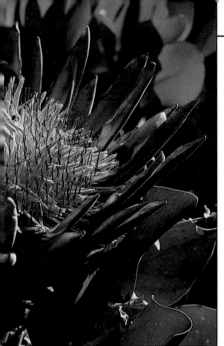

ABOVE: the King protea is most spectacular in late winter–early spring, when its nectar forms the diet of the Cape sugarbird, one of eight species endemic to fynbos habitat.

BELOW: aloes andother succulents flourish in South Africa, and you will see them growing wild in the Table Mountain National Park.

THE CAPE FLORAL KINGDOM

With its parched summers and damp winters, the so-called Mediterranean climate that characterises the southwestern coastal belt is an inversion of the summer rainfall pattern in the rest of southern Africa. And the borders of this isolated winter rainfall region also define those of what is by far the smallest of the world's six recognised floral kingdoms, an ecological island that extends over some 90,000 sq. km (3,475 sq. miles) yet supports a tally of almost 9,000 flowering plant species, most of which occur nowhere else in the world.

To place this in some perspective, although just one-tenth of these species occur within the 75-sq. km (29-sq. mile) Cape of Good Hope Nature Reserve on the southern tip of the Cape Peninsula, this still amounts to more than half the species indigenous to the entire European subcontinent.

Just north of the Cape Floral Kingdom, starting about 100 km (60 miles) inland of Cape Town, the Karoo is a flat, dry semi-desert. Superficially it seems bereft of life. Yet it is one of the world's top biodiversity hot-spots, dominated by succulents – a full 1,700 species, accounting for 10 percent of the global total. And in August and September, when the Karoo receives its meagre annual allocation of precipitation, its 400 species of spring annuals erupt into a riot of colour.

RIGHT: South Africa's most famous orchid, *Disa uniflora*, is known as the Pride of Table Mountain.

THE CAPE PENINSULA

The Cape Peninsula is one of South Africa's great natural landscapes, a stunning sequence of glorious mountains and gorgeous sandy beaches culminating at Cape Point

A trip around the coast of the Cape Peninsula will take you a day by car – that's if you want to stop along the way and swim, picnic or eat at a restaurant, admire a view, take in the flora and see animals, birds and historic buildings. There's all this, and more. You could do parts of it on one day, and other parts on another. You could just travel to Cape Point for a swim, or to Scarborough for lunch on Sunday. But wherever you decide to go, and whatever you decide to see, the one constant is an epic chain of mountains that runs from Table Mountain in the city to Cape Point. On the way it passes all the famous peaks of the Peninsula – including the Twelve Apostles, the Constantiaberg, the Noordhoek Peak, the Swartkop Mountains, Kalk Bay Peak and Steenberg.

The landscape

For the most part, the route around this famous spit of land jutting out into the Atlantic at the bottom of Africa hugs the shoreline. Occasionally it rises to great heights, as at Chapman's Peak, and gingerly skirts a sheer cliff face which plunges some 200–300 metres (650–1,000 ft) into the sea. The topography of the Cape Peninsula is stunning, and even if you set out

simply to admire the various views, you'll return to base more than satisfied that you've seen one of the great sights of Africa. On the way you'll see a great variety of fynbos plant species, many of them endemic, and if you visit the nature reserve at Cape Point you'll see some of the fauna which once roamed this part of the world.

Around the coastline are coves, inlets and sandy beaches popular with the locals not for swimming, because the water's mostly too cold,

Map on page 150

LEFT: the cloud-clad Twelve Apostles above Camps Bay.
BELOW: on the rocks at Camps Bay.

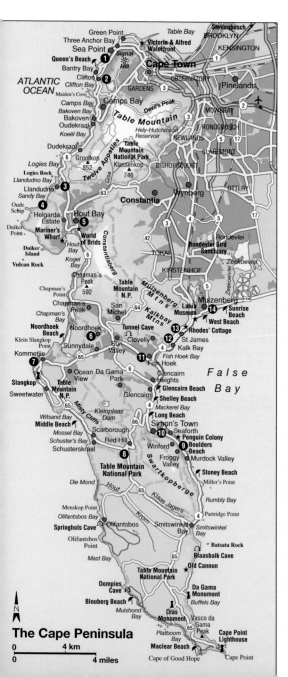

The Cape Peninsula

0   4 km

0   4 miles

but for surfing, sunbathing and walking the dog. Some places, like the Atlantic Seaboard from Sea Point to Camps Bay, are built up. Indeed, Clifton, where Capetonians go to bare their beautiful bodies, has some of the most expensive real estate in Africa – even for a very small property. Some R22 million for a clapboard cottage with two bedrooms and 150 steps to get to it? Come and see.

Other parts of the Peninsula are quiet and empty, and you can be quite alone on your walk – visit the coastline from Kommetjie via Scarborough to Cape Point. Other places, such as Simon's Town, are filled with historic buildings and museums, while Kalk Bay has a concentration of antique and bric-a-brac shops.

The False Bay coast is warmer than either the Atlantic Seaboard or Hout Bay, Noordhoek or Kommetjie. At Fishhoek, St James and, best of all, Muizenberg, you can swim for hours. And all along the coast there are places to eat or relax over a drink, and there are many great hotels and guest houses if you want to spend the night.

This route starts at Table Bay, rounds the tip of the Peninsula and ends in False Bay at Muizenberg. In all, it's about 100 km (60 miles).

Sea Point

Between the seaward side of the rump of Lion's Head and the coastline of Table Bay, just before it merges with the Atlantic Ocean, is **Sea Point ❶**, a busy, brash, noisy and slightly seedy section of town noted for its apartment blocks, takeaways, dodgy nightclubs and porn shops. In the 19th century wealthy Capetonians built holiday villas here, surrounded by gardens of exotic palms and pungent, scented shrubs. Most of these have now gone, and today prostitutes,

Map on page 150

both male and female, drug dealers, drunks and assorted riff-raff congregate along its two main arteries, Main and Beach Roads.

But the neighbourhood is changing for the better. The widespread installation of street cameras has made it a much safer area in which to live, and in the wake of the recent property boom in Cape Town, Sea Point's old apartment blocks, Victorian terraces and modern villas are suddenly shooting up in value. The upgrading of Sea Point has begun.

Along the seafront, under the various apartment blocks lining the landward side of Beach Road, some of them art deco, you'll also see joggers and cyclists making use of the wide promenade, nannies with prams, old ladies and their nurses, couples with dogs, and children from the townships playing football. **Graaff's Pool**, a wide, natural rock pool protected from view by a whitewashed wall, is a nudists' haven in the heart of the city. Gay men cruise the area until the early hours of the morning.

Sea Point has an urban character entirely alien to the rest of the city. Along Main Road, at night a strip of flashing billboards, you can find something to eat virtually 24 hours a day, as well as the city's best video-rental stores. There are banks, supermarkets, delis, pubs, restaurants, chemists, hotels, guest houses and backpackers' lodges, clothing and liquor stores, locksmiths, DIY centres and garages.

Sea Point even has the occasional stretch of beach where you can swim. There are some old tidal pools here, which at the weekend are very busy indeed. The newly restored **Sea Point Public Pool** has changing rooms and showers.

Bantry Bay and Clifton

From Beach Road, the seaside drive enters Queen's Road and then Victoria Road, passes through Bantry Bay, overlooked from on high by one of the city's best hotels, Ellerman House, and continues on to Clifton, all the time hugging the steep mountainside beneath Lion's Head – which looks at its most monumental from here. This is known as

Between Bantry Bay and Clifton is a promontory (signposted) where igneous and sedimentary rock meets, thus forming the continental shelf. Charles Darwin stopped off to inspect the site on his round-the-world voyage on the Beagle *in 1836.*

BELOW: surveying the scene at Sea Point.

Kloof is originally an Afrikaans word for ravine or cliff, though it has now passed into English. You will come across it frequently in place names. The term "kloofing" refers to the adventure sport of following a river through a gorge, jumping into pools from great heights.

BELOW: Lion's Head marks the start of the Atlantic Seaboard.

the "lower road". The so-called "upper road", Kloof Road, can be entered by continuing to the top of Queen's Road and turning right, continuing until you descend to Victoria Road above Glen Beach on the approach to Camps Bay. The views from the upper road are some of best in Cape Town.

Bantry Bay is a lovely, small seaside neighbourhood characterised by sedate Victorian villas and old gardens filled with palms and bougainvillea. Its neighbour, **Clifton ❷**, is somewhat brasher. It has four little wind-free coves, each one an amphitheatre lined with characteristic bungalows. Don't be deceived, however. Bungalows they may be, simple they're not. Many have been redeveloped, and are luxurious. Clifton is a millionaire's playground, and if you can afford a pad here you've made it.

In summer, the stretch of Victoria Road running through Clifton is virtually impassable and parking impossible to find. Everybody wants to come to the beach here for a piece of the action, even though it is far

too cold to swim anywhere along this coastline – except in the heated pools of the locals.

Choose your beach

The four coves have become popular with different types of people. **Fourth Beach**, the furthest away, on the Camps Bay side, is longer and wider than the others, and generally packed with families with their nannies and dogs. The water is shallow for the first few metres, then slopes away gradually. It's safe to bathe here, if you can stand the icy-cold water, and there are lifeguards on duty during summer. A little further offshore, private yachts are at anchor and water-skiing and canoeing are on offer. You can also hire umbrellas and beach chairs, and there are little booths for cool drinks and ice cream.

Next door, at **Third Beach**, you'll find the city's most beautiful bodies on display. Tanned and taut, they parade up and down, with every curve and bulge on show. Capetonians are very body-conscious, and nowhere more so than here.

Third Beach is again popular with gays, all of whom seem to know each other. If you're an out-of-towner, this is where you'll make your friends. During the holidays there's a continuous round of beach, clubs and parties to go to, none of it worth much unless you are a regular at the gym. As on Fourth Beach there are umbrellas and chairs for hire, and ice cream and water sellers beat their weary path down here too.

At **Second Beach** you'll find quieter, fatter gays, straight men playing ball, dogs gambolling in the waves and couples napping under their umbrellas. **First Beach** is much the same, but less busy, not least because it is accessed via 100 steps, which make for a long and arduous climb after a lazy day on the beach. If it's peace and quiet you're after, First Beach is where you should go.

Camps Bay

From the beaches at Clifton you can see Table Mountain in profile. To the right you get your first view of the **Twelve Apostles**, which, by the time you've rounded the wide bend of Victoria Road above Glen Beach on the approach to Camps Bay, are in full view. From the wide – and very windy – beach at Camps Bay, the sweep of mountains and sea is magnificent. Again, the water is so cold that it is hard even to dip your toes into the water, but brave souls do when the summer heat becomes too hot to handle.

Camps Bay is a popular beach all year round. It's wide, backed by lawns dotted with palms, and is easily accessible from the road. There are cold showers and toilets at either end. Everybody comes here, from families to singles, from beauties to those who couldn't give a damn, and there are umbrellas and chairs to rent. There is also a big tidal pool, which is great for a gentle wave-free swim.

There's plenty of parking up in the streets of Camps Bay, and all along the front are lots of popular, busy cafés, bars and restaurants, some simple, some swanky, for breakfast, lunch and dinner – or just a drink with a view. One hotel, the

Map on page 150

TIP

If you have your own transport, Camps Bay is one of the best places to come for a sundowner. There are several good cocktail bars with ringside views of the sunset and the youthful passing scene.

BELOW: the beach at Camps Bay.

Bay Hotel, is attached to the Rotunda, built in 1903 as a roller-skating rink and dubbed the "best dance floor in South Africa". Today it's the hotel's function room. There are plenty of guest houses and B&Bs with their own swimming pools, all within easy distance of the beach.

Camps Bay itself is again a very expensive suburb, which isn't surprising given the panoramic views of the coastline from virtually every vantage point. Up on the Lion's Head side is the early-19th-century Round House, which was built on the circular foundations of one of the small batteries which guarded one of the approaches to Cape Town. As the building stands now, it was Lord Charles Somerset's shooting box; inside it is still kitted out with four gun cupboards. At the time wild animals, including lion and leopard, still roamed the mountainsides here – which is hard to believe when you take your dog for a walk up the "glen" surrounding it. The Round House and the neighbouring youth hostel, Stan's

Halt, have magnificent views out over the Camps Bay coastline to Llandudno.

Llandudno and Sandy Bay

Between Camps Bay and Llandudno, Victoria Road continues on its way, skirting the last stretch of beach in the vicinity where the mountain launches an uninterrupted sweep down to the sea. At **Oudekraal**, just before Victoria Road rounds a corner and passes the Twelve Apostles Hotel, you can skin dive at an old wreck, and there are places to picnic or *braai*. There is also a tidal pool (entrance fee). It's very popular in summer, so go early.

From here the road continues to **Llandudno ❸**. As it climbs towards the "nek" which opens the way to Hout Bay, take the right-hand fork and corkscrew your way down to a junction which, to the right, leads to Llandudno beach, and to the left, Sandy Bay. Llandudno is another expensive suburb of lovely modern beach houses built to maximise the view. Parking is minimal; be prepared to walk down the steep roads

TIP

The Cape Peninsula offers some of the best surfing in South Africa. Visit www.wavescape.co.za. For the latest surf report, tel: 082 234 6370.

BELOW: waiting for the big one at Llandudno.

Map on page 150

to the beach. This is a quiet beach, great for sitting and dreaming, or sunbathing. People come here to surf, although again the water is icy. There are no shops in Llandudno, and rarely do the ice-cream sellers make it this far, so make sure you bring snacks and drinks.

Sandy Bay ❹ is also busy, frequented by sun-worshippers who prefer to do it in the nude. The only way to reach Sandy Bay is to park in the small area at the end of the road, then walk, for up to 3 km (2 miles), along the wonderful long white beach. On the way, a section filled with enormous boulders and little private inlets and overhangs is popular with naked gays. But if you go early on a weekday morning you could have the whole area to yourself. It's a magical place. Take your clothes off, oil yourself up, and settle down with a book or have a nap. When it gets too hot, take a dip in a rock pool. The beach itself is popular with couples, same-sex and straight, who make a day of it, taking an umbrella, a coolbox for food and drink, and the dogs. It's never too busy here, as the walk puts people off.

Hout Bay

Victoria Road sweeps down into **Hout Bay ❺**, a seaside district that takes its name from the fact that it was an important source of timber for the Dutch East India Company since the very earliest date of the colony (*hout* is an Afrikaans word meaning wood). There was an early farm here. A Cape Dutch house called Kronendal, dated 1800 or so, still stands there today, the only surviving example in the Cape Peninsula of an H-shaped house.

Hout Bay has been a fishing village for many years and has a busy little harbour and informal places to buy and eat fresh fish. **Mariner's Wharf** (open daily 9am–5pm; tel: 021 790 1100) is the best place to

come. There are also little shops selling T-shirts, shells, postcards and buckets and spades, as well as self-service and takeaway restaurants.

Ask at the tourist information office (tel: 021 790 1264) about boat trips out to nearby **Duiker Island** to see the 7,000-strong colony of Cape Fur Seals. Diving and snorkelling can be arranged.

Also here is the **World of Birds** (daily 9am–5pm; admission charge), the largest bird park on the continent. Its walk-through aviaries are home to some 3,000 indigenous and exotic birds of 350 different species.

There's not much left of the village's old character, and few traditional buildings have survived. However, there's a pretty stone-built Anglican church of St Peter the Fisherman dating from 1895, and, as you leave town and enter Chapman's Peak, passing the popular Chapman's Peak Hotel on the left, you can visit what remains of the **East Fort**, erected to protect the bay when hostilities broke out between the Dutch and the British in 1781. Two batteries were built to

Llandudno, one of a string of expensive suburbs stretching south of Camps Bay.

BELOW: long alfresco lunches are an essential part of summer.

Look out for African black oystercatchers and other waders at Noordhoek.

protect the bay and a third was later added by the British. The site was abandoned in 1827 and partially dismantled, but enough remains for you to get an idea of what the complex looked like. It has tremendous views out over Hout Bay to Kapteinspiek and The Sentinel, its beach (popular with mothers and their children, and dog-walkers) and the harbour.

As you leave Hout Bay, Chapman's Peak Drive hugs the foothills of the **Constantiaberg** and **Noordhoek Peak** above **Kogel Bay**. The drive is one of the most impressive stretches of road in the country. It's a cliff road (also known as the M6), the construction of which defied all the odds in 1915. Joining Hout Bay and Noordhoek, it was built by convicts over the course of seven years. Rockfalls have marred it since the day it was built, and after expensive remedial work in 2000, it reopened in 2004 as a toll road (one-way fee is about R20 for an ordinary car). At its summit there are wonderful panoramic views out over the coastline above Chapman's Point.

Noordhoek

As you round the final curve of Chapman's Peak Drive, look straight ahead and you will see the vast expanse (4 miles/6 km) of **Noordhoek Beach**, a location used in the filming of *Ryan's Daughter*, and perfect for horse-riding. At its landward side, wetlands attract wild birds. This section, including Noordhoek Beach, is now owned by South Africa National Parks, ensuring its future protection.

If you want some idea of what the Peninsula must have been like before anyone settled here, visit **Noordhoek ❻**. There is little or no building on its edge, and the only humans you're likely to see are dog-walkers. There are a few shipwrecks to be seen on the sand. However, the isolation of this beautiful spot has attracted muggers, so leave your valuables at home and tell someone where you are going.

At the furthermost (southern) end past Klein-Slangkop Point, is **Kommetjie ❼**, another seaside village, reached at the junction of the M6 and M65. Once a village of holiday

Map on page 150

homes, it is becoming increasingly popular with commuters. It's sufficiently distant from the city to be a quiet haven, yet within reasonable commuting distance. Its beach, Long Beach, is lovely, white and wide, but as at Noordhoek, swimming is dangerous. There is a strong undercurrent that can carry you out to sea immediately.

A lovely walk takes in both beaches. On the way look out for African black oystercatchers, African sacred ibis, lapwings, plovers, egrets and other waders. Do this walk when the tide is out so that you can make use of the harder sand at the shoreline.

The M65 continues on around the coast, passing the **Slangkop Lighthouse**, built in 1919, Witsand Bay, Misty Cliffs and on to the village of **Scarborough** which has two restaurants – Cobbs at the Cape and Camel Rock. If you want a simple lunch on your drive, this is the place to make a stop. Cobbs has a terrace with beautiful views over the surrounding area, including the beach, which is popular with surfers and Sunday dog-walkers. But, again beware: the currents are strong and swimming is very dangerous.

Cape Point

From Scarborough, the M65 continues on its way across the Peninsula to the gates of what used to be known as the Cape of Good Hope Nature Reserve at Cape Point – it includes the southernmost tip of the Cape Peninsula. From Scarborough to Cape Point, and from the M65 to the sea in the west, it is is now known as the **Table Mountain National Park** ❽ (open daily Apr–Aug 7am–5pm, Sept–Oct 6am–6pm; admission charge), part of the wider park area that includes the Table Mountain range, the Constantiaberg, the land behind Sand Bay and Silvermine. Altogether, this is a vast area, continually being made larger by the addition of other tracts of land when they become available.

You won't be disappointed, and it is worth coming for the day. The reserve has pristine original landscape and vegetation. Fashioned

False Bay on the east side of Cape Point reputedly got its name on account of it being mistaken for Table Bay by early mariners.

LEFT: taking the funicular down to the view site at Cape Point.

Cape of Storms or Cape of Good Hope?

All the romance of the sea route around the Cape of Storms to the east is vested in this tongue of land jutting out into a fierce, stormy ocean. Somewhere at Cape Point Bartolomeu Dias, who set sail from Lisbon in 1487 with three small ships, erected a *padrão*. Its location is uncertain, but only recently a small cross was found engraved on a rock, and it is thought this could be the location.

Dias called the Peninsula the Cape of Storms, while his contemporary, the Portuguese King João renamed it the Cape of Good Hope in anticipation of opening a sea route to the east. Vasco da Gama came later, reaching India in 1498. Sir Francis Drake also sailed by in 1580, and on a clear, still day you can see why he called it "the most stately thing and the fairest cape we saw in the whole circumference of the earth".

But on a wild and windy day it is very much the Cape of Storms, as testified by the many shipwrecks littering the Cape, each one documented at the museum in Simon's Town *(see page 161)* and at the Maritime Museum in Cape Town *(see page 98)*.

Two members of the baboon population at Cape Point.

from two old farms, Buffelsfontein and Blaauberg Vlei, it was formed in 1939. Today 77 sq. km (30 sq. miles) is covered in fynbos – the major vegetation type of the Cape Floral Kingdom, the smallest, and for its size, the richest of the world's six floral kingdoms.

Wildlife includes baboons, Cape mountain zebra, eland, bontebok, grey rhebok and grysbok. The beaches are magnificent (in what other city could you see wild game wandering along the beach as you lie in the sun and picnic?), and the the Two Oceans Restaurant is to hand for breakfasts and lunch. The restaurant has a magnificent terrace looking out over False Bay. There's also a visitor's centre with maps of the reserve and information about walks, things to do and the various wild animals and birds that can be seen (tel: 021 780 9402).

Boulders Beach

From the gates of the reserve, the M65 continues east towards False Bay, and as it bears north, it becomes the M4 on its way to Boul-

ders and Simon's Town. **Boulders Beach** ❾ is well known for its rare (listed as "vulnerable" in the Red Data Book listing threatened species) jackass penguins (also known as African penguins) which colonised the beach in 1982. Africa's only penguin, they have bred prolifically since then (there are more than 3,000 birds living here today), and Boulders Beach is now a National Park.

The beach itself is stunning. Huge boulders protect it from wind, and at one time it was possible to swim. Not so any more, as it's all about the penguins. If you want to see them it will cost you the price of ticket to take a walk along the specially con-structed boardwalks, as they bray at each other and play on the sand (daily 8am–6.30pm). This is the only place in the world where you can get close to them.

Simon's Town

Boulders Beach lies on the outskirts of **Simon's Town** ❿, the head-quarters of the South African Navy. This is a seaside village rich in

history and filled with character.

Simon's Town acquired its name from the visit Simon van der Stel paid to the area in 1687. It was originally an alternative anchorage for ships in Table Bay, which in winter were often driven ashore and wrecked by the prevailing north-west wind. Only after 1814, after the Second British Occupation, did it become a naval base. Simon's Town has one of the densest clusters of old buildings in the country, and many of them are still used, Admiralty House, the Residency, the Martello Tower and the British Hotel among them.

There's plenty to do and see here, with the main attractions easily accessible from the main road running through the town. At the centre of town is **Jubilee Square 🅐** with its tall palm trees and statue of Able Seaman Just Nuisance, a famous Great Dane. The mascot of the Royal Navy during World War II, Just Nuisance befriended and inspired the visiting sailors. His birthday is 1 April – known as Just Nuisance Day, which is celebrated with a parade of Great Danes and other dogs through the town to Jubilee Square. You can even visit the dog's grave *(see page 162)*.

The waterfront below Jubilee Square overlooks the yacht basin and the town pier. Boat trips along the shore and into the naval harbour provide an interesting introduction to the town and its rich history as well as a glimpse of the South African Navy at work.

The **Simon's Town Museum 🅑** (open 9am–4pm Mon–Fri, 10am–1pm Sat, 11am–3pm Sun; tel: 021 786 3046; admission charge), in the historic Residency, built in 1777 as the winter residence for the Dutch East India Company Governor at the Cape, is one of the best museums of its kind in South Africa and well worth visiting. It encapsulates

the history of the town and its people, and their connection both to the Dutch East India Company and the Royal Navy, in great detail. The museum also arranges guided walks around the more historic parts of the town, including both the mosque and the churches.

The Residency was used over the years as a hospital, post office, school, customs house, police station, gaol and magistrate's court, and the exhibits reflect the composite functions of this lovely old building. They begin with artefacts relating to the earliest inhabitants of the area, and tools and equipment of the Khoisan people of the South Peninsula are also exhibited. The early history of the Company and van der Stel is well documented. Displays point out the earliest buildings in the area – some the early farm buildings that still dot the mountain slopes around Simon's Bay. Many of these original buildings have been declared National Monuments.

Simon's Town also played a strategic role in the aftermath of

Map on page 160

Wardens keep a watchful eye on the penguins of Boulders Beach.

BELOW: an African or jackass penguin on Boulders Beach.

TIP

If you don't have your own transport, you can travel all the way to Simon's Town by rail from Cape Town's railway station *(see page 204)*. It is a lovely ride along the False Bay coast, with sea views and stops at Kalk Bay, St James and Fish Hoek. However, for safety reasons, be sure to take a train with a restaurant car and sit there.

BELOW: shopping in Simon's Town.

Napoleon's rampage across Europe in the 18th century. Britain took the colony at the Cape from the Dutch at the Battle of Muizenberg in 1795 to prevent it falling into the hands of the French. They erected a small fort known as a Martello Tower in St George's Street to reinforce their defence (1796).

The British handed the Cape back to the Batavian Government in 1803. Three years later they were back, this time for good, after the Battle of Blaauwberg in 1806. The Royal Navy established the South Atlantic base at Simon's Town in 1814, thus beginning its 143-year occupation of the port. The tiny settlement expanded rapidly from a far-flung winter anchorage to a strategic naval port that played an important role in the expansion of the British Empire.

Elsewhere, displays highlight the early development of schools (the first was Cradock's Dutch School,

opened in the Residency in 1813) and the building of the town's churches and hospitals. The oldest church in Simon's Town is the Wesleyan Chapel (1828), which served the Anglicans as well as the Dutch Reformed Church congregation until their own church was built in 1856. The Roman Catholic Church of SS Simon and Jude was built in 1850, while the local Muslims completed the Noorul Islam Mosque in 1926. The latter had formerly been a house in which the faithful had met since 1888. The exhibition forms part of an attempt to record and preserve the history of some 7,000 people who were forcibly relocated to other parts of the Cape Peninsula and beyond under the Group Areas Act by the apartheid government in the 1960s.

Of the many hospitals in Simon's Town, the most impressive was the Dutch East India Company Hospital, with its three sea-facing gables.

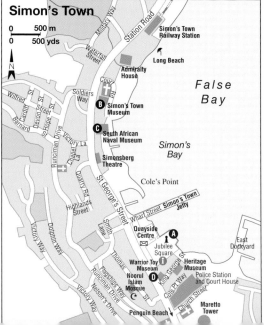

It was built on the mountainside above the Residency in 1764. More famous though, and of greater interest, is Old Hospital Terrace, built in 1814 for the Royal Navy. Here Lord Lister's new antiseptic methods were used for the first time in South Africa. The old Military Hospital was where Edgar Wallace, poet, author and playwright, served as a medical orderly in the late 1890s.

The new Royal Naval Hospital, built in 1901, had a very good reputation during World War II for treating patients with severe burns. Other local history displays refer to the Old Burying Ground, the oldest extant cemetery in South Africa (1813). A walk around here is a roll call of the many and varied communities who, down the centuries, made Simon's Town their home. There are also those who were just passing through and those who were lost at sea. Royal Navy matelots lie beside Russian sailors. There are slaves and aristocrats, Italian artisans and Boer prisoners-of-war. And there are generations of townspeople.

Most interesting of all are the town's links with the Boer War and the two world wars. There are displays illuminating the horrors of the Anglo-Boer War prison ships, and the Boer prisoner-of-war camp at Boulders near by, now known for its penguins. Then there are the heroic stories of the hunt in the Rufigi River Delta for the German raider SMS *Konigsberg* (World War I) using the Curtis seaplane in 1914, and the Royal Navy's search from Simon's Town for the German ship, the *Graf Spee* (World War II) on the River Plate in 1939. At least 125 Allied ships were sunk by the Germans, Japanese and Italians in relatively close proximity to Simon's Town.

Also look out for memorabilia of royal visits to Simon's Town. The British royals were visitors, the Aborigine prince Metarai came in 1808, and Louis-Napoleon's corpse rested here on its way to Britain after this Prince Imperial's death in Natal in the Zulu wars. The Zulu king, Cetshwayo, also dropped in briefly en route to his imprisonment near Cape Town.

Map on page 160

TIP

In March each year the Navy holds a festival in Simon's Town, when dockyard and naval vessels are opened to the public. The Penguin Festival in spring is another highlight in the town's events calendar.

BELOW: Simon's Town has loads of old-style charm.

TIP

The Battery in Simon's Town is a good place from which to spot the southern right whales who come to breed here between May and December. Other good places on False Bay are Kalk Bay and Fish Hoek.

The shipwrecks around this stormy coast are of particular interest – their remains are often revealed at low tide, and legends abound right the way around the Cape Peninsula. Look in at the cells built to house the slaves of the colony's governor in the 18th century, the gaol, the stocks – generally used to hold women – and the punishment cell with whip marks on the ceiling.

Less interesting, but worth a look if you have a special interest in the subject, is the **SA Naval Museum** (open daily 10am–4pm; admission charge) in West Dockyard, which has interesting displays on shipwreck off the Peninsula, and the **Warrior Toy Museum** in St George's Street (open Mon–Sun 10am–4pm; admission charge), which may reawaken the child in you. It has Dinky toys, luxury doll's houses, Meccano sets and model boats, cars, trains, planes, toy soldiers, etc.

The are plenty of shops and cafés in the main street, George Street, and on Jubilee Square, the main hub of Simon's Town. On the

BELOW: Fish Hoek's pretty beach.

way out of town, you may want to call in at the **Bronze Age Art Foundry, Gallery & Sculpture Garden** (open Mon–Thur 10am–5pm, Fri 10am–4pm, Sat and Sun 10am–3pm; admission charge), a wharf-side complex where you can see artists at work. A serious working foundry, it is well worth a look. The adjoining gallery displays work by top local artists.

Further on (turn left up Dido Valley Road) is **Mineral World & Topstones** (open Mon–Fri 8.30am–4.45pm, Sat and Sun 9am–5.15pm – Mineral World only; admission charge), a larger version of Scratch Patch at the V&A Waterfront in Cape Town. Visitors can choose and buy a variety of minerals and precious stones either in polished or unpolished form, or in jewellery and other artefacts. A good range of fossils is also on display. You can leave the children at the Scratch Patch, where they can play in the offcuts of smooth, polished gemstones, while you peruse the more precious objects upstairs.

Just above Simon's Town, on Redhill Drive, is the grave of the Great Dane Just Nuisance (open daily 9am–3.30pm), a Royal Navy mascot who died in 1944. His reputation was such that he was given the rank of Able Seaman and finally buried with full military honours. A statue of him by Jean Doyle stands in Jubilee Square in the town below (*see page 159*).

Fish Hoek

Beyond Simon's Town, the M4 meanders around the coast through Glencairn to **Fish Hoek**. The lovely beach is cut off from the town by a railway line and poor development, but persevere and you can spend a delightful day on the sand here. Take care when entering the water. Shark attacks have happened here and the danger remains.

It's a beautiful spot, though, and very quiet during the week.

There are two museums to visit. One, the **Fish Hoek Valley Museum** (open Tues–Sat 9.30am–12.30pm; admission charge), documents the history of whaling in the town, and displays stone-age implements relating to nearby Peers Cave. Excavated in 1926, the cave was found to contain nine ancient burial chambers. The skull of one of them, so-called Fish Hoek Man, was found to have the largest brain cavity of any other skull of similar age.

The **Heritage Museum** in **Amlay House** (open Tues–Fri 11am–4pm, Sat and Sun by appointment; tel: 021 782 1752; admission charge) is the private home of Zainab Davidson, a Fish Hoek resident who, because of her colour, was forced to move out of her home in 1975 under the Group Areas Act. But she moved back 20 years later, and today she has turned her home into a museum of local Muslim culture. She'll take you around and chat to you as though she's known you all her life. You could be one of the family.

Apart from the museum and the beach, Fish Hoek is quite a bland place. More interesting is Kalk Bay.

Kalk Bay

After Fish Hoek, the road runs through **Clovelly** and then **Kalk Bay ⑫**, a pretty seaside village that acquired its name from the lime kilns located here in the early days of the colony. Capetonians come here for a lazy day ferreting through bric-a-brac shops and then lunching on freshly caught fish. It's well worth poking around through the furniture, books, ceramics, curios and a variety of other things old and not so old, because real treasures have been known to turn up from time to time. Beware of the silly prices though: Kalk Bay is in danger of becoming over-commercialised. There are also art galleries filled with the work of Sunday afternoon painters, potters' shops and so on, and you can buy fresh fish at the quaint little harbour.

Kalk Bay is a busy weekend destination, particularly on Sundays when sleepy locals turn up at

Map on page 150

TIP

If you are interested in seeing great white sharks (from a distance), several companies run excursions to seal island, a feeding ground for the sharks about 6 km (4 miles) offshore. Enquire at the tourism office in Cape Town or Simon's Town.

BELOW: crashing waves at Kalk Bay.

Kalk Bay is a happy hunting-ground for bric-a-brac and old furniture, especially on weekends.

BELOW:
inspecting the day's catch at Kalk Bay.

Olympia Café and Deli for the best brunch in Cape Town. Chaotic, busy and small, this café-restaurant – whose kitchens occupy an old theatre (ask to have a look) – is also noted for its bakery.

Kalk Bay evolved in the middle of the 19th century. Its little fishing harbour became a very successful whaling station. During the whale-watching season (May–December) the Brass Bell restaurant here is a good place to enjoy a meal while observing them. The harbour is still the focus of the colourful local fishing fleet.

Victorian St James

Kalk Bay runs into **St James** ⓭, which has the same seaside character. Victorian villas line the sea-front, and narrow cobbled alleys link the houses on the vertiginous slope beneath Ridge Peak and St James's Peak. There are lovely warm tidal pools at Dalebrook and St James, the latter recognisable for its brightly painted beach huts lining the sands. The tidal pools here are great for small children.

Muizenberg

St James merges with **Muizenberg** ⓮ a little further on. Here the coastline bears east, and a magnificent sweep of beach heads all the way to Gordon's Bay, 25 km (15½ miles) away. The town itself has seen better days, but the beach is fantastic. The water is safe for swimming and its temperature is relatively warm. Surfers particularly love it here, but Capetonians of every description come here to ride the waves, paddle and picnic. You can buy surfing equipment, boogie boards and so on, have a meal, order a takeaway or simply relax over a drink.

Muizenberg has long been a favourite getaway for Capetonians. From 1882, when the suburban railway arrived, people came here in droves to sample the warm waters of the bay and the town quickly grew. Beach houses went up and it became a popular Sunday destination. Before that, Muizenberg was a military outpost which protected the back door to Cape Town from invasion through False Bay. However, in

1795, at the Battle of Muizenberg, the British succeeded in breaking through the defences, and thus began the First British Occupation of the Cape.

Architectural landmarks

The stretch of coast from Muizenberg to Kalk Bay is particularly interesting architecturally. In the late 19th century wealthy South Africans, including several mining magnates such as Oppenheimer, had their holiday homes here. Cecil John Rhodes loved this spot too, and owned the cottage at 246 Main Road. A very simple building under thatch, it was originally intended as a temporary home until Herbert Baker could build him his mansion at what is now Rust-en-Vrede at 244 Main Road. But Rhodes loved this cottage, and died here in 1902 aged 49. The cottage is now a museum (open daily 9.45am–4.30pm; free) about Rhodes's life.

Rust-en-Vrede was in the end built for Abe Bailey, another mining magnate, in 1905. It is considered one of Baker's best works, but a private residence and therefore not open to the public.

At 190 Main Road is The Fort, built in 1929 by Frederick Mackintosh Glennie as a holiday home for Count Natale Labia, the Italian ambassador to South Africa. Now known as the **Natale Labia Museum** (open Mon–Fri 10am–5pm; free), it gives an insight into a grand seaside lifestyle now vanished. It has original furniture and paintings on display, many of which were imported from Venice, the count's home. At 182 Main Road is the **Posthuys**, the old toll-keeper's house which dates from around 1730. Today it is a small maritime museum (open daily 10am–4pm; admission charge).

Another Herbert Baker seaside home is on display at the Muizenberg waterfront. Now known as the **Joan St Leger Lindbergh Arts Foundation**, it is in fact four houses containing a library of Africana. Concerts are held here, and there are art exhibitions and lectures (coffee shop open Mon–Fri 9am–3.30pm, Centre open Mon–Fri 9am–4.30pm; tel: 021 788 2795; free). ❏

Map on page 150

Cecil Rhodes's simple cottage at Muizenberg, now a museum.

BELOW: family-friendly St James, where a tidal pool offers safe bathing for children.

RESTAURANTS & BARS

Restaurants

The following listing is arranged in geographical order, beginning at Sea Point and then following the Peninsula round to False Bay.

Sea Point

Harvey's
Winchester Mansions Hotel, 221 Beach Road, Sea Point. Tel: 021 434 2351. Open: B, L & D daily. $$
If there is such a thing as Euro-African food, you will

find it here. New takes on South African dishes are the order of the day, plus simple staples such as fresh line-fish. The venue is pretty and quiet, in the courtyard of an old-fashioned seaside hotel.

La Perla
Beach Road, Sea Point. Tel: 021 434 2471. Open: L & D daily. $$
The most famous restaurant on the Atlantic seaboard, La Perla is always busy whatever day of the week, so be sure to book. Good fish, meat and poultry, massive salads and sorbets. It's the neighbourhood haunt for swanky locals who want to let their hair down.

Camps Bay

Blues
The Promenade, Victoria Road, Camps Bay. Tel: 021 438 2040. Open: L & D daily. $$
Long a popular seaside venue for locals and visitors alike, Blues attracts a smart-casual set who like to see and be seen. There's lots of seafood here, an extensive wine list and a great terrace overlooking Camps Bay.

Codfather Seafood Emporium
37 The Drive, Camps Bay. Tel: 021 438 0782. Open: L & D daily. $$
Come here for the seafood and sushi. Customers select what they fancy from the counter, where it is weighed and then cooked while they wait. Very popular, so make a reservation. There's a good, accessible wine list too.

Paranga
Shop 1, The Promenade, Victoria Road, Camps Bay. Tel: 021 438 0404. Open: B, L & D daily. $$
Hip and happening, this restaurant-bar faces the ocean across busy Victoria Road. Salads, pastas and other light dishes feature on the menu, but its more about the people than the food.

Tides
The Bay Hotel, 69 Victoria Road, Camps Bay. Tel: 021 438 4444. Open: B & D daily. $$$
A seaside venue with magnificent views of the ocean. The terrible service is more than made up for by favourite basics such as burgers and fresh line-fish.

Hout Bay

Chapman's Restaurant
Chapman's Peak Hotel, Chapman's Peak Drive. Tel: 021 790 1036. Open: L & D daily. $
Chapman's is a very popular hotel restaurant with a good seafood menu. It is most famous for its calamari, fries and seaside views. Also good for weekend lunches when it is okay to come in wearing shorts and flip-flops.

La Cuccina
Victoria Mall, Victoria Road. Tel: 021 790 8008. Open: B, L & D. Unlicensed. $
This is a great brunch venue. Choose from a huge buffet of Italian-style dishes. There are endless pots of coffee and great cakes.

Fish on the Rocks
Hout Bay Harbour. Tel: 021 790 0001. Open: B, L & D 9.30am–8pm. $
Very basic, but serving

LEFT: a photo opportunity in Hout Bay.
RIGHT: a light lunch in Camps Bay.

superb fish and chips.
The calamari and kingklip
are especially good. Sit
inside or out on the grass.

Wharfside Grill

Mariner's Wharf, Hout Bay
Harbour. Tel: 021 790 1100.
Open: B, L & D daily. $
A very busy venue right
in the harbour. Eat your
fish or calamari while
you watch fish being
unloaded on the quay.
The waiters are dressed
like sailors. Easy, laid-
back and cheap.

Scarborough

Camel Rock

Main Road. Tel: 021 780
1122. Open: L & D
Wed–Mon. $
Camel Rock has been
around for years. It has a
weather-beaten look
about it and serves big
portions of seafood,
grills and curry.

Cobbs at the Cape

Main Road. Tel: 021 780
1480. Open: B & L 9am–
6pm Tues–Sun, D 6.30pm
until late Tues–Sat. $
The best venue on the
Peninsula for a weekend
lunch, and one of only two
restaurants you'd want to
go to between Kommetjie
and Simon's Town.
Serves big portions of
seafood, burgers and
grills. Down a bottle of
wine and look out to sea
from the top terrace.

Simon's Town

Bertha's

1 Wharf Road. Tel: 021 786
2138. Open: B, L & D daily. $
Specialising in seafood,

this harbourside restau-
rant is also good for burgers, pasta and salads.
Customers are attracted
by the big open deck
overlooking the water.
Very busy at the
weekends.

Kalk Bay

Brass Bell

Kalk Bay Station. Tel: 021 788
5456. Open: L & D daily. $$
If you want to see the
whales (May–Nov), come
to the Brass Bell. To get
here, pass under the
railway line and climb up
some old-fashioned
steps to a warren of old
station buildings, and
ask to be seated in the
non-smoking section.
The views are amazing,
even if the food's only
passable. Ask them to
grill the fish and serve it
with oil and lemon.

Cape to Cuba

Main Road. Tel: 021 788
1566. Open: L & D daily. $$
Serves a mixture of
Cuban and seafood
dishes. More important,
though, is the location –
practically straddling the
railway line. It tries to
evoke the shabby mad-
ness of Havana and is
great for a theatrical-
style night out.

Harbour House

Kalk Bay Harbour. Tel: 021
788 4133. Open: L & D daily. $
Excellent, inexpensive
dining in the heart of the
harbour. Expect fresh
fish imaginatively pre-
pared, good salads and
great wines.

Olympia Café and Deli

134 Main Road. Tel: 021 788
6396. Open: B, L & D daily. $
Really great food in a
bohemian atmosphere.
For brunch, take the
papers, order a jug of
coffee and settle down
with poached eggs and
smoked salmon. Every-
thing here from the shell-
fish to the cakes is
first-class.

Muizenberg

Gaylords

65 Main Road. Tel: 021 788
5470. Open: L, D Wed–Sun.
D only Mon. Closed Tues.
An Indian restaurant
frequented by families
who've been coming back
again and again for years.
Hardly any wines but good
Indian beer.

Railway House

177 Main Road. Tel: 021 788
3251. Open: L & D. Closed
Mon and Tues. $

Another restaurant in a
defunct station, featur-
ing contemporary South
African cuisine and
really good line-fish.

Bars

For cocktails there is a
host of buzzing possibilities in Camps Bay, such
as **Paranga** (see restaurants), **La Med**, another
fashionable hang-out
between Clifton and
Camps Bay, and **Baraza**,
Victoria Road, a relaxed
lounge cocktail bar.

For a pub-like atmos-
phere, Kalk Bay has two
options: the **Brass Bell**
(the waves practically
wash over it on a stormy
night) and the **Polana**,
also right on the ocean,
where you can eat or
simply hang in an old
leather armchair. This
one's open until 3am, so
settle in for a long haul.

FURTHER AFIELD

There is plenty to see and do within a short distance of Cape Town. You can tour the wineries of the Boland, visit the picturesque towns of Stellenbosch and Franschhoek, or, in winter, enjoy land-based whale-watching from Hermanus

Cape Town's reputation as an outdoor-oriented city is enhanced by the beauty of the surrounding coastline and its mountainous hinterland. Scenically, the far southwest of the Western Cape Province is utterly magnificent – hazy blue peaks and heath-covered hills sloping down towards wide green valleys planted with leafy vineyards, quaint thatch-and-whitewash villages, and a seemingly endless stock of uncrowded and idyllically framed beaches.

Day trips from Cape Town

The part of the Western Cape that lies within realistic day-tripping distance of the provincial capital splits neatly into three tourist circuits, each with its own distinct character. Centred on the historic towns of Stellenbosch, Franschhoek and Paarl, the Cape Winelands of the Boland (literally "upland") is undoubtedly the most popular of these circuits, consisting of more than half a dozen different wine routes, each of which offers the opportunity to sample the produce of one of South Africa's oldest and most economically important agricultural industries. By contrast, the Overberg, a sheep-and-grain farming region situated to the southeast of Cape Town, is best-known for

the excellent whale-viewing out of Hermanus and as the site of Africa's most southerly point, Cape Agulhas. Finally, there is the West Coast, which attracts relatively few international tourists, yet offers those who do make the effort a winning combination of marine wildlife, low-key wine estates and fabulous mountain scenery.

In practice, with a rented vehicle, you could loop between all three of these circuits over the course of five or six days – the optimum route

Map on page 172

PRECEDING PAGES: the Vergelegen Estate on the Helderberg Wine Route. **LEFT:** hitting the open road near Stellenbosch. **BELOW:** a Cape Dutch cottage, Stellenbosch.

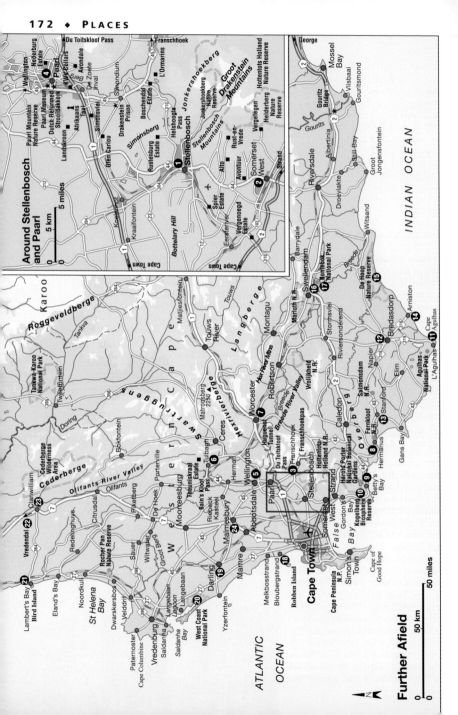

Further Afield

Around Stellenbosch and Paarl

would entail following the R27 along the West Coast to Saldanha, then cutting east along the R45 through Malmesbury to Paarl, Stellenbosch and Franschhoek, before taking the R45/43 through Caledon to Hermanus and the Overberg. Equally, most individual destinations along these circuits would make for a straightforward day trip out of Cape Town, the one exception being the somewhat far-flung Cape Agulhas.

Using public transport, your options are more limited, although Stellenbosch and Paarl – the former arguably being the highlight of the whole region – are both connected to Cape Town by regular passenger trains. Another possibility is to join one of the organised wine-tasting day tours offered by numerous operators based in and around Cape Town, or to undertake other activities (ranging from hiking and kayaking to caged shark dives and bungee jumping) with specialist operators. Any hotel or backpacker hostel in Cape Town can provide details and make bookings at short notice.

THE CAPE WINELANDS

The second-oldest town in South Africa, **Stellenbosch ❶** is 27 years junior to Cape Town, yet its compact, low-rise town centre projects a far more overt sense of architectural cohesion and antiquity than the Mother City, 45 km (27 miles) to the east.

Founded on the banks of the Eersterivier (First River) by Governor Simon van der Stel in 1679 and accorded its own magistracy six years later, Stellenbosch started life as something of a frontier town, an isolated outpost of European urbanity. It lay days away from the Cape by ox-wagon, and was bounded to the north by mile after uncharted mile of lawless African wilderness.

Today, by contrast, it is the site of the country's premier Afrikaans university, as well as the epicentre of the burgeoning Cape wine industry. And it's less than an hour away from Cape Town by road or train.

Shaded by stately trees (some planted back in Van der Stel's day) from which its nickname "Eikestad" (Oak Town) derives, Stellenbosch is well worth a few hours' exploration, ideally on foot. There's no better place to start than Dorp (Village) Street, which runs roughly parallel to the Eersterivier at the southern end of the town centre, and contains what is probably the longest row of pre-20th-century buildings anywhere in South Africa. These include the quaint **Oom Samie's se Winkel** (Uncle Samie's Shop; open Mon–Fri 9am–6pm, Sat and Sun 9am–5pm; tel: 021 887 0797) and a Lutheran Church of 1851.

Immediately to the north, entered via Rymeveld Street, the **Dorp Museum ❹** (open Mon–Sat 9.30am–5pm, Sun 2–5pm; tel: 021 887 2902; admission charge) consists of an entire block of impressive antique

Map on page 172

Uncle Samie's Shop, a traditional general store, typifies the olde-worlde atmosphere of Stellenbosch.

BELOW: Cape Dutch architecture abounds in Stellenbosch.

The University of Stellenbosch has provided higher education to two students who later became prime ministers of South Africa, Jan Smuts (1870–1950) and Daniel François Malan (1874–1959), who defeated Smuts in 1948 and was one of the main architects of apartheid.

buildings, most notably the unpretentious Schreuderhuis, the oldest surviving townhouse in the country, which was built in 1709. Others in the row include the elegant **Cape Dutch Blettermanhuis** (1789), the Georgian-styled **Grosvenor House** (1803) and the fine mid-Victorian **Murray House** (1850).

Near by, on Alexander Street, the H-shaped **Burgherhuis** 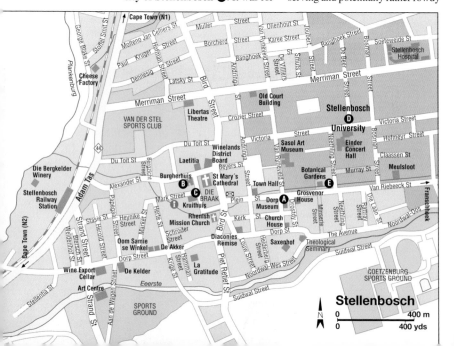, built in 1797 and now listed as a National Monument, is one of the town's finest examples of traditional Cape Dutch architecture. It overlooks **Die Braak** – literally, "The Fallow", a commonage equivalent to the English village green – which is also where you will find the **Kruithuis** (Powder House; Mon–Fri 9am–1pm), a whitewashed munitions magazine that was built in 1777, and now serves as a low-key military museum.

Also situated in the town centre, off Ryneveld Street, is the **University of Stellenbosch** . It was formally established by Act of Parliament in 1918, but it started life 60 years earlier as the Theological Seminary of the Dutch Reformed Church. As of 1866, it became the secular Stellenbosch College (renamed Victoria College in 1887 in honour of the English queen's silver jubilee). Campus highlights include the Victorian Ou Hoofgebou (Old Main Building), which now houses the Faculty of Law, the **Sasol Art Museum**, and the small but beautiful **Botanical Garden** (open daily 9am–4pm; free) that encloses the tranquil Katjiepiering Tea Garden.

Lively nightlife

The significant student population of the town ensures that the sleepy olde-worlde ambience that engulfs Stellenbosch by day is complemented by an unexpectedly lively nightlife when the sun goes down, at least during term time. One long-serving and potentially rather rowdy

Stellenbosch

pub, called De Akker, and the more upmarket and wine-oriented De Kelder, both on Dorp Street, are reliable standbys, and the latter occasionally hosts live music. Several other, mostly more ephemeral, drinking holes line Bird Street as it runs north from Dorp Street.

If "popular with students" isn't a recommendation in your book, the town centre is also liberally studded with classier restaurants serving fine Continental and Cape Malay fare accompanied by a varied selection of Cape wines. Revellers who are in the Cape area at the right time of year might want to ensure that their visit coincides with one of the local festivals, such as the Student Rag Carnival (February), the Stellenbosch Wine Festival (August), Stellenbosch Street and Music Festival (September) or the Van der Stel Food Festival (October).

Trekking in the mountains

Situated less than 20 km (12 miles) inland of False Bay as the crow flies, Stellenbosch lies at the relatively modest elevation of 110 metres (360 ft) above sea level, but it is encircled by several impressive mountain ranges. Notable among these is the 1,608-metre (5,275-ft) **Groot Drakenstein** (Large Dragon's Rock), the 1,490-metre (4,889-ft) **Stellenbosch Mountains** and 1,390-metre (4,560-ft) **Simonsberg** (both named after Simon van der Stel), and the 1,224-metre (4,016-ft) **Helderberg** (Clear Mountain).

In addition to providing a memorable backdrop to the town and the surrounding Winelands, the upper slopes of these mountains all support significant strands of indigenous fynbos, characterised by a wealth of proteas and colourful wild-flower displays in the spring.

Opportunities for a leg stretch range from the relatively undemanding circular 6-km (4-mile) Swartboskloof–Sosyskloof Trail through the **Jonkershoek Nature Reserve**, which lies 8 km (5 miles) east of the town centre along the Jonkershoek Road, to the more challenging 24-km (15-mile) **Vineyard Trail** connecting the Papegaaiberg (Parrot Mountain) to the Kuils River, starting on the western outskirts of town behind the railway station. Several more arduous overnight hikes can be undertaken in the majestic **Hottentots Holland Nature Reserve**, the entrance to which lies off the R321 between Grabouw and Villiersdorp.

Exploring the wineries

The most popular attraction around Stellenbosch, however, is the Wineland – more than 100 wine-producing farms and estates that nestle in the surrounding valleys and foothills. Divided informally into several different "wine routes", the first of which was established in 1971, most of these estates have a public wine-tasting room open from around 9am–4pm daily, though some operate shorter hours and may

Map on page 172

This way to one of the many wineries around Stellenbosch.

BELOW: dawn over the Drakenstein Mountains.

You will find that many of the region's restaurants and wineries like to capture the Cape Dutch cosiness of a bygone age.

BELOW: picture perfect on the Helderberg Wine Route.

close altogether on Saturday or Sunday. Admission to most estates is free, but the more popular ones charge a nominal tasting fee. Full details of the opening times and charges for individual estates are provided in a free booklet issued at the tourist offices in Stellenbosch and Cape Town. It is perfectly possible to explore the Winelands under your own steam in a rented vehicle, but inadvisable to so without a spittoon-trained or teetotal designated driver in your party. Otherwise, if your whole party wants to enjoy a varied selection of wines with a clear conscience, it's best to hook up with one of the many inexpensive wine-tasting tours that run out of Cape Town or Stellenbosch every day.

Those who are touring independently are faced with some tough decisions regarding which of the plethora of different estates to visit. That selection will depend on your objectives and circumstances. If it's a genuine Cape Dutch atmosphere and mountain scenery you're after, there is no better place to start than the lovely **Rustenberg Estate** (tel:

021 809 1200) on the northeastern outskirts of Stellenbosch. However, if you're travelling with children in tow, head southwest out of town for about 10 km (6 miles) along the R310 to the fun-for-the-family **Spier Estate** (tel: 021 809 1100), where fine wines and a quality Cape Malay restaurant are complemented by horse-riding, a small zoo and playground, a picnic site, and regular steam-train connections to and from Cape Town.

Serious buyers may find that a better option than hopping between individual estates might be to sample the more varied wines on offer at a specialist wine exporter, such as the Wine Export Cellar (Dorp Street, tel: 021 883 3814) or Die Bergkelder (Adam Tas Road; tel: 021 809 8492) in Stellenbosch town centre, or the out-of-town Vineyard Connection (on the R44; tel: 021 884 4361).

Justifiably voted South Africa's "top winery" and its "most beautiful winery" by readers of *Wine* magazine, **Vergelegen** (open 9.30am–4.30pm; tel: 021 847 1334; www.vergelegen.co.za) is a highlight of the **Helderberg Wine Route**, which centres on **Somerset West ❷**, some 20 km (12 miles) south of Stellenbosch and 40 km (24 miles) southeast of Cape Town. The farm of Vergelegen, which translates as "Far Away", was founded in 1700 by William van der Stel (son of Simon), and the first vines were planted there shortly afterwards. The Cape Dutch manor house, now a private museum decorated in period style, is set in tranquil gardens with a great little coffee shop, and the estate's multi-award winning wines are equally inviting.

Other outstanding wineries along the Helderberg Wine Route include the venerable and very pretty **Vergenoegd Estate** (tel: 021 843 3248), founded in 1696, as well as **Avon-**

tuur (tel: 021 855 3450), **Alto** (tel: 021 881 3884) and **Rust-en-Vrede** (tel: 021 881 3881).

For those who prefer walking to imbibing, there are seven trails, ranging from 15 minutes to three hours in duration, running through the **Helderberg Nature Reserve** (open daily sunrise to sunset). The entrance is 4 km (2½ miles) north of Somerset West and is signposted. Its floral wealth is capped by the endemic disa orchid, an exquisite red flower that blooms between January and March.

Franschhoek

Arguably the most scenic drive out of Stellenbosch is the R310, which skirts the northern slope of the Groot Drakenstein Mountains via the evocatively named **Helshoogte** (Hell's Heights) **Pass**, before descending via the R45 into the attractively sprawling village of **Franschhoek ❸**.

Situated 28 km (17 miles) from Stellenbosch by road, Franschhoek was initially named Olifantshoek after the prodigious elephant herds that foraged the valley, and acquired its present name (which means French Corner) in reference to the Huguenots who left France in the early 18th century and settled here. Completed in 1943, the **Huguenot Memorial Museum** (open Mon–Sat 9am–5pm, Sun 2–5pm; tel: 021 876 2532; admission charge) recounts the history of these French Protestant refugees, who were persecuted by the Catholic King Louis XIV following the revocation of the Edict of Nantes in 1685.

Encircled by tall, craggy peaks, Franschhoek is blessed with the most spectacular setting of any Boland town, and while the elephants that once roamed the area are long gone, the town is distinguished by the tangible French influence that remains here, not least in its impressive tally of eight restaurants listed in the country's top 100 *(see page 186 for some of them)*. The French settlers also did much to develop Franschhoek's wine industry, as you'll see from the names of the estates. These include Chamonix, Dieu Donné, La Bri and La

Map on page 172

BELOW: the Huguenot Memorial Museum.

Paarl's name dates from 1657, when Abraham Gabbema followed the Berg River inland as far as the glistening granite-domed mountain he christened Peerlbergh – Dutch for "Pearl Mountain".

Couronne, and you can sample more than 100 wines produced by these and other local wineries at the **Franschhoek Vineyards Co-op Cellar** (open Mon–Fri 9.30am–5pm, Sat and public holidays 10am–4pm, Sun 11am–3pm; tel: 021 876 2086) in the town centre.

Visitors prepared to venture a little further afield can follow the highlights of the **Franschhoek Valley Wine Route**, which includes the Cape Dutch-style manor house at **L'Ormarins** (tel: 021 874 1026), whose Optima Reserve is a full-bodied Bordeaux-style blend that merits 10–15 years' cellaring. **Cabrière** (tel: 021 876 2630), which produces five different sparkling wines, is another highlight of the tour.

Best of all, though, is the 300-year-old **Boschendal Estate** (open daily 8.30am–4.30pm, closed Sun May–Oct; tel: 021 870 4200; www.boschendal.com). Set below the tall peaks of the Groot Drakenstein along the R310 about halfway back towards Stellenbosch, its attractive Cape Dutch manor house is reached along a sweeping drive lined by ancient trees. It has a good restaurant and also offers the option of a "pique-nique" between November and April. Boschendal is best-known for its iconic Blanc de Noir, a popular off-dry salmon-pink "white" wine blended from pinot noir and merlot grapes. Lovers of champagne might also want to sample the estate's bone-dry sparkling brut, and dry-red enthusiasts are pointed to the highly-rated shiraz or a cabernet sauvignon-based blend called Lanoy.

Paarl

The township of **Paarl** ❹ was founded on the banks of the Berg River in 1720, but much of the surrounding farmland (including the extant Laborie Estate) was given to Huguenot settlers as early as 1687. Paarl is a 45-minute drive from Cape Town along the N1 Highway, and a similar driving distance north from Stellenbosch or Franschhoek.

The town centre is unmemorable, even dreary, by Boland standards, and the 11-km (7-mile) main road – for what it's worth, vaunted by the local marketing machine as the longest in the country – takes ages to drive along. No original 1720s buildings survive, but the Oude Pastorie (Old Parsonage) on Main Street, now the **Paarl Museum** (open Mon–Fri 9am–5pm, Sat 9am–3pm; tel: 021 872 2651; admission charge), was constructed in 1787, and the nearby **Dutch Reformed Strooidakkerk** (Thatched Roof Church) was consecrated in 1805.

Of greater interest than the town itself is the adjacent **Paarl Mountain Nature Reserve**, with a trio of lunar domes that can be reached via a relatively easy walking trail through slopes draped in protea-studded fynbos. A relatively modern landmark, set on the southern slopes of Paarl Mountain, is the obelisk-

BELOW: Boschendal vineyard, picturesquely situated below the peaks of the Groot Drakenstein.

Map on page 172

like **Afrikaans Taal (Language) Monument**, which was erected in 1975 to commemorate the centenary of the local movement that led to the recognition of Afrikaans as the world's youngest official language.

Also situated just outside Paarl is **Drakenstein Prison**, formerly Victor Verster Prison, where Nelson Mandela was held captive for the last two years of his imprisonment.

The Paarl Wine Route

The Paarl Wine Route offers access to some of the country's most venerable wine estates, as well as a range of quality restaurants. A good place to start is the central **KWV Cellars** (tel: 021 807 3900) or the more outlying **Nederburg Estate** (tel: 021 862 3104). The latter, probably the best-known of all South Africa's wine producers, has received many awards for its reserve range, while its everyday drinking wines are ubiquitous restaurant fare.

Other prominent local cellars include **Avondale** (tel: 021 863 1976), **Landskroon** (tel: 021 863 1039) and **Glen Carlou** (tel: 021 875

5528), while **Simonsvlei** (tel: 021 863 3040 and the **Du Toitskloof Winery** (tel: 023 349 1601) both offer an extensive range of well-priced wines for everyday sipping, boosted in the latter case by a magnificent location below **Du Toitskloof Pass**, 16 km (10 miles) east of Paarl.

A little further afield, the small town of **Wellington ❺**, on the R44 about 12 km (7 miles) north of Paarl, is notable for its Dutch Reformed Moederkerk built in 1838 and imposing Town Hall.

Another 50 km (30 miles) north of Wellington, crossing the Slanghoek (Snake Corner) Mountains via the magnificent **Bain's Kloof Pass**, is the small town of **Tulbagh ❻**. It was founded on the banks of the Little Berg River in 1795, and is a rare architectural gem. Historic Church Street was completely restored in Cape Dutch style following a series of earthquakes that virtually demolished the town and claimed the lives of nine of its residents in 1969–70. Designed by the French architect Louis Michel Thibault in 1804, the gracious

Nelson Mandela spent the last two years of his imprisonment (1988–90) in Victor Verster Prison, near Paarl. Unlike Robben Island, where conditions were harsh, Victor Verster was a comfortable and spacious villa, in his words "a gilded cage". Indeed, when he later had a new house built for himself, he based its design on that of Victor Verster.

LEFT: the Afrikaans Language Monument in Paarl.

Afrikaans

A derivative of the Dutch spoken by the earliest Europeans to settle the Cape, Afrikaans, though readily intelligible to any Hollander today, is classified as a language in its own right thanks to its simplified grammar, pronunciation quirks and magpie vocabulary. It is rooted in the pidgin Dutch that formed the lingua franca of the early colonists and their Malay and indigenous subjugates. It was only in 1875, however, that the fledgling language's grammar was formalised.

In 1925 Afrikaans replaced Dutch as the country's second official language (alongside English), and it is now one of 11 official languages. Perceptions of Afrikaans in the New South Africa are sometimes tainted by apartheid-era associations – it was, for instance, the Nationalist Party's insistence on using Afrikaans as a teaching medium that sparked the Soweto riots of 1976 – but Afrikaans is not an exclusively "White" language. Ironically, perhaps, roughly half of the six million South Africans who call Afrikaans their mother tongue are so-called Coloureds of mixed racial descent.

A southern right whale comes up for air. Hermanus is the best spot on the Cape for land-based whale-watching.

RIGHT: Hermanus's official "whale crier".

Oude Drostdy (open daily, closed Sun am; admission charge), 4 km (2½ miles) outside the village, now serves as a storeroom and sales floor for several nearby vineyards.

Further out of town is the **Theuniskraal Estate** (tel: 023 230 0687), in the possession of the Jordaan family since 1927, which produces some excellent white wines, including an iconic dry Riesling.

Founded in 1820 and named after the Marquis of Worcester, the elder brother of then Governor of the Cape, Lord Charles Somerset, the attractive Boland town of **Worcester ❼** lies in the Breede River Valley at the base of the Hex River Mountains. Rising to 2,250 metres (7,382 ft), they form the highest peaks in the Western Cape. Some 50 km (30 miles) southeast of Tulbagh, the town is notable for its elegant **Drostdy**, regarded by experts as the country's finest example of Cape Regency architecture. There's also a neo-Gothic Dutch Reformed **Moederkerk**, built in 1824.

The oldest wine producer along the Worcestor Wine Route, the De Wet Wine Cellar (tel: 023 341 2710), was founded as recently as 1946, so while the wines are good, the architecture doesn't compare to the more historic estates around Stellenbosch or Paarl.

The **Karoo National Botanical Garden** (open daily 8am–5pm; admission charge), on the northern edge of town, is known for its flowering succulents, which bloom most vividly after the spring rains. From Worcester, a straight 100-km (60-mile) drive southwest along the N1 leads back to Cape Town.

THE OVERBERG

Roughly 120 km (72 miles) southeast of Cape Town via the N2 and R44, **Hermanus ❽** is the main focus for tourism in the otherwise rather low-key and rustic region called the Overberg (literally, "beyond the mountain"). The town was founded in 1857 by German settlers who named it Hermanuspietersfontein (Hermanus Pieter's Spring) in remembrance of an itinerant shepherd who once used the

Whale-watching off Hermanus

Hermanus's main claim to fame is as the world's top site for land-based whale-viewing. Every year, between June and November, up to 100 southern right whales congregate in Walker Bay for the mating and calving season, together with a smaller and less reliable number of humpback whales, and they often breach and lobtail in the water just 30 metres (100 ft) below vantage points such as Castle Rock, which lies in the town centre overlooking the Old Harbour.

Whale activity generally peaks over September and October, when a wander along the 11-km (7-mile) cliff walk leading west from Castle Rock is almost certain to yield whale sightings in the crystal-clear water. At this time of year, the tourist office (tel: 028 312 2629) hires a special "whale crier" to keep visitors up to date on where the whales are best seen, and an underwater microphone transmits their strange "songs" live back to a room in the Old Harbour Museum (open daily, but closed Sun am; admission charge). Boat-based whale-viewing in Walker Bay is permitted but strictly regulated – the only two licensed operators are Southern Right Charters (tel: 082 353 0550) and Hawston Fishers (tel: 082 396 8931).

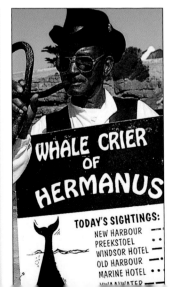

Map on page 172

site as his regular summer encampment. The fledgling resort town gained municipal status in 1904, two years after the official abbreviation of its name, and for much of the 20th century it served as a fashionable fishing, boating and beach retreat for a wealthy elite of holiday-home owners.

In recent years, this formerly rather exclusive resort town has assumed an altogether more egalitarian character – indeed, Hermanus can get quite crowded, especially at Christmas – but its clifftop setting near the mouth of the Klein (Small) River remains inspirational, and the town itself, all cobblestone alleys and open-air restaurants, retains the quaint feel of an olde worlde fishing village.

Whale-watching aside *(see facing page)*, Hermanus boasts an attractive sandy beach, and a good range of marine activities can be organised locally, from scuba dives and caged shark dives to sailing and kayaking. The 1,400-hectare (3,459-acre) **Fernkloof Nature Reserve** (open daily dusk to dawn; free), on the northern outskirts of town, protects the pretty fynbos-strewn slopes of the Kleinriviersberg, and is criss-crossed with a rewarding network of day trails.

Two other places are also worth a diversion – **Betty's Bay ❾**, a pretty resort town on the R44 back towards Cape Town, also known for the prodigious colony of African penguins at Stony Point, and the waterfall-strewn fynbos of the **Harold Porter National Botanical Gardens** (open daily 8am–6pm; tel: 028 272 9311; admission charge), below the Kogelberg Mountains.

For dedicated hikers and botanists, the vast **Kogelberg Biosphere Reserve ❿** (open summer 7.30am–7pm, winter 8am–6pm; tel: 028 271 5138; admission charge) is said to protect the most diverse montane fynbos habitat in the Cape, with

more than 1,500 plant species identified, a full 10 percent of which occur nowhere else. The reserve, which lies 6 km (4 miles) from Kleinmond on the R44 between Hermanus and Betty's Bay, also harbours a wide variety of birds, a healthy Chama baboon population and a herd of wild horses, probably descended from beasts abandoned by soldiers of unknown affinities in the Anglo-Boer War of 1899–1902. Four hiking trails run through the reserve, from 6 km (4 miles) to 23 km (14 miles) in length, and there's canoeing on the Palmiet River.

The end of the continent

Situated in the **Eastern Overberg** almost 200 km (120 miles) from the Cape of Good Hope as the crow flies, **Cape Agulhas ⓫** is not only the official meeting point of the Indian and Atlantic Oceans, but also, somewhat less arbitrarily, the most southerly point on the African continent. Geographical significance aside, Agulhas can be rather underwhelming by comparison to, say, Cape Point, consisting of a flat,

One of the nicest ways of exploring the Kogelberg Biosphere Reserve is on horseback.

BELOW: on the lookout.

A bontebok in Salmonsdam Nature Reserve.

BELOW: Swellendam, the third-oldest town in South Africa, has many fine examples of Cape Dutch architecture.

rocky, windswept peninsula punctuated by South Africa's second-oldest lighthouse (open daily, but closed Sun am; admission charge).

The name Agulhas, which translates as "Needles", was coined by one of the more prescient Portuguese navigators to enter the Indian Ocean in the 16th century: the treacherously jagged rocks that lie offshore have subsequently accounted for at least 250 shipwrecks. By contrast, the altogether more benign beach at nearby Struisbaai is magnificent, with its turquoise-blue sea and colourful fishing boats.

Diversions and backwaters

Agulhas lies about 100 km (60 miles) southeast of Hermanus by any of several backroads, of which the most straightforward option is probably the R326/R316/R319 via **Napier** and **Bredasdorp ⑫** – the latter notable for its Shipwreck Museum (daily, but am only Sat and Sun; admission charge), with treasures from ships wrecked off the Agulhas coast.

Various diversions are possible en route between Hermanus and Agul-

has. For a gentle ramble, several undemanding walking trails run through the **Salmonsdam Nature Reserve** (open daily; tel: 028 314 0062; admission charge), which lies near **Stanford ⑬**, some 45 km (28 miles) west of Hermanus. It protects a hilly area coloured by red fields of proteas and inhabited by bontebok, klipspringer and numerous birds. Altogether different is the small village of **Elim**, founded as a Moravian Mission in 1824 and now consisting of several picturesque, albeit increasingly run-down, whitewashed thatched dwellings, as well as a wooden waterwheel dating to 1828.

Just as rewarding is a detour from Bredasdorp to **Arniston ⑭**, named in memory of a ship that ran aground there in 1852, claiming 352 lives. The fishing village, with its thatched, whitewashed 19th-century fishermen's houses, has been declared a National Monument.

The village is also sometimes referred to by its pre-1852 name Waenhuiskrans (Wagonhouse Cliff), in reference to a nearby cavern which is large enough to house sev-

eral ox-wagons but is accessible only at low tide.

Running for some 50 km (30 miles) along the coast east of Arniston, the **De Hoop Nature Reserve** ⓫ (open daily; tel: 028 542 1126/7; admission charge) protects the largest remaining contiguous coastal fynbos habitat. Walking trails range from the two-hour Klipspringer Trail to the 55-km (34-mile), five-day Whale Trail. The offshore marine reserve offers great snorkelling, and forms a breeding ground for an estimated 120 southern right whales between June and November.

Some 60 km (37 miles) north of Bredasdorp, you can rejoin the N2 near **Stormsvlei**, from where it's another 12 km (8 miles) to **Swellendam** ⓰, the third-oldest town in South Africa (founded 1743). The town's Cape Dutch buildings include the **Town Hall** and a fine period-furnished **Drostdy** (open daily; admission charge), the latter built in 1746. An old prison and two other Victorian buildings form part of the same complex. Also of interest, on Voortrek Street, is the magnificent **Dutch Reformed Church** built in 1911. Just 6 km (4 miles) south of Swellendam, the **Bontebok National Park** ⓱ (open daily; tel: 028 514 2735) is home to graceful bontebok, a fynbos-endemic antelope that was hunted to near-extinction in the early part of the 20th century, as well as springbok and the rare Cape mountain zebra.

THE WEST COAST

The Atlantic coastline north of Cape Town is characterised by relatively chilly and rough waters, making it a poor bet for a sedentary beach holiday. However, its combination of unspoilt beaches, sleepy fishing harbours, magnificent spring wildflowers and superb marine birdlife should recommend itself to more active travellers seeking relief from the more popular tourist hotspots. The main road servicing this region is the N7, which runs about 50 km (31 miles) inland for most of its length, but the more scenic option would be the coastal R27 via **Bloubergstrand** ⓲. The long sandy beach here offers a

Map on page 172

BELOW:
Bloubergstrand, with Table Mountain just across the bay.

superb (and much photographed) view of Cape Town with Table Mountain in the background.

Darling

Some 50 km (31 miles) further north, the small town of **Darling**  pirouetted from obscurity in 1996 when gay icon Pieter Dirk Uys converted a former railway building into the cabaret theatre **Evita se Perron**. Evita Bezuidenhout is the name of Uys's Dame-Edna-esque alter ego, while "Perron" is an Afrikaans word for a railway platform. Uys's satirical one-man show (open Fri, Sat and Sun evening; tel: 022 492 2851) has not only put Darling (named after Lt-Gen Sir George, not an itinerant "luvvie") on the tourist map, but also forms a worthwhile if rather irreverent introduction to contemporary South African politics.

Cape cormorants at Lambert's Bay.

BELOW: a colony of Cape fur seals at Lambert's Bay.

West Coast National Park

The **West Coast National Park** ❷ (open daily 9am–5pm; tel: 022 772 2144; admission charge), situated 20 km (12 miles) further north, protects a 30-km (18-mile) stretch of coast dominated by the **Langebaan Lagoon**, one of the world's most important conservation areas for migrant marine birds, and home to significant breeding colonies of 10 species of marine bird. Even more impressive as natural phenomena go is the glorious eruption of spring wild-flowers in August – the best displays are usually in the Postberg sector of Langebaan, which also harbours large mammals such as springbok, bontebok and gemsbok.

Langebaan Lagoon flows into **Saldanha Bay**, South Africa's deepest natural harbour, which is of limited interest to tourists since the eponymous town is also an important naval base, industrial centre and railway link. In contrast is **Paternoster**, some 30 km (18 miles) further north, an as yet unspoilt fishing village famed for its crayfish, which can be sampled at the local restaurants.

Continuing north for 100 km (60 miles) will bring you to the lonely fishing port of **Lambert's Bay** ❷. It has a picturesque harbour, but is best-known for **Bird Island** (open daily 9am–5pm; tel: 022 931 2900;

admission charge), with a nesting colony of around 14,000 Cape gannets and a few hundred African penguins. They can be viewed from an observation tower linked to the town by a short causeway.

In the **Olifants River Valley**, lying inland from Lambert's Bay, **Vredendal** ㉒ is an emergent centre of viticulture. For wine-tasting, the best starting point is the vast **Vredendal Estate**, now the largest single wine producer in the southern hemisphere, whose Gôiya export range is instantly recognisable by the stylised bushman painting that adorns its label.

Further south along the N7, **Clanwilliam** ㉓ is an orchard town that was founded at the beginning of the 18th century. It is the springboard for excursions into the craggy **Cederberg Wilderness Area**, with a 2,000-metre (6,500-ft) peak covered with snow during the winter. Several short walks on the lower slopes are particularly suitable for day visitors; one of the most worthwhile leads to a rock face bearing a well preserved example of rock art

(see Rock Art of the San, page 81) depicting an elephant herd.

The Black Land

Back down in the Olifants River Valley, the drive along the N7 south of Citrusdal passes through a region known as the Swartland (Black Land) since the earliest days of European settlement, most probably in reference to the renosterbos (rhinoceros bush) that once grew here prolifically and turns black seasonally. Today, it might more accurately be known as the *geel* (yellow) land, since it produces about 15 percent of the national wheat crop.

The Swartland Cellar on the outskirts of **Malmesbury** ㉔ is the country's third-largest co-op, using grapes grown on almost 100 different farms to produce more than 20 everyday wines. Their Shiraz and Columbard deserve singling out, and there's also a more limited selection of reserve reds in good years.

If you're heading onward to the Cape Winelands, the R45 south of Malmesbury leads to Paarl after about 50 km (24 miles). ❑

Map on page 172

BELOW: the beautiful and remote Cederberg Wilderness Area.

RESTAURANTS

The Winelands

Stellenbosch & Surrounds

De Kelder
63 Dorp Street, Stellenbosch. Tel: 021 865 2330. Open: L & D daily. $$
Established in 1791, this popular wine-tasting cellar in the heart of historic Stellenbosch also boasts a lively beer garden and serves decent Cape and Continental fare.

De Oewer
Aan-de-Wagen Road, Stellenbosch. Tel: 021 886 5431. Open: L & D daily. $$
Idyllically situated on the willow-lined banks of the Eersterivier. The light, alfresco Mediterranean meals here are accompanied by good local wines.

D'Ouwe Werf
30 Church Street, Stellenbosch. Tel: 021 887 4608. Open: B, L & D daily.$$$
This atmospheric small restaurant is located in South Africa's oldest inn (founded 1802). It serves quality Cape and

PRICE CATEGORIES

Prices for three-course dinner per person with a half-bottle of house wine:
$ = under R140
$$ = R140–200
$$$ = R200–300
$$$$ = more than R300

Continental food, complemented by an excellent wine list.

Mugg & Bean
Mill Street, Stellenbosch. Tel: 021 883 2972. Open: B, L & D daily. $
Serves good coffee and inexpensive pastries and snacks – especially recommended for a leisurely breakfast.

Neethlingshof Estate
M12 west of Stellenbosch. Tel: 021 883 8988. Open: L Mon–Sat. $$–$$$
Reached via a long avenue lined with venerable pines, this three-century-old estate has two restaurants, both of which offer the opportunity to enjoy the Cape Dutch ambience. Wash down a tasty meal with their award-winning range of wines.

Spier Estate
R310 south of Stellenbosch. Tel: 021 809 1100. Open: L & D daily. $–$$
www.spier.co.za
Family-oriented wine estate with a popular Cape Malay restaurant, as well as a takeaway delicatessen ideally suited for stocking up for a lakeside picnic.

Vergelegen
Off the R44 near Somerset West. Tel: 021 847 1334. Open: L Mon–Fri. $$–$$$
Arguably the most

beautiful wine estate in the Cape, Vergelegen has a superb Continental restaurant as well as a cosy coffee shop, both annexes of the stately manor house.

Volkskombuis
Aan-de-Wagen Road. Tel: 021 886 2121. Open: L, D daily. $$$
An upmarket neighbour to De Oewer, the Volkskombuis – People's Kitchen – serves tasty traditional Cape and Malay dishes in a riverside Victorian Cape Dutch building with a beautiful view towards the mountains.

Wijnhuis Stellenbosch
Cnr Church and Andringa streets, Stellenbosch. Tel: 021 887 5844. Open: L, D daily. $$$
Top-notch Continental cuisine complemented by legendarily varied wine list – connoisseurs can sample up to six different wines over the course of a meal for a sensible set fee. Many of the wines are from the Stellenbosch area.

Franschhoek & Surrounds

Boschendal Restaurant
R310 towards Stellenbosch. Tel: 021 870 4274. Open: L Mon–Sat. $$$
Situated on the lovely wine estate of the same name, this fine-dining

restaurant offers first-class South African cuisine amid elegant surroundings.

Bread & Wine
Moreson Winery, Happy Valley Road, La Motte, Franschhoek. Tel: 021 876 3055. Open: L & D Wed–Sun. $$$
www.moreson.co.za
Idyllically set among vineyards and orchards of the Moreson wine estate, Bread & Wine is an excellent place to stop for lunch. It has a courtyard and covered terrace, and the eclectic, Mediterranean-inspired menu features a good range of meat and seafood, homemade sausages, pastas, etc. The emphasis is on freshly prepared dishes made with top-quality ingredients.

French Connection Bistro
Huguenot Road, Franschhoek. Tel: 021 876 4056. Open: L daily. $$
Reasonably priced Continental snacks, pastry and coffee in the heart of the historical town centre.

La Petite Ferme
North of town on the Franschhoek Pass Road, Franschhoek. Tel: 021 876 3016. Open: L & D Mon–Sat. $$
Here you can enjoy a hearty meal or mid-afternoon coffee and cakes

on an attractive terrace overlooking the Franschhoek Valley.

Le Quartier Français
16 Huguenot Street, Franschhoek. Tel: 021 876 2151. Open: L & D daily. $$$$
This well-established, award-winning restaurant has a superb wine list complementing an equally inviting menu. The cooking here reflects the influence of the region's original French settler families. As an alternative, the adjoining bar serves affordable but classy pub grub.

Paarl

Kostinrichting Coffee Shop
19 Pastorie Avenue, Paarl. Tel: 021 871 1353. Open: L Mon–Sat. $$
The aromatic aroma of fresh coffee permeates the oak-shaded courtyard of this restored Victorian school hostel adjacent to the Paarl Museum. Its menu offers a range of light meals.

Laborie Wine House
Taillefert Street, Paarl. Tel: 021 807 3095. Open: L & D daily. $$$
Olde-Worlde-style restaurant set on a 1691 estate on the outskirts of town, serving gourmet Cape and Mediterranean cuisine alongside a lengthy wine list dominated by Paarl's leading vintners.

Wagon Wheel Steakhouse
57 Lady Grey Street. Tel: 021 872 5265. Open: L Tues–Fri, D Tues–Sat. $$$
This award-winning steakhouse also offers a good range of salads and seafood dishes.

Tulbagh

Paddagang Restaurant
23 Church Street. Tel: 023 230 0242. Open: B, L daily. $$$
Known for its excellent wine list, the Paddagang – literally, and oddly, "Frogmarch" – serves wholesome traditional South African fare in an attractive restored Cape Dutch building.

The Overberg
Hermanus

MacRib
Village Square, Market Street, Hermanus. Tel: 028 312 4122. Open: L, D daily. $$$
The name offers a hint. Good spare ribs and other steakhouse fare, as well as fresh seafood and a busy pub, all with a superb view over cliffs that offer reliable seasonal whale-watching.

Milkwood Restaurant
Onrus Beach, Hermanus. Tel: 028 316 1516. Open: L, D daily.$$$$
This smart beachfront restaurant, serving traditional Cape fare and seafood, is renowned for its award-winning wine list.

Savannah Café
Marine Drive. Tel: 028 312 4259. Open: L daily, D Sat–Sun. $$
Offers affordable café-style snacks and meals in a beachfront setting alongside the popular Victoria Theatre.

Agulhas

Agulhas Tearoom
In the lighthouse. Tel: 028 435 7506. Open: L Mon–Sat. $
The tearoom's inexpensive light meals and snacks are accompanied by a perfect vantage point over the southern tip of Africa. An ideal spot for a modest lunch.

Swellendam

Zanddrif Restaurant
Swellengrebel Street. Tel: 028 514 1789. Open: B, L daily. $$
All-day breakfast and other typical café fare

are served in a restored 18th-century building next to the museum.

The West Coast
Darling

Evita se Perron
Tel: 022 492 2851. Open: usually D Fri–Sun only. $$
Light snacks with a traditional Cape touch accompany the one-man show performed most weekends by the legendary drag artist and socio-political satirist Pieter Dirk Uys.

Langebaan

Die Strandloper
Saldanha Road. Tel: 022 772 2490. $
This is one of a clutch of great little West Coast restaurants serving delicious grilled, smoked and curried seafood in the open air, right on the beach.

RIGHT: Evita se Perron in Darling.

THE GARDEN ROUTE

Wild forests and unspoilt beaches lead past hidden
valleys and majestic mountains to the forested
shores of Tsitsikamma National Park

L ush and bountiful, the relatively short stretch of coastline
between Mossel Bay and Tsitsikamma is popularly referred to as
the Garden Route, and its timeless
appeal both to foreign travellers and
to South African holidaymakers is
reflected in a booming guest house
and hotel industry, not to mention
the region's ever-escalating property
prices. This, however, is a distinctly
African garden – no European-style
manicured lawns with neat and formal layouts, but an exhilaratingly
rugged coastline flanked by indigenous rainforests, blue lagoons, parallel rows of serrated mountain
peaks and fields bright with fynbos.

Mossel Bay and George

Coming from Cape Town, the east-
bound N2 runs inland through
Swellendam *(see page 183)* and
Riversdale to reconnect with the
coast after some 400 km (240 miles)
at **Mossel Bay ❶**. Generally regarded as the beginning of the Garden Route, Mossel Bay also has the
distinction of being the place where
Portuguese navigator Bartolomeu
Diaz dropped anchor in 1488,
becoming the first European on
South African soil. The **Bartolomeu
Diaz Museum Complex** (open:
Mon–Fri 9am–5pm, Sat and Sun
9am–4pm; admission charge; tel:

044 691 1067; http://diasmuseum.
museum.com), housed inside a converted granary, is dedicated to his
memory. Displays include exhibitions of shells and shipping; best of
all is the full-scale replica of Diaz's
surprisingly small caravel.

The first permanent settlement at
Mossel Bay didn't begin until about
300 years later, though passing ships
often stopped for water and to trade
with the local Hottentots. The town
is still a popular holiday resort
thanks to its many beaches and calm

Map
on page
192

PRECEDING PAGES:
Roberg Nature Reserve,
Plattenberg Bay.
LEFT: the Garden
Route, a riot of wild
flowers in spring.
BELOW: an evening
round a *braii*.

swimming pools between rocks. It has also become a sprawling industrial centre since the discovery of oil and natural gas off the coast.

Write postcards, nevertheless, because the local mail system has a long tradition – in 1500 Pedro d'Ataidea, a Portuguese sailor, placed a letter inside an old boot and hung it beneath a milkwood tree. A year later, another sailor found the letter and was kind enough to forward it. The tradition continued as the tree became a message board for passing sailors. Today the tree is part of the Diaz Museum, and if you post your cards in the boot-shaped letterbox provided (with a suitable stamp), the "oldest post office in South Africa" will process them promptly.

If Mossel Bay has sacrificed something of its former charm to industrial development, there's no doubt that it also offers some of the most alluring marine activities in the region, full details of which can be obtained from the tourist office next to the old post office. Most popular, and relatively inexpensive, is a boat excursion to nearby **Seal Island** (hourly departures 9pm–5am; tel: 044 690 3101), where hundreds of Cape fur seals can be seen basking on the rocks and foraging in the surrounding waters.

Rather more daunting (and not just financially) are the caged shark dives arranged by Shark Africa (tel: 044 691 3796; www.sharkafrica.co.za) to view predatory great whites in their natural habitat. More conventional dives can be arranged too, as can kayaking expeditions, while back on terra firma – or, more accurately, suspended above it – the **Gouritz Bridge bungee jump** from the N2, 35 km (22 miles) back towards Swellendam, is popular with adrenaline junkies.

Leaving Mossel Bay, the scenery grows increasingly wild as the N2 continues east towards the former

Posting a letter in Mossel Bay's unique boot-shaped postbox.

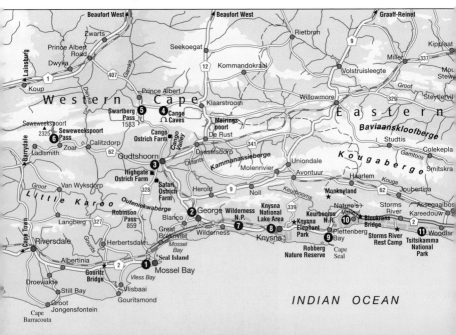

lumber village of **George** ❷, founded in 1811 at the base of the Outeniqua Mountains and described a few decades later by Anthony Trollope as "the prettiest village on the face of the earth". A few kilometres inland, George today is anything but a village – indeed, its population of 150,000 is twice that of any other town on the Garden Route – and few would regard it as especially pretty. On the plus side, George does offer a good range of tourist facilities at lower prices than you'll find elsewhere in this popular area, and it's well placed as a base for numerous day trips along the Garden Route or the Little Karoo.

Within George's historic town centre stand several fine buildings. These include the **Dutch Reformed Moederkerk** with its magnificent carved stinkwood pulpit, and the elegant **Public Library** (1840) – although the latter's books have sadly all been moved to Cape Town. Out-side the library is the mighty **Slave Tree**, one of the broadest oak trees in the southern hemisphere, beneath which a slave market was once held. And since we're touching on a dark chapter of South African history, the **George Museum** (open Mon–Fri 9am–4pm; tel: 044 873 5343; admission charge) on Courtenay Street has an exhibition devoted to the years of apartheid rule under President P. W. Botha, the last of the hard-liners. He retired here in 1989.

Rather jollier times are to be had on the local **Outeniqua Choo Tjoe** (24-hour information and reservations: 082 234 6332), a popular narrow-gauge railway. Here, a steam locomotive dating from 1928 takes passengers from George through several attractive, wooded ravines along the coast to Knysna. The trip takes 2½ hours, and can be linked to a return shuttle-bus service. Around 115,000 passengers travel the line annually.

Map on page 192

BELOW: life on the farm in the Karoo.

The Garden Route

50 km

50 miles

N

At speeds of up to 78 km/h (48 mph), the ostrich can outrun most of its enemies.

The Outeniekwa Mountains to the north of George offer some excellent hiking possibilities, while motorists can explore the fynbos- and forest-covered slopes along a road loop via the sensational Outeniqua and Montagu passes to Oudtshoorn.

The Little Karoo

Situated roughly 60 km (36 miles) north of George via the N12 and Outeniqua Pass, **Oudtshoorn** ❸ is an increasingly popular day or overnight trip out of the Garden Route proper. It is the principal town of the Little Karoo, a rather arid region whose name derives from a Khoi word for dry. It can get blisteringly hot in summer, but it also has an austere beauty that comes in many guises – the serenity of far horizons, a black eagle soaring above a silent plain, a cool breeze after a stifling day, or just a donkey-cart crunching slowly along an old farm road.

Oudtshoorn was once a celebrated ostrich-feather centre. Between 1880 and 1910 Jewish traders from eastern Europe came here, set up ostrich farms and made a small fortune

exporting the feathers to fashion-conscious Europe. The trade brought vast riches – 1 kg (2 lb) of feathers could fetch up to R200. The **C. P. Nel Museum** (Baron van Rheede Street; open Mon–Sat 9am–5pm; tel: 044 272 7306; admission charge) has displays on the history of the ostrich boom. All this revenue pouring into what had hitherto been nothing more than a remote hamlet helped build a number of "feather palaces", several of which have survived the decline in the market. One, the **Le Roux Townhouse** (admission included in museum ticket), stands on the corner of Loop and High streets, complete with period fittings and furnishings.

Today, the ostrich industry still thrives, but the feathers are used more for dusters than millinery, and today it's the skins that are sought after in the world of high fashion. Ostrich skins for expensive shoes, handbags and purses now command prices comparable to the highly prized skins of baby crocodiles. Farms where the ostriches are bred form the lynchpin of an increasingly

lucrative tourist industry. Why Oudtshoorn? Ostriches are happiest in a hot, dry climate, like a type of alfalfa that grows here, and find here some of their favourite dietary supplements – sand, stones and insects.

Several farms are open to the public, including **Safari Ostrich Farm** (open daily 8am–5pm; tel: 044 272 7311; www.safariostrich.co.za; admission charge), which lies just outside town on the Mossel Bay road. The homestead was built to a high standard, with teak from Burma, Belgian roof tiles and marble floors. Lunchtime at an ostrich farm usually means dining on an ostrich steak; you can also try riding on the back of the world's largest bird, or watch jockeys take part in a mock Ostrich Derby. Similar entertainment is offered at other ostrich farms, such as **Highgate** (tel: 044 272 7115) and **Cango** (tel: 044 272 4623), the latter situated 15–20 km (9–12 miles) from town along the R328 towards the Cango Caves.

About 2 km (1¼ miles) from the town centre along the R328, **Cango Wildlife Ranch** (open daily 9am–5pm; tel: 044 272 5593; admission charge) was established in the 1980s to breed endangered wildlife. One of the world's most productive breeding centres for cheetah, it has also successfully bred serval, aardwolf, African wild dog and pygmy hippo (the latter a West African rainforest species). Essentially, the ranch comes across as a zoo – albeit a very good one – offering the opportunity to hold hand-reared cheetahs and to see a variety of indigenous and exotic animals, including white Bengal tigers, pumas, jaguars and meerkats. There's a snake park, curio shop and restaurant attached.

The fascinating **Cango Caves** ❹ (open daily, guided tours hourly; tel: 044 272 7410; admission charge) lie 32 km (20 miles) north of Oudt-

shoorn, and are part of a massive cave system that extends into the Swartberg Mountains. The caves once sheltered San bushmen whose paintings *(see page 81)* were found on the walls. A guided tour introduces three of the biggest caves, after which you can either turn back or continue on a route that involves squeezing through narrow, hot, damp and stifling shafts where the seat of your trousers will get as much wear as your shoes.

Past the caves, the R328 continues towards the whitewashed village of **Prince Albert** over one of the most beautiful of all the mountain passes in South Africa – the 1,436-metre (4,700-ft) **Swartberg Pass** ❺. Built between 1881 and 1888 and now a National Monument, the gravel road climbs 1,000 metres (3,281 ft) in 12 km (7 miles) over the mighty Swartberg Range, with very sharp, blind hairpin bends. The views are magnificent, but not for those who suffer from vertigo.

If that's not challenging enough, you could take an alternative route via the **Seweweekspoort Pass** ❻,

Map on page 192

The native aloe plant has renowned medicinal properties.

BELOW: exploring Wilderness National Park.

TIP

Wheelchair access in Wilderness National Park is limited. Ebb and Flow Restcamp (South) has one accessible chalet and one accessible forest hut. Most of the board-walk along the Touw River is wheelchair-friendly, although the access ramps are intimidating. A bird hide at Rondevlei is harder to reach (the pathway is a mixture of sandy soil and thick grass).

BELOW:
fishing from the rocks.

across the mountains, or by the main road (the R29) through Meir-ingspoort. First opened in 1857, this pass crosses the River Groot some 30 times along its 17-km (11-mile) length, snaking through bare walls of vertical rock which at times stretch hundreds of metres high. Twisted bands of red sandstone and milky quartz loom above the road, their yellow-lichened crags glowing in the sun. Check the status of the road before you set out to drive through the gorge, though – it's often closed after heavy rains.

Most visitors approach Oudt-shoorn via the N12 from George, either returning the way they came, or using the R328 to Mossel Bay via the 859-metre (2,818-ft) **Robinson Pass**, or the rougher **Montagu Pass** to the east. Coming to or from Cape Town, however, a rewarding alter-native is to travel between Swellen-dam and Oudtshoorn on the R324 through Tradouw Pass to **Barry-dale**, then follow the R62 through fertile valleys and pretty orchard vil-lages like Ladysmith and Calitzdorp.

Wilderness National Park
Heading east from George, the rail-way and the N2 both pass through **Wilderness**, a bustling little resort town fringed on one side by a mag-nificent 8-km (5-mile) sandy beach and on the other by the Wilderness National Park. Shortly before the N2 enters Wilderness, it offers a superb view over a photogenic riverine gorge spanned by the Out-eniqua Choo Tjoe's railway bridge. Immediately after this, you can pull up at a viewpoint from where dol-phins are regularly observed play-ing in the surf below.

Wilderness National Park ❼ (open daily 8am–5pm; tel: 044 877 1197) protects a series of freshwater pans – the largest are Swartvlei, Langvlei, Groenvlei and Rondevlei – connected by various tributaries of the Touws River, which empties into the ocean in the town. It's a beauti-ful park, and the combination of open waterways, reed beds and marshes provides a rich source of food and varied habitats for a wide array of birdlife, as does the sur-rounding bush and forest. Most attractive of all are the large wading birds that scour the shallows for food. Pink flamingos drift across the shimmering water, straining the sur-face for tiny algae and crustaceans, and African spoonbills rake the mud with their broad, wide beaks. Of the 95 waterbird species recorded in South Africa, 75 have been seen bobbing about on the lakes here.

Understandably popular with birdwatchers, Wilderness National Park also offers some great ram-bling opportunities in the form of a network of non-strenuous day trails, each of which is named for one of the park's six kingfisher species. The Half-Collared Kingfisher Trail is a good one to begin with, an 8-km (5-mile) circuit that leads through riparian woodland fringing the Touws River to an attractive water-

fall that tumbles over a group of gigantic round boulders. Forest birds such as the beautiful Knysna loerie and yellow-throated warbler are likely to be seen here, and bush-buck and duiker are present too. A similar route can be followed on the water by renting a canoe from the main rest camp and paddling gently upstream to the base of the falls.

A short distance east of Wilder-ness lies the busiest resort on the Garden Route: **Knysna ❸**, founded at the beginning of the 19th century by George Rex, who was rumoured to be an illegitimate son of King George III. Wooded hills, dotted with holiday homes, surround pretty **Knysna Lagoon**, connected to the ocean by a single narrow waterway. The mouth of this canal is flanked by two huge sandstone cliffs known as **The Heads**, which ensured that Knysna never became a harbour town. Access by sea was simply too dangerous. The eastern cliff is the only one open to cars (along George Rex Drive), and the view from the top is fantastic. The western cliff can only be reached by taking a ferry

excursion across the lagoon mouth to the private **Featherbed Nature Reserve** (open daily excursions; tel: 044 382 1693/7), home to the shy blue duiker, various birds and the endangered Knysna sea horse.

A good place for crafts, such as pottery and woven fabrics, is **Thesen House**, a historic townhouse named after one of Knysna's oldest and most influential families. However, the area is chiefly known for natural wood products, especially hardwood furniture. The best-quality products are made by hand by master crafts-men, using yellowwood, dark stinkwood and ironwood judiciously culled from the surrounding forests.

Another popular photo opportu-nity – albeit a rather surreal one for Africa – is the **Holy Trinity Church** in the leafy settlement of Belvedere, looking much like an 11th-century Norman implant. In contrast, in the last week of May Knysna hosts a four-day gay, lesbian, transsexual and transgender carnival, the Pink Loerie Mardi Gras, the only one of its kind on the African continent.

Like Mossel Bay, Knysna is a

Map on page 192

BELOW:
the Holy Trinity Church
at Belvedere, Knysna.

The strong cheek teeth of the Cape clawless otter make short work of bones and crab shells.

popular base for a wide range of marine and other adventure activities, including scuba diving, sailing, hiking, mountain biking, canoe trips, whale and dolphin safaris, and abseiling down the Knysna Heads. The excellent **tourist office** (Main Road; tel: 044 382 5510) can provide details of costs and booking contacts. There are also several excellent overnight hikes through the surrounding hills, details of which can be obtained from the Department of Forestry office on Main Road.

Don't leave Knysna without sampling the product of the legendary **Mitchell's Brewery** on Arend Street (tour Mon–Fri 10.30am; tastings Mon–Fri 8am–5pm, Sat 9am–1pm) or the sumptuous oysters served fresh from the lagoon at dockside restaurants.

Thus fortified, you'll be ready to visit **Plettenberg Bay ❾**, South Africa's most upmarket seaside resort, 32 km (20 miles) east of Knysna. Although the town lacks Knysna's charm, the perfectly rounded Baia Formosa (Beautiful Bay), with its golden beaches, has long been a favourite. Sadly, a hideous multi-storey hotel, the Beacon Isle, now dominates Plettenberg's Bay beachfront from its rocky promontory. A better option for those who like their beaches relatively unspoilt is the lengthy **Keurboomstrand**, 10 minutes' drive east near the Keurbooms River mouth. During the Christmas holiday, "Plett" is extremely popular, but out of season it can be surprisingly quiet.

Nature reserves

A bracing day hike leads through the **Robberg Nature Reserve** (open daily 7am–6pm; admission charge) some 9 km (5 miles) south of Plettenberg Bay. The centrepiece of the reserve is the Robberg ("seal mountain") Peninsula, where dramatic cliffs rise almost vertically from the choppy blue sea, interspersed with several small sandy coves. The full circuit covers an undulating 11 km (7 miles), but shorter variations are available. As its name suggests, the peninsula is home to an impressive colony of Cape fur seals – along with marine birds such as the African black oystercatcher. Look out, too, for the whales and dolphins that pass by seasonally.

Another scenic gem is the **Keurbooms Nature Reserve** (open daily; tel: 044 532 7876; admission charge), the entrance to which lies along the N2 about 7 km (4 miles) east of the town centre, immediately before it crosses a bridge over the forest-fringed Keurbooms River. Ferry cruises run along the river three times daily, and it's also possible to follow a hiking trail into the spectacular wooded gorge. But for those who have the time and the energy, there is no more satisfying way to explore this reserve than to take one of the overnight canoe trips that terminate at a rustic riverside hut deep in the forested gorge. The

tourist office in the town centre can provide full details.

About 10 km (6 miles) west of Plettenberg Bay on the Knysna Road, the **Knysna Elephant Park** (tours daily 8.30am–4.30pm; tel: 044 532 7732; admission charge) does not – as might be expected – protect the few survivors of the wild herds that once roamed these coastal forests, but instead offers the opportunity to touch and feed a few semi-domesticated tuskers relocated from elsewhere in the country.

Equally contrived, but great fun all the same, is the private primate sanctuary called **Monkeyland** (open daily 8.30am–5pm; guided tours hourly; tel: 044 534 8906; www.monkeyland.co.za), which lies 16 km (10 miles) east of Plettenberg Bay, shortly before the turn-off to **Nature's Valley ❿**. The forested sanctuary hosts about 200 monkeys of a dozen species, ranging from the South American spider monkey to various Madagascan lemurs, which were rescued from domestic captivity. A visit can be combined with one to the neighbouring **Birds of Eden**, where a 1-km (⅔-mile) walkway and suspension bridge leads through a huge free-flight aviary. All these places are open daily, offer guided tours, and charge admission.

Tsitsikamma National Park

From Plettenberg Bay you can take either the fairly straight N2 toll road through forests and across the high coastal plain, or the byway (the R102) winding down past the Grootrivier and Bloukrans gorges and through sleepy Nature's Valley on the western boundary of the **Tsitsikamma National Park ⓫** (open daily 5.30am–9.30pm; admission charge). One of the Garden Route's best-kept secrets, Nature's Valley is a tiny forested village overlooking a wonderfully isolated beach that remains practically undeveloped for tourism – there are few more attractive places to pitch a tent than at the magical National Park campsite on the edge of town.

Taking the back road is a rewarding experience, sinking deep into the forest's cool microclimate. Beneath giant yellowwoods, the shaded floor

Map on page 192

BELOW: the coastline has many moods.

Map on page 192

is thick with proteas, arum lilies and watsonia; vividly coloured lourie birds dart through the dense forest canopy, while shy duiker and bushbuck hide in the undergrowth. Back on the N2, the concrete bridges over the Storms, Groot and Bloukrans rivers each had the distinction when they were new of being the biggest such structures in the world. The **Bloukrans Bridge**, 215 metres (710 ft) above the river, is also the site of the world's highest bungee jump.

Either option – the N2 or the R102 – will bring you to the turn-off to **Storms River Mouth**, with its forests and unspoilt, rocky shore, its log cabins and intimidating suspension bridge at the eastern border of the beautiful Tsitsikamma National Park. Stretching 35 km (20 miles) between Nature's Valley and Storms River, this scenic park protects coastal lagoons, dunes, cliffs, beaches and coral reefs, with an interior of steep ravines, thickly clothed with ancient yellowwoods up 50 metres (164 ft) high.

The well-run **Storms River Rest Camp**, in the National Park 1.5 km (1 mile) west of the river mouth, has chalet lodgings and campsites, and forms a good base for swimming, snorkelling and hiking. The short walk from the rest camp to the bridge across the river mouth is a must (look out for seals below the bridge), and you can ascend from here to a viewpoint on the surrounding cliffs. Another justifiably popular day hike effectively follows what would be the first day of the longer Otter Trail along the rocky coast for about 4 km (2½ miles) to a small waterfall.

For dedicated hikers, the **Otter Trail**, which follows the coast all the way from Stormsriver to Nature's Valley, is renowned as one the most scenic and challenging hikes in South Africa. The 41-km (25-mile) trek takes five days (staying at overnight huts along the way) and crosses 11 rivers – sometimes you will need to swim rather than just wade. Only 12 people are allowed to start the trail daily, and because it is so popular it should be booked through South African National Parks (www.sanparks.org) up to 13 months in advance. ❑

BELOW: relaxing on the beach.

RESTAURANTS

Restaurants

Mossel Bay

Gannet Restaurant
Church Street. Tel: 044 491 3738. Open: L & D daily. $$
Part of the Bartolomeu Diaz Museum Complex, this popular restaurant is known for its excellent and good value seafood, including oysters, mussels and sole all delivered fresh from the harbour daily.

Post Tree Restaurant
3 Powrie Street. Tel: 044 691 1177. Open: L Mon–Fri, D daily. $$$
Mossel Bay's finest eatery, the Post Tree specialises in local seafood, but it also serves a wide selection of excellent meat and other dishes.

Rose & Vine Restaurant
5 Amy Searle Street, Great Brak River. Tel: 044 442 3590. Open: L daily $–$$
Set in a mid-19th century cottage in the village of Great Brak River, just five minutes from the N2 between Mossel Bay and George, this friendly family-run restaurant specialises in country cooking, light lunches, and teas accompanied by scones, muffins, cheesecakes and so on.

George

Reel 'n' Rustic
Corner Courtney and York streets. Tel: 044 884 0708. Open: L Sun–Fri, D daily. $$$
Set in a stately and elegantly decorated building from 1885, this award-winning restaurant specialises in fresh seafood as well as prime meat cuts, all complemented by a superb wine list.

Oudtshoorn

Bandella's
9 Ruddslane. Tel: 082-920 9230. Open: D daily, booking essential.
$$–$$$
This hilltop restaurant, with its commanding views of the Klein Karoo Mountains, is a great place for a sundowner or to sample a buffet-style *braai* – selected ostrich cuts, beef, chicken and vegetables – beneath a glittering African night sky.

Knysna

Roland's Restaurant
Pledge Square, 48 Main Street. Tel: 044 382 6641. Open: L Tues–Sun, D daily. $$$
Formerly Oysters Restaurant, this cosy, intimate restaurant in central Knysna specialises in fresh seafood, but also serves an extensive range of Cajun/Creole dishes and grills. The wine list is top notch.

Long Barn Tavern
Nelson St. Tel: 044 382 3839. Open: L & D daily. $
Known for its English pub atmosphere, complete with 12 draughts on tap and DSTV sport on the big screen, this welcoming drinking hole, set in a mid-19th century building with a friendly ghost, serves filling pub grub as well as pizzas.

Knysna Oyster Company/ Oystercatcher Oyster Bar
Thesens Island, Knysna Quays. Tel: 044 382 6941. Open: daily, 10am–7pm winter, 10am–9.30pm summer. Established in 1949, the Knysna Oyster Company is renowned for its oysters, cultivated in the Knysna river estuary, and this venue, great for waterside sundowners (oysters with champagne) as well as seafood, grills and game meals. The affiliated alfresco Oystercatcher Oyster Bar around the corner is open in summer only.

East Head Café
Knysna Heads. Tel: 044 384 0933. Open: B & L daily. $
A memorable location on the waterfront makes this a great spot for a relaxed and inexpensive breakfast or a lunchtime sandwich accompanied by crisp white wine.

Plettenberg Bay

Blue Bay Restaurant
Lookout Centre, Main Street. Tel: 044 533 1390. Open: L & D daily. $–$$$
Set in a shady courtyard, this smart Mediterranean restaurant serves a good variety of seafood, grills, sandwiches and light meals to suit most budgets.

Mugg & Bean
Market Square. Tel: 044 533 1486. Open: B, L & D daily. $
This casual and affordable coffee house has a great sandwich and snack menu and plenty of tempting cakes and pastries – a good breakfast spot, it also stays open until late.

Lookout Deck
Lookout Beach. Tel: 044 533 1379. Open: L & D daily. $$
One of the Garden Route's most popular eateries for over a decade, this superb beachfront restaurant offers great views of the sea, and there is a good chance of spotting dolphin's frolicking in the waves while you dine. Specialities include seafood and prime steak matured on the premises, accompanied by a wide selection of wines.

PRICE CATEGORIES

Prices for three-course dinner per person with a half-bottle of house wine:
$ = under R140
$$ = R140–200
$$$ = R200–300
$$$$ = more than R300

TRANSPORT

GETTING THERE AND GETTING AROUND

GETTING THERE

By Air

Cape Town International Airport is operated by the **Airports Company of South Africa** (ACSA, tel: 086-727 7888; www.airports.co.za). It is located 22 km (15½ miles) east of Cape Town along the N2 highway, and it takes between 15 and 20 minutes to reach the city centre from the airport outside rush hours. These are 7–9am and 4–6pm, and during these hours your journey time will increase to around 30–45 minutes (bear this in mind when returning to catch a flight).

From UK, USA & Europe

International airlines that fly daily to Cape Town include:
South African Airways, tel: 021-936 1111; www.flysaa.com
British Airways, tel: 021-936 9000; www.ba.com
Air France, tel: 086-134 0340; www.airfrance.com
Singapore Airlines, tel: 021-674 0601; www.singaporeair.com
KLM Royal Airlines, tel: 021-689 9876; www.klm.com
Lufthansa, tel: 086-184 2538; www.lufthansa.com
Swiss International Airlines, tel: 086-004 0506; www.swiss.com

Internal

Domestic airlines flying into Cape Town include:
South African Airways, tel: 021-936 1111
SA Airlink, tel: 021-936 1111
BA/Comair, tel: 086-001 1747
Nationwide, tel: 086-173 7737
Kulula, tel: 086-158 5852
There are daily flights to Cape Town from Durban, Johannesburg, Bloemfontein and Port Elizabeth. Tickets can cost anything from R600 to R2,500 for a return ticket to Johannesburg. Kulula.com (www.kulula.com) and 1 Time (www.1time.co.za) are online-based, low-cost airlines that offer great-value deals on flights around South Africa.

By Rail

The state-owned long-distance rail passenger operator, **Spoornet's Shosholoza Meyl**, offers a daily Trans-Karoo service linking Cape Town to Johannesburg and Pretoria, and the weekly Trans-Oranje from Cape Town to Bloemfontein, Pietermaritzburg and Durban. For bookings and timetables, tel: 086-000 8888 or visit www.spoornet.co.za.

For extreme luxury there is the privately owned **Rovos Rail** (tel: 021-421 4020; www.rovos.com). Its beautifully restored trains consist of four royal suites and 32 de luxe

suites, accommodating a maximum of 72 passengers, and its variety of routes includes a two-day trip between Cape Town and Pretoria, and a 24-hour journey between Cape Town and George.

Another alternative is the famous and recently revamped **Blue Train** (tel: 021-449 2672; www.bluetrain.co.za), with its swish sleeper compartments. It offers two scheduled routes: Cape Town to Pretoria or vice versa (one day, one night) and Cape Town to Port Elizabeth (the Garden Route), taking one day and two nights.

By Bus

Luxury coaches linking major cities across the country every day are run by **Greyhound** (tel: 021-505 6363; www.greyhound.co.za), **Translux** (tel: 0861-589 282; www.translux.co.za or www.computicket.com) or **Intercape Mainliner** (tel: 021-380 4400; www.intercape.co.za). The trip from Cape Town to Johannesburg is about 1,400 km (870 miles), and takes about 18 hours by bus. Expect to pay about R450 on Greyhound and R310 with Intercape Mainliner and Translux.

The **Baz Bus** (tel: 021-439 2323; www.bazbus.co.za) runs less frequently from Cape Town to Johannesburg via KwaZulu–Natal and the Drankensburg. It's popular among backpackers and younger travellers who want the hop-on/hop-off option of getting around the country. Tickets cost about R1,800 (one way from Cape Town to Johannesburg) – and you can get on and off as much as you like along the route.

By Car

Roads in and around the Western Cape are good and generally well signposted. Vehicles of all types can be rented from major car companies such as **Avis** (tel: 086-1021 111), **Budget** (tel: 086-001 6622), **Hertz** (tel: 021-400 9650), **Europcar** (tel: 021-934 2263) and **Imperial** (tel: 086-113 1000). Car-rental desks can be found inside the International and Domestic Arrival terminals at the airport.

Driving conditions

The roads in the Cape area are excellent and some of the best in the country. In South Africa you drive on the left-hand side of the road. Speed limits are generally 60–80 km/h (35–50 mph) in towns and up to 120 km/h (75 mph) on national highways. Each province operates independently in terms of law enforcement, and some are stricter than others when it comes to speed limits, parking limitations and so on. Always beware of speed traps (and pedestrians) as you approach smaller country towns and big housing developments alongside the highways.

The journey between Johannesburg and Cape Town should take about 15 hours via Bloemfontein through the Karoo. For those who want to take it at a more leisurely pace, it is best to make a one-night stop-over at a bed-and-breakfast in Colesburg or Beaufort West.

If you are following the Garden Route from Port Elizabeth to Cape Town your journey should take about eight hours, including a quick meal break.

ABOVE: Cape Town's railway station.

By Ship

There are a number of shipping companies offering passage to the Cape. **Safmarine**, a container-ship operator, offers berths for up to 10 fare-paying passengers on its Tilbury (England) to Cape Town, Port Elizabeth or Durban route (via Le Havre or Zeebrugge). The service is year-round, with two sailings in each direction every month. Book through travel agents or, in the UK, contact Captain Richard Hellyer (tel: 01703-334415; www.safmarine.co.uk). In Cape Town, tel: 021-425 2470.

RMS *St Helena* carries up to 128 passengers on its Cardiff (Wales) to Cape Town route, via Tenerife, Ascension Island and St Helena. There are four sailings in each direction every year. In the UK, contact Curnow Shipping Ltd (The Shipyard, Porthleven, Helston, Cornwall TR13 9JA, UK, tel: 01326-563434; www.rms-st-helena.com). In South Africa, contact St Helena Line (PTY) Ltd (2nd Floor, BP Centre, Thibault Square, Cape Town 8001, tel: 021-425 1165; fax: 021-421 7485).

A number of cruise companies offer Cape Town as a port of call, including Crystal Cruises, Peter Deilmann Cruises, Princess Cruises and Silversea Cruises.

GETTING AROUND

From the Airport

There is no rail or bus service from Cape Town International Airport, so you will either need to take a taxi or one of the shuttle buses. **Touch Down Taxis** (tel: 021-919 4659) is the official taxi company for the airport. Taxis are licensed and display regulated charges on a meter.

The other way of getting into town is to use one of the shared shuttle services. These include **Magic Bus** (tel: 021-505 6300), **Citi Hopper** (tel: 021-934 4440) and **Way 2 Go** (tel: 021-934 2503). They will drop you outside your hotel. Tickets can be bought in the arrivals hall.

By Bus

The city bus service is fairly basic, but if you don't have your own transport and don't want the continual expense of taking taxis, buses can be useful. **Golden Arrow** (tel: 0800-656463; www.mti.co.za) runs bus services within the city as well as around the Peninsula. You can pick up a timetable at their terminus in Strand Street.

ACCOMMODATION

ACTIVITIES

A – Z

ABOVE: the Cape Town Explorer links the essential sights.

Cape Town Explorer

The open-top **Cape Town Explorer** (tel: 021-511 1784) links the main places of interest within the city centre. It leaves the V&A Waterfront (Ferryman Pub or, 10 minutes later, the Clock Tower) at 45-minute intervals from 9.30am–3pm (until 3.30pm from mid-Oct to mid-Apr). Stops include all the major museums, the Convention Centre on the Foreshore, Cape Town Tourism on Burg Street, the Cableway, Camps Bay and Sea Point. Tickets cost R90 (adult), R40 (child), and you can hop on and off as you wish.

By Car

Although the city centre is best explored on foot, to get the most out of the Cape Peninsula you will need to rent a car. The driver must be at least 25 years old and have a valid driver's licence (an international licence is not necessary). If you are planning to rent in Cape Town, shop around, as the rental companies have different ongoing deals and special rates for foreign tourists.

Parking is always a problem, so ensure that your hotel has guarded parking places and check the cost. When parking on the street look out for official, uniformed parking attendants whom you pay per hour (you'll also find unofficial parking guards looking for money). The City of Cape Town is very strict about cars parked illegally, and tows them away to the local pound; retrieving them costs about R1,000–5,000 for tow-and-release, and R500 for a parking ticket. *See also Driving conditions, page 203.*

By Train

Metrorail (tel: 0800-656 463; www.capemetrorail.co.za) is another transport option, especially for getting down to Kalk Bay and Fish Hoek on the False Bay Coast, but it has been associated with unreliable schedules and crime issues. That said, most commuters use the train every day to and from Cape Town, and trains are jampacked at peak hours during the week. If you do take the train, always travel in the first-class coach (Metroplus) – a third-class ticket costs less but you're more at risk of being mugged or pickpocketed, especially at off-peak times when security is less tight.

The railway station is at the junction of Adderley and Strand streets.

By Taxi

Sedan taxis

These can be hired by telephone or at designated taxi ranks, but cannot be hailed on the street. They are more expensive than the minibus taxis *(see below)*, and it is best to ask the driver for a quote before getting in. Your hotel concierge or guest-house owner will be able to recommend a reliable taxi service. If you're stuck, **Rikki's Intercity** (tel: 021-423 4888) operates in the city centre and V&A Waterfront.

Minibus taxis

The legendary minibus taxi is South Africa's trademark method of transport. However, the vehicles are often overcrowded and their drivers have a reputation for driving recklessly. That said, they transport thousands of people to and from the surrounding townships and from Cape Town to the Southern Suburbs, and can cost as little as R5 for a one-way journey. Simply flag one down in the street, or go to a designated taxi rank in Adderley Street, or the upper deck of the Cape Town railway station. Take care if you are travelling alone, especially if you are a woman, and make sure you know exactly where you are going. Don't carry any valuables.

Cycling

For those fit enough to cycle around the Cape Peninsula, **Daytrippers** (tel: 021-511 4766; www.daytrippers.co.za) offers half-day tours on mountain bikes or extended tours around the Cape. **Downhill Adventures** (tel: 021-422 0388; www.downhill adventures.com) also offers mountain bike rentals and tours through the Cape Point Nature Reserve, Constantia Winelands, Tokai Forest and Table Mountain.

Motorbike/Scooter Hire

If you want to zip around the city on a funky Vespa, contact **Café Vespa** (tel: 021-426 5042) for daily, weekly and monthly specials and rentals. For a more sophisticated ride on a BMW motorbike or Honda 100cc scooter, **Moto Berlin** (tel: 021-415 7080) is a reliable company that rents out bikes on a daily, weekly and monthly basis.

ACCOMMODATION

SOME THINGS TO BEAR IN MIND BEFORE YOU BOOK THE ROOM

Choosing a Hotel

Cape Town has a wide range of accommodation, which includes luxury hotels, smaller boutique hotels that have all the frills of the larger establishments, comfortable bed-and-breakfasts and guest houses, self-catering apartment and villa rentals, and youth hostels for the young at heart. Whether you are looking for a hip hang-out or a snug home-from-home with sea views, you won't be disappointed. Cape Town has also become known for its excellent standards of service in all areas of accommodation.

In Cape Town, hotels range from new and funky to old and traditional, with style, charm and pizzazz. Most of the big luxury hotels are centrally located in the City Bowl, on the V&A Waterfront and along the Atlantic seaboard, and are relatively pricey. However, a number of smaller boutique hotels, often with no more than 20 rooms, have sprung up over the last few years in the City Bowl and such Southern Suburbs as Bishopscourt and Constantia. They offer everything you would expect from a larger-chain hotel, but are often better priced and a little bit more intimate. Of course, the location is important, too. If you want the the best

cosmopolitan experience, close to a wide range of restaurants and all the popular beaches, find a place in the City Bowl or Atlantic Seaboard. For a more tranquil environment, where you can take it easy in leafy, more homely surroundings, head for the Southern Suburbs, on the other side of Table Mountain but still only a 20-minute drive to the city (depending on traffic).

Some of the guest houses can be quite luxurious, too, and there are plenty of less expensive bed-and-breakfasts for total informality, plus basic backpacker retreats. For greater freedom and your own front door, there are some excellent villa and apartment rentals, which are also ideal if you plan to stay in the city for an extended period of more than three weeks.

Always negotiate prices, especially in low season when there's greater availability. At any time of year, though, published rates are never cast in stone, so it's worth shopping around.

Low season is, of course, over the winter months, from early May to mid-September. High season can occupy the whole of the remaining months, when the weather is generally good, but the peak season is from mid-December to the end of January.

If you plan to visit at this time, make reservations well in advance, as hotels fill up quickly with both local and international guests. You'll be most likely to get the best peak-season rates by booking early, too.

For good last-minute, value-for-money accommodation, visit www.lastminute.co.za, where you'll find fantastic specials that are perfect if you're not on a fixed itinerary.

Rates given in the listings provide an indication of the price of a double room. However, some smaller establishments (like bed-and-breakfasts and youth hostels) have a per-person rate (based on two people sharing a room); single travellers will usually be charged a supplement.

INFORMATION

The following websites are worth checking for a range of accommodation, from luxury hotels to self-catering apartments and villas, in and around Cape Town:
www.sa-venues.com
www.portfoliocollection.com
www.bookabed.co.za
www.cape-venues.co.za
www.wheretostay.co.za
www.capestay.co.za

If you're looking for a place of your own for a long or short rental, there is no shortage of agencies and private companies in Cape Town that will organise anything from luxury, seafront villas that are serviced daily to small, economical bachelor lofts in the city centre.

Village & Life
Tel: 021-422 2371
www.villageandlife.co.za
This company rents out holiday accommodation across the city, including Waterfront, Camps Bay, Mouille Point and De Waterkant. They have more than 80 properties that range from luxurious beachside villas on Camps Bay to small garden studios in De Waterkant.

Icon Villas & Vistas
Tel: 021-424 0905
www.icape.co.za
Private and luxurious self-catering luxury accommodation, from city penthouses to small cottages, is available on a daily, weekly or monthly basis from this company.

Townships

For a truly African experience, try to spend at least one night at a township bed-and-breakfast in Langa or Khayelitsha, where you'll enjoy warm and modest accommodation with welcoming hosts. We suggest that you enter the townships either with an arranged transfer, or accompanied by a recognised tour operator or guide. Please note: quoted rates are estimated and may be subject to change.

Malebo's B&B
Khayelitsha. Tel: 021-361 2391; double rooms from R360. Host, Lydia Masoleng, offers comfortable beds and a traditional African breakfast with the family in the morning.

Ma'Neos
Langa. Tel: 021-694 2504; doubles from R360. Thandi Peter is your warm and welcoming host here.

For a traditional African buffet with local dishes and beer, eat at **Eziko Cooking School**, where trainee chefs destined for some of the leading hotels and guest houses in Cape Town have the opportunity to show off their skills. For further information and bookings, tel: 021-694 0434.

If you would like to enjoy a typical township supper, try out **Igugu Le Africa** in Khayelitsha, tel: 021-364 3395.

CITY CENTRE AND THE CITY BOWL

Mount Nelson Hotel
76 Orange Street, Cape Town 8001
Tel: 021-483 1000 **$$$$**
www.mountnelsonhotel.orient-express.com
Traditionally one of the "Big Five" luxury hotels in Cape Town, and still the grande dame of Cape Town's historic hotels. Illustrious past visitors include Sir Winston Churchill and Lady Colefax. Luxury, opulence, world-class service and out-of-this-world food make this a favourite among celebrities, world leaders and royalty. Recently renovated suites are a modern take on 1950s glamour. A new funky addition is the Planet Cocktail Bar and Lounge, where Cape Town's hip crowd spend their Friday and Saturday evenings.

Alta Bay
12 Invermark Crescent, Higgovale, Cape Town 8001
Tel: 021-487 8800 **$$$**
www.altabay.co.za
This six-bedroomed guesthouse (sleeps 12) is a real find. On the slopes of Table Mountain in the leafy suburb of Higgovale, its designer-chic ambience blends contemporary style with comfort, and the classic modern furniture is in neutral, warm colours. This is a place that's both smart and relaxing, with a lovely pool area and a first-floor terrace. Available on an exclusive basis for longer stays.

ArabellaSheraton Grand Hotel
1 Lower Long Street, Convention Square, Cape Town, 8000
Tel: 021-412 9999 **$$$**
www.sheraton.com/capetown
Opposite the Cape Town International Convention Centre with views of the V&A Waterfront and Table Mountain, this hotel, with its ultra-cool glass-and-granite structure, conforms to the luxury and style of the worldwide Arabella-Sheraton brand. At the end of the day, cool down at the spa or swim in the heated pool.

Four Rosmead
4 Rosmead Ave, Oranjezicht, Cape Town 8001
Tel: 021-480 3810 **$$$**
www.fourrosmead.com
This boutique guest house, built in 1903, has been stylishly renovated to its former glory. It's a Cape contemporary classic with a rich history. Accommodation includes four de luxe and three luxury en-suite bedrooms that exude a sophisticated African feel. Upstairs bedrooms

ABOVE: one of two pools at the Mount Nelson Hotel.

have views across the city, Table Mountain and Lion's Head, whilst the rooms downstairs lead onto a quiet landscaped garden. Spend the day lounging around the pool, or enjoy one of many spa treatments on offer.

Hemingway House
1–2 Lodge Street, Gardens, Cape Town 8001
Tel: 021-461 1857 **$$$**
www.hemingwayhouse.co.za
Holidaymakers who are looking for a colonial, bohemian-style home in Cape Town's City Bowl need look no further. Days and nights are spent around the sun-baked central court-yard, with its sparkling pool and loungers. For alfresco dining there's a long wooden table shaded by a twisted bough of bougainvillea, or you can chill out in the separate covered nook with an open fire-place and sofas. The four double bedrooms are at the four corners of the house.

The Metropole
38 Long Street, Cape Town 8001
Tel: 021-424 7247 **$$$**
www.metropolehotel.co.za
This is the latest hip addition to Long Street. Set inside an Old Victor-ian building, the upbeat interiors are Manhattan-glam meets sassy Afro-chic. The M Bar is were you'll find a funky crowd chilling out on comfy red sofas, and the elegant Veranda restaurant offers simple, fusion-style cuisine.

Inexpensive

Abbey Manor
3 Montrose Ave, Oranjezicht, Cape Town 8001
Tel: 021-462 2935 **$$**
www.abbey.co.za
Set against the slopes of Table Mountain in the City Bowl suburb of Oranjezicht, this was once the home of an early-20th-century ship-ping magnate. It has lovely views across the city, and each spacious en-suite room has been

individually decorated in rich, textured fabrics and with a mix of contempo-rary and traditional furnishings. Rooms are air-conditioned, and have a minibar and free access to wireless internet (laptops are available for hire). There's a large heated swimming pool in a landscaped garden, as well as a spa bath on the upper terrace.

The Cape Cadogan
5 Upper Unions Street, Gardens, Cape Town 8001
Tel: 021-480 8080 **$$**
www.capecadogan.co.za
Close to vibey Kloof Street, with its selection of restaurants, decor boutiques, cinemas and café society, this hotel has an equally bohemian yet contempo-rary feel. It occupies a stately two-storey Geor-gian and Victorian build-ing that has left its farmhouse origins far behind, and provides many comforts and luxuries that you would expect of a bigger hotel.

Cape Heritage Hotel
90 Bree Street, Cape Town 8001
Tel: 021-424 4646 **$$**
www.capeheritage.co.za
This hotel is centrally located in Cape Town's Heritage Square, an 18th-century courtyard that's alive with bars, restaurants and bou-tiques. It's small, but the 15 spacious rooms all feature high ceilings, hardwood floors and stylishly individual decor. The range of services include free internet access and valet parking, and the hotel is convenient for all the major sights and entertainments.

The Cape Milner
No. 2A Milner Road, Tamboers-kloof, Cape Town 8001
Tel: 021-426 1101 **$$**
www.capemilner.co.za
Situated in Tamboers-kloof, between Table Mountain and the City Bowl, this hotel offers a peaceful, Zen-inspired setting with contem-porary furnishings, impressive views and tranquil surroundings. There's a swimming pool, restaurant and outside bar.

Cape Riviera Guest House
31 Belvedere Ave, Oranjezicht, Cape Town 8001
Tel: 021-461 8535 **$$**
www.caperiviera.co.za
Ideally located in the City Bowl, this period

PRICE CATEGORIES

Price categories are for a double room (some include breakfast):
$ = under R500
$$ = R500–1,000
$$$ = R1,000–2,000
$$$$ = over R2,000

home set at the foot of Table Mountain is perfect for a one-night stay, or it can be rented out as a whole guest house. It comes with everything from internet connection to reliable baby-sitting services. Decor is modern, with dark wood veneers and clean, simple lines, and luxurious accessories include goose-down duvets and faux-fur throws. Generous breakfasts are served. There's a comfortable lounge, well-stocked reading room and a 9-metre swimming pool.

Hiddinghof
22 Hiddingh Ave, Gardens,
Cape Town 8001
Tel: 021-465 2929 **$$**
www.hiddinghof.com
A beautifully restored Cape Dutch-style house situated in the heart of

the City Bowl, featuring five luxury apartments. They are furnished with a Cape-Provençal theme, and include a wonderful collection of antique French cupboards, embroidered linen and an impressive art collection. All of the self-catering units are completely self-contained, and have a fully equipped kitchen, satellite TV, internet connections and an alarm system. The small apartments sleep two, while the larger two-bedroomed units can accommodate up to six people. A real boon during the hot summer months is the on-site swimming pool, and if you stay here you're only minutes away from shopping centres and beaches.

Budget

Ashanti Lodge
11 Hof Street, Gardens,
Cape Town 8001
Tel: 021-423 8790 **$**
www.ashanti.co.za
You won't be roughing it at Ashanti – they offer a laundry service, internet facilities, travel consultants and a vibrant bar and restaurant. Rates are a little higher than other backpackers' in the area, but you're getting small home comforts you wouldn't normally find at this end of the market.

Long Street Backpackers'
209 Long Street, Cape Town
Tel: 021-423 0615 **$**
www.longstreetbackpackers.co.za
Cheap and cheerful for the young adventurous spirit on a tight budget, it's central and close to

all the happening hotspots on Long Street.

The Village Lodge
49 Napier Street, De Waterkant, Cape Town 8001
Tel: 021-421 1106 **$**
www.thevillagelodge.co.za
Comprises two boutique guest houses in trendy De Waterkant Village, close to a good range of shops, bistros, restaurants and more. All of the 12 en-suite bedrooms are simply decorated and come with internet access, telephone, air conditioning and safes. The rooftop swimming pool is a great feature, with panoramic views across the harbour and city, and the SOHO restaurant serves Thai style meals at lunch and dinner, plus a hearty English-style breakfast to start your day.

VICTORIA & ALFRED WATERFRONT

Luxury Hotels

Cape Grace Hotel
West Quay Road,
Cape Town 8001
Tel: 021-410 7100 **$$$$**
www.capegrace.com
As a member of the Leading Small Hotels of the World, the Cape Grace combines world-class service and standards with understated elegance and charm. Surrounded by water, with views of the harbour and Table Mountain, it includes a spa that incorporates various facets of African traditional healing. In the restaurant – called one.waterfront – executive chef Bruce Robertson produces a fresh

take on contemporary African flavours.

The Table Bay
Quay 6 , Cape Town 8003
Tel: 021-406 5000 **$$$$**
www.suninternational.com
Another member of the Leading Small Hotels of the World, this hotel is perfect for those who want big service, big views and big rooms. The services on offer range from a personal butler to a fully equipped state-of-the-art gymnasium. Little wonder that it attracts so many international celebrities. Take time out in the Camelot Spa after a day's sightseeing followed by a sumptuous meal at the Atlantic Restaurant.

Moderate

Radisson Waterfront
Beach Road, Granger Bay,
Cape Town 8001
Tel: 021-441 3000 **$$$**
www.radissonsas.com
Sipping a gin and tonic at the water's edge at the Radisson's own marina in Granger Bay, right next door to the V&A Waterfont, is rather like being on a cruise liner. It's comfortable, stylishly decorated and has plenty of modern amenities to suite both holidaymakers and business travellers.

Victoria & Alfred Hotel
Cnr Dock and Alfred roads,
Cape Town 8001
Tel: 021-419 6677 **$$$**
www.vahotel.co.za

Located at the heart of the Waterfront Complex, the V&A Hotel is a welcoming and comfortable place in a lovely setting. Views extend across the marina and its yachts to Table Mountain. The hotel has 68 spacious, air-conditioned en-suite bedrooms, and a wide selection of restaurants including the hotel's own brasserie-style eatery, the Waterfront Café downstairs.

Inexpensive

Breakwater Lodge
Portswood Road,
V&A Waterfront
Tel: 021-406 1911 **$$**
www.breakwaterlodge.co.za
Those who wouldn't relish spending time in a prison should think again. This distinctive hotel is in a beautifully restored and converted 19th-century prison building that now offers great value-for-money accommodation and good, friendly service. The decor and furnishings are fairly standard modern-hotel-style, and the light, airy rooms couldn't be less cell-like, with en-suite bathrooms, TV and some good views. There are some suites, too, plus a pleasant restaurant and a bar with a terrace.

City Lodge Waterfront
Cnr Dock and Alfred roads,
Cape Town 8001
Tel: 021-419 9450 **$$**
www.citylodge.co.za
Revamped and refurbished, this hotel now has a fitness room, an internet café and a jacuzzi-pool for guests. It's in a central location, and though there's nothing special about the decor, it's a clean and comfortable place, and is well priced.

Davids
12 Croxteth Road, Green Point,
Cape Town 8005
Tel: 021-439 4649 **$$**
www.davids.co.za
This Victorian terrace home in trendy Green Point has light and airy rooms with individual balconies or charming gardens. The lounge, TV room and breakfast room are modern and stylish, with masses of

ABOVE: the Cape Grace Hotel on the V&A Waterfront.

pictures on the walls. There's also a lovely wooden sun deck. There are lots of nice personal touches here, and it's in a good location for trestaurants, shops and attractions.

La Splendida
121 Beach Road, Mouille
Point, Cape Town 8005
Tel: 021-439 5119 **$$**
www.lasplendida.co.za
Situated on the Mouille Point beachfront promenade opposite the Mouille Point Lighthouse, this small hotel is ideally placed between Sea Point and the V&A Waterfront (with the best views of sunrise and sunset in town). Interiors feature a pleasing blend of art deco and African style, with lovely warm tones. Rooms and suites are comfortable and spacious, each with a fridge, bar and safe, and there's a luxurious two-storey penthouse with two balconies. The Bravo restaurant, which serves Italian food, is buzzing in the evening.

Budget

Braeside Bed & Breakfast
15 Braeside Road, Green
Point, Cape Town 8005
Tel: 021-439 7909 **$**
www.braesidebnb.co.za
Conveniently situated on a quiet road in Green Point, this is a turn-of the-20th-century home with high pressed ceilings and beautiful Oregon pine floors. The large and comfortable bedrooms have private bathrooms, television and tea tray, and some even have a fireplace – great for off-season visits. When it's fine you can enjoy breakfast on the patio shaded by bougainvillea. There's easy access to the V&A Waterfront, the city and Sea Point.

Launic House
10 Romney Road, Green Point,
Cape Town 8005
Tel: 021-434 4851 **$**
www.launichouse.co.za
There's a relaxed and comfortable atmosphere at this pleasant place in the heart of

Green Point, within walking distance of the Waterfont, restaurants and Cape Town's vibrant nightlife. Decor is ethnic with a colonial twist, and all rooms have television and safes. Breakfast is served on the terrace.

The Villa Rosa
277 High Level Road, Sea
Point, Cape Town 8005
Tel: 021-434 2768 **$**
www.villa-rosa.com
At the foot of Lion's Head, this is a restored Victorian mansion, with friendly service and delicious breakfasts. Rooms are comfortable, with telephone, TV, ceiling fans and safe, and it's close to shops, restaurants and beaches.

PRICE CATEGORIES

Price categories are for a double room (some include breakfast):
$ = under R500
$$ = R500–1,000
$$$ = R1,000–2,000
$$$$ = over R2,000

SOUTHERN SUBURBS

Luxury

The Cellars-Hohenort
93 Brommersvlei Road,
Constantia
Tel: 021-794 2137 $$$$
www.collectionmcgrath.com
A Cape colonial building, quietly tucked away in Constantia, the Cellars-Hohenort is a charming and stylish hotel set in lush gardens with mountain views. Enjoy the excellent menu at the Green House restaurant, looking out to the gardens through enormous plate-glass windows.

Moderate

The Bishops' Court
18 Hillwood Avenue,
Bishopscourt, Cape Town
Tel: 021-797 6710 $$$
www.thebishopscourt.com
An exclusive residence with jaw-dropping views of Table Mountain. If the beach is not your thing, this is a perfect location to stay. Each of the five luxury suites features king-size beds, huge marble bathrooms and private sitting areas that are separate from the bedroom. For recreation there's a rim-flow swimming pool and tennis court. A full English breakfast is served every morning.

The Constantia
Spaanschemat River Road,
Constantia 7864
Tel: 021-794 6561 $$$
www.theconstantia.com
Spacious, well-appointed rooms are a feature of this hotel in the heart of Constantia's winelands. Here you can enjoy country-style accommodation with all the frills, from air conditioning to heated towel rails and a full English breakfast (and rates include both breakfast and drinks). It's just a short drive to local shopping centres and beaches.

The Vineyard Hotel & Spa
Colinton Road, Off Protea,
Newlands
Tel: 021-657 4500 $$$
www.vineyard.co.za
A recent expansion to this hotel has provided 10 new "Riverside De Luxe Suites", which feature a modern, Zen-style of decor that contrasts with the more traditional rooms within the main building. Other rooms are arranged around a Japanese-style courtyard, and Mountain rooms are named for their lovely views. Interiors are understated, with natural stone tiles, muted fabrics and mahogany wood furnishings. Wall-length sliding doors front each ground-floor unit, with a sunny outdoor terrace. An added bonus is that you're only steps away from a mind-blowing, authentic Thai massage available at the Angsana Spa next door.

Inexpensive

Alphen Cottages
2 Spilhaus Avenue, Constantia
Tel: 021-794 2989 $$
www.alphencottages.co.za
Situated in the scenic green belt of the Constantia Valley, surrounded by vineyards, the two newly built Alphen Cottages feature spacious living quarters that are perfect for families wanting to self-cater. The Gate House offers two bedrooms, satellite TV, DVD, ADSL and a fully equipped Italian-design kitchen. There's also a patio with a barbecue area and a private garden. The Stables has one bedroom, a fully equipped kitchen and access to the garden. There's also a swimming pool for cooling down during the hot summer months. There are mountain views, and beaches, golf courses and shopping centres are near by.

Hunters Moon Lodge
Southern Cross Drive,
Upper Constantia
Tel: 021-794 5001 $$
www.huntersmoonlodge.co.za
This Tuscan-inspired guest house, set high up in the Constantia Valley, has breathtaking views across the vineyards, and is extremely well priced for what you get. En-suite rooms are luxurious, with four-poster beds and fine linen, and overlook gardens of lavender with fountains and pools. Each has satellite TV, ADSL and a mini-bar. This is the perfect retreat for honeymooners who want time away from the bustle of the city.

Medindi Manor
4 Thicket Road, Rosebank,
Cape Town
Tel: 021-686 3565 $$
www.medindi.co.za
This renovated Victorian home is well suited to

both business travellers and holidaymakers who want easy access to the Cape's main attractions. It offers a relaxed and informal setting filled with a collection of Cape antiques and three inviting fireplaces. Rooms have bar fridges, and there's a pool if you fancy a dip on a warm summer's day. Bathrooms are kitted-out with Victorian baths.

Budget

The Green Elephant
57 Milton Road, Observatory
Tel: 021-448 6359 $
www.capestay.co.za/greenelephant
Set in Cape Town's lively Observatory area, near the city centre, this backpackers' lodge has lots of luxuries, including a heated swimming pool and hot tub, internet access and four-poster beds, yet it's really well priced. Run by a backpacker, it's a very sociable place.

Paradiso Bed & Breakfast
6 Purcell Way, Kreupelbosch,
Constantia
Tel: 021-715 8701 $
In a tranquil garden setting with views of the Constantiaberg Mountains, this B&B has spacious rooms, two with a self-catering option. All have satellite TV, fridges and tea tray.

ATLANTIC SEABOARD
(BANTRY BAY, CAMPS BAY, CLIFTON, HOUT BAY)

Luxury

The Bay Hotel
69 Victoria Road, Camps Bay
Tel: 021-430 4444 **$$$$**
www.thebayhotel.co.za
This Miami-style hotel is on Cape Town's prime strip of beachfront in Camps Bay. Decor is cool, crisp and minimalist, but there's nothing minimal about the amenities, which include a hair salon, boutique shops, and restaurants. The beach bar, Sandy B, is great for sundowners on a hot summer's evening.

Twelve Apostles Hotel & Spa
Victoria Road,
Oudekraal, Camps Bay
Tel: 021-437 9000 **$$$$**
www.12apostleshotel.com
One of the world's top 100 new hotels, according to *Condé Nast Traveler*, this laid-back hotel is set between mountain and sea on the Atlantic coast and has a variety of chic sea-view rooms. The spa offers indulgent body-and-health treatments inside a cave-like space, with flotation tanks and steam rooms. South African food is served at the Azure restaurant, overlooking the ocean, and the service is friendly.

Moderate

Atlantic House
20 St Filians Road, Camps Bay 8005
Tel: 021-437 8120 **$$$**
www.atlantichouse.co.za
A luxury hideout in Camps Bay offering

wonderful sea views and exceptional service for its modest size. Within the modern-contemporary interior, comfortable en-suite bedrooms are well equipped. The heated pool has underwater music.

Atlantic View
31 Francolin Road, Camps Bay
Tel: 021-438 2254
(London reservations:
020-7724 9800) **$$$**
www.atlanticviewcapetown.com
A contemporary villa set high above Camps Bay, with spectacular views of the Atlantic Ocean. Luxurious suites have queen- or king-sized beds, fine cotton linen, bar fridges, high-speed internet and TV. For the active there's a gym, or you can arrange for a relaxing massage. There are beaches and restaurants very close by. Rates include breakfast, aperitifs and hors d'oeuvres. No smoking.

O on Kloof
92 Kloof Road,
Bantry Bay 8005
Tel: 021-439 2081 **$$$**
www.oonkloof.co.za
Situated in a quiet spot in the lovely, sheltered Bantry Bay, this trendy boutique hotel is nevertheless convenient for the beach and local shops. A new addition to the accommodation scene, it has high-tech modern finishes, huge bathrooms, an indoor swimming pool, views across to Lion's Head, and seriously comfortable beds.

Winchester Mansions Hotel
Beach Road, Sea Point
Tel: 021-434 2351 **$$$**
www.winchester.co.za
This is a stylish and elegant hotel right on the Sea Point promenade, with a colonnaded courtyard and rooms that combine traditional decor and ultra-modern facilities. The personal attention to detail is exemplary, and a good range of treatments is offered at the adjoining Gingko Spa. A huge bonus is that this hotel is only minutes away from the V&A Waterfront.

Inexpensive

Bali Bay Apartments
113 Victoria Road, Bantry Bay
Tel: 021-438 1893 **$$**
www.balibay.com
Set against the Twelve Apostles Mountains along the Atlantic coast, Bali Bay is a luxury retreat offering a studio with kitchenette (perfect for the business traveller), a spacious apartment that sleeps six people, and a penthouse with its own private pool deck. All accommodation offers fully equipped kitchens, underfloor heating, air conditioning in the main bedrooms, satellite TV, music systems and telephones. Sliding doors open out onto small balconies right above the sea. Shops and restaurants are within walking distance. Accommodation is serviced daily.

Craigrownie Guest House
10 Craigrownie Road, Bantry Bay 8005
Tel: 021-439 5688 **$$**
www.craigrowniehse.co.za
Set in a quiet cul-de-sac only a few steps from Saunders Rock Beach, this private guest house offers lovely sea views with six stylish and spacious bedrooms, each with a balcony overlooking the sea and with a view of Lion's Head. You can relax on the sun deck or in the guests' lounge, and choose between an English or Continental breakfast.

Hout Bay Manor
Main Road, Hout Bay
Tel: 021-790 0116 **$$**
www.houtbaymanor.co.za
Built in 1871, this hotel is one of many national monuments in Hout Bay. Individually decorated rooms offer comfortable accommodation with satellite TV and coffee/tea-making facilities. The brasserie serves up delicious country cuisine,

ACCOMMODATION

ACTIVITIES

A – Z

ABOVE: the Twelve Apostles overlooking Camps Bay.

and you can relax around the pool or enjoy a night cap in the Voorkamer lounge. The hotel is only 20 minutes from the city and waterfront, with beaches and restaurants a short stroll away.

Tarragona Lodge
Disa River Road, Hout Bay
Tel: 021-790 5080 **$$**
www.tarragona.co.za
Situated in the Hout Bay valley surrounded by forest and lush vegetation, Tarragona Lodge is reminiscent of a Swiss chalet. Spacious en-suite bedrooms have private balconies with a view to the mountains. Mouthwatering country breakfasts are served in the dining room overlooking the gardens. Later, you can enjoy the heated swimming pool or relax in the cocktail lounge with a drink in hand. Activities include mountain walks and horseriding through the forest.

Budget

Camps Bay Chalet
14 Chas Booth Avenue,
Camps Bay
Tel: 021-438 1047 **$**
This self-contained chalet is child-friendly and can be rented completely to ensure you have total privacy. It sleeps a maximum of five people, and consists of a lounge, dining room, fully equipped kitchen, two large bedrooms, two bathrooms and a swimming pool. There is air conditioning, a dishwasher, a microwave and a stove. A thoughtful extra service is that you can arrange to have a full breakfast served in your chalet.

The Lavender Lodge
Cnr Ave Fresnaye and De Longueville, Fresnaye
Tel: 021-439 8328 **$**
www.lavenderlodge.co.za
This is a very friendly and hospitable place, offering comfortable Provençal-style rooms that all have private patios. Each room has a fridge, satellite TV, tea tray and fan, and the bathrooms have heated towel rails for added comfort during the chilly months. Lavish buffet breakfast spreads are served every morning.

FALSE BAY (MUIZENBERG, KOMMETJIE, KALK BAY, SIMON'S TOWN)

Luxury

The Beach House
No. 7 The Point, Kommetjie
Tel: 083-461 8419 **$$$$**
www.littleruo.co.za
Eat, sleep and entertain at this romantic beach villa perched on the water's edge in Kommetjie, a 45-minute drive from Cape Town. A very laid-back self-catering seaside retreat, it has four en-suite double bedrooms and a spacious living area that leads into a nice eat-in kitchen area. It is chic and unfussy. White shuttered folding doors open onto a timber deck, complete with a 12.5-metre (41-ft) pool. You'll feel completely removed from all the bustle of Cape Town, but still close enough to get there easily when you do want to visit.

Moderate

Colona Castle
1 Verwood Street, Off Boyes Drive, Lakeside
Tel: 021-788 8235 **$$$**
www.colonacastle.co.za
Located between Sandvlei Lake and Muizenberg, on sheltered False Bay, this Tuscan-style villa built in the 1920s is lavishly furnished with antiques and paintings. Three luxury en-suite rooms are kitted out with satellite TV, heated towel rails, minibar and safe. Delicious gourmet breakfasts and dinners are served on the patio when the weather permits.

The Long Beach
No. 1 Kirsten Avenue, Kommetjie
Tel: 021-783 4183 **$$$**
www.thelongbeach.co.za
In the quaint fishing village of Kommetjie on an 8-km (5-mile) stretch of white beach with

turquoise waters, you'll feel a million miles from city life, which makes this the perfect getaway. Accommodation is available on an individual daily room basis or as an entire beach villa to share with family and friends. There are five stylishly appointed suites, all with sea views, and each room includes a safe, satellite TV, air conditioning, heated towel rails, and underfloor heating during the cooler months.

Inexpensive

The Inn at Castle Hill
37 Gatesville Road,
Kalk Bay 7945
Tel: 021-788 2554 **$$**
www.castlehill.co.za
This inn occupies a restored Edwardian villa overlooking the pretty little fishing village of Kalk Bay. Rooms are clean and comfortable, and the inn is close to some fabulous antiques shops and restaurants on the Kalk Bay strip.

Simon's Town Quayside Hotel
Off Jubilee Square, St George's Street, Simon's Town
Tel: 021-786 3833 **$$**
www.quayside.co.za
If you don't mind the slightly dated nautical decor, you can wake up to the sound of the sea in one of this hotel's comfortable rooms overlooking the harbour. There are some great restaurants within walking distance.

Whale View Manor
402 Main Road, Murdock Valley, Simon's Town
Tel: 021-786 3291 **$$**
www.whaleviewmanor.co.za
On the Main Road in Simon's Town, overlooking a secluded beach,

Whale View Manor is authentically decorated with a colourful mix of exotic and ethnic fabrics, scultpure and accessories. Six rooms have sea views, while the other two look towards the mountains. Leisurely breakfasts are served in the dining room, from where you can watch whales and penguins splash about in the bay.

Budget

Cape Point Cottage
59 Cape Point Road, Castle Rock, Simon's Town
Tel: 021-786 3891 **$**
www.capepointcottage.co.za
Only five minutes from

the Cape Point Nature Reserve, this cottage can be taken as a self-catering cottage or on a bed-and-breakfast basis. It's a perfect spot for nature-lovers.

Clovelly Lodge
40 Montrose Avenue,
Clovelly, Fish Hoek
Tel: 021-782 3000 **$**
www.clovellylodge.com
Bordering the Cape Peninsula National Park, you'll find yourself in a tranquil setting surrounded by lush greenery and birdsong, with mountain and sea views. The lodge has comfortable double bedrooms, a separate TV room and a lounge with a fireplace.

FURTHER AFIELD

STELLENBOSCH

Devon Valley Protea Hotel
Devon Valley Rd,
Stellenbosch 7600
Tel: 021-865 2012 **$$**
www.protea-hotels.co.za
Set on Sylvanvale, a boutique estate known for its pinotage reserve and vine-dried Chenin blanc, this medium-sized hotel has a scenic Winelands ambience, a fine restaurant, good facilities for disabled guests, and many other facilities, including a swimming pool.

D'Ouwe Werf
30 Church Street,
Stellenbosch 7600
Tel: 021-887 4608 **$$$**
www.ouwewerf.com
Established in the heart of old Stellenbosch in 1802, this plush inn is

a real gem – notable for its authentic Cape Dutch architecture, period decor, personal service, sumptuous traditional Cape cuisine and quality wine list.

Lanzerac
Jonkershoek Road,
Stellenbosch 7600
Tel: 021-886 5641 **$$$$**
www.lanzeracwines.co.za
Established in 1692 on what now forms the eastern outskirts of Stellenbosch, this renowned wine estate, complete with restored manor house, is also one of the most sumptuous small hotels in the Winelands, with a restaurant to match.

Rolands Uitspan
1 Cluver Rd, Stellenbosch
Tel: 021-883 2897 **$$**
www.rolands.co.za
Neat, central guest house with pleasant pool and sundeck offer-

ing en-suite accommodation at very reasonable rates.

Stellenbosch Protea Hotel
Techno Park, off the R44 about 5 km (3 miles) south of Stellenbosch.
Tel: 021-880 9500 **$$**
www.protea-hotels.co.za
This efficient modern hotel, consisting of 176 spacious rooms, lies in the vicinity of the award-winning Blaauwklippen and Kleine Zalze Estates, in the shadow of the craggy Helderberg.

Stumble Inn
12 Market Street, Stellenbosch 7699
Tel/fax: 021-887 4049 **$**
Lively, central backpacker hostel sprawling over two houses. Facilities include a swimming pool, satellite TV and discounted wine-tasting tours.

FRANSCHHOEK

Auberge La Dauphine
Excelsior Road,
Franschhoek 7690
Tel: 021-876 2606 **$$$**
www.ladauphine.co.za
Cosy and attractively

PRICE CATEGORIES

Price categories are for a double room (some include breakfast):
$ = under R500
$$ = R500–1,000
$$$ = R1,000–2,000
$$$$ = over R2,000

located accommodation in the former wine cellar of La Dauphine Estate in the Franschhoek Valley on the southeastern outskirts of town.

Le Quartier Francais
16 Huguenot Road, Franschhoek 7690
Tel: 021-876 2151 **$$$$**
A small but exceptional guest house in the heart of the Winelands' most scenic village. Its focus is an award-winning restaurant.

Roche Hotel
Plantasie Street, Paarl 7622
Tel: 021-863 2727 **$$$$**
www.granderoche.co.za
A superb vineyard setting, luxury accommodation, good service, fine food and prize-winning cellar (plus swimming pool, tennis and gym) put this among the best hotels in South Africa.

Roggeland Country House
Roggeland Road, Northern Paarl 7623
Tel: 021-868 2501 **$$$**
www.roggeland.co.za
This superb eight-room Cape Dutch-style guest house, in the shadow of

the Drakenstein Mountains, has been rated as one of the 50 best country-house hotels in the world and features excellent South African regional cuisine.

HERMANUS & THE OVERBERG

Bontebok National Park Rest Camp
Tel: 012-428 9111 **$$**
www.sanparks.org
This tranquil camp outside Swellendam consists of a campsite and some inexpensive six-berth "chalavans" with wooden ante-room and basic kitchen, using communal washrooms.

De Hoop Nature Reserve
Tel: 028-425 5020 **$**
www.capeconservation.org.za
Low-key and inexpensive dotted around this reserve, includes 11 self-catering cottages and a campsite.

Die Herberg
Arniston
Tel: 028-445 9420 **$–$$$**
This resort-like hotel in sleepy Arniston offers

comfortable en-suite accommodation and good facilities. There are also basic dorms and rooms under the pseudonym South of Africa Backpackers.

Marine Hermanus
Marine Drive, Hermanus 7700
Tel: 028-313 1000 **$$$$**
www.marine-hermanus.com
Expanded and renovated since it spearheaded Hermanus's first tourist boom back in 1902, this cliffside hotel now has 42 individually decorated bedrooms and suites with views across Walker Bay or the Kleinriviersmond Mountains.

Salmonsdam Nature Reserve
Tel: 028-314 0062 **$**
www.capeconservation.org.za
Basic hutted accommodation here has a wonderful location and is very inexpensive.

Zoete Inval Lodge
23 Main St Hermanus
Tel: 028-312 1242 **$**
www.zoeteinval.co.za
Excellent backpacker hostel on the west side of town. Good facilities and local day tours.

WEST COAST

Kagga Kamma
Near Citrusdal
Tel: 021-872 4343 **$$$$**
www.kaggakamma.co.za
A private reserve, with craggy scenery, ancient rock art and a San village, offering lodging in luxury chalets or tents, and there's a restaurant and swimming pool.

Lambert's Bay Protea
Voortrekker, St Lambert's Bay 8130
Tel: 027-432 1126 **$$**
www.protea-hotels.co.za
Bland but comfortable accommodation faces the old harbour of a quaint village known for its bird colonies and fine seafood.

Cederberg Lodge
67 Voortrekker St Citrusdal 7340
Tel: 022-921 2221 **$$**
www.cedarberglodge.co.za
A comfortable place to stay in the Olifants River Valley, with air conditioning, telephone in rooms, restaurant and pool.

Columbine Beach Camp
Columbine Nature Reserve
Tel: 082-926 2267 **$**
www.ratrace.co.za
This private camp offers tented and A-frame accommodation, plus organised sea-kayaking, diving, boat trips to seal and seabird colonies, and hiking.

Saldanha Bay Protea
51B Main Road, Saldanha, 7395
Tel: 022-714 1264 **$$$**
www.protea-hotels.co.za
This recently refurbished harbour-front hotel forms a good base from which to explore the nearby West Coast National Park.

BELOW: Kagga Kamma on the West Coast.

GARDEN ROUTE

MOSSEL BAY

Old Post Office Tree Manor
Tel: 044-691 3738
Fax: 044-691 3104 **$$$**
Email: book@oldposttree.co.za
www.oldposttree.co.za
Built as a warehouse in 1846, this historic hotel has an attractive waterfront location in the town centre and has 30 smart rooms with modern amenities.

Santos Express Train Lodge
Tel/fax: 044-691 1995 **$**
Email: santos_express@mweb.co.za
This unusual and popular backpacker lodge is in a genuine train carriage, set above lovely Santos Beach, with a pub and restaurant.

GEORGE

Protea Hotel Landmark Lodge
123 York Street, George 6529
Tel: 044-874 4488
Fax: 044-874 4428 **$$–$$$**
Email: reservations@
proteageorge.co.za.
This comfortable 50-room hotel is in the historic heart of town.

OUDTSHOORN

Eight Bells Mountain Inn
PO Box 436, Mossel Bay 6500
Tel: 044-631 0000 **$$$**
www.eightbells.co.za
Family-run country inn amid stunning scenery on the R328 between Mossel Bay and Oudtshoorn. It has a variety

of sports facilities.

Riempie Estate Hotel
Baron Van Rheede Street,
PO Box 370, Oudtshoorn 6620
Tel: 044-272 6161
Fax: 044-272 6772 **$$**
Cosy country atmosphere and tranquil setting in the heart of ostrich country.

WILDERNESS

Ebb & Flow Rest Camp
Tel: 044-877 1197 (bookings through SANParks) **$$**
Camping sites and inexpensive cabins and chalets are available at this idyllic rest camp on the Touws River.

Fairy Knowe Hotel
Dumbleton Road, PO Box 28,
George 6560
Tel: 044-877 1100
Fax: 044-877 0364 **$–$$**
Email: fairybp@mweb.co.za
Built in 1874, this homely resort on the Touws River offers basic but comfortable hotel-style rooms and backpacker accommodation.

KNYSNA

Eden's Touch
Tel: 083-253 6366
Fax: 044-532 7655 **$$$**
Email: info@edenstouch.co.za
www.edenstouch.co.za
This idyllic retreat has large wooden chalets with kitchen, satellite TV and lots of activities. It's fringed by privately protected indigenous forest.

Knysna Backpackers
42 Queen Street, Knysna 6570
Tel: 044-382 2554 **$**
Email: knybpack@netactive.co.za
This Victorian manor

houses one of the more sedate of the half-dozen hostels around central Knysna. It offers private rooms as well as dorms.

Knysna Quays Protea
51 Main Street, PO Box 33,
Knysna 6570
Tel: 044-382 2127
Fax: 044-382 3568 **$$$**
Quality hotel, with air conditioning, telephone in rooms, facilities for disabled guests and swimming pool.

Knysna River Club
Sun Valley Drive, Knysna 6570
Tel: 044-382 6483
Fax: 044-382 6484 **$$$$**
Email: knysna.riverclub@pixie.co.za
www.knysnariverclub.co.za
This small, award-winning resort has 35 fully equipped and serviced self-catering log chalets on the grassy verge of Brenton Lagoon. Facilities include a restaurant, swimming pool and canoeing.

PLETTENBERG BAY

Albergo
6–8 Church Street,
Plettenberg Bay 6600
Tel: 044-533 4434 **$**
Email: albergo@mweb.co.za
This hillside backpacker hostel, within walking distance of the town centre and beach, has camping, dorms and private rooms.

Bitou River Lodge
Tel/fax: 044-535 9577 **$$$**
Email: info@bitou.co.za
www.bitou.co.za
Voted South Africa's Best B&B/Guest House in 2003, this luxurious owner-managed guest house with five rooms is on the forested banks of

the Bitou River.

The Plettenberg
40 Church Street, PO Box 719,
Plettenberg Bay 6600
Tel: 044-533 2030
Fax: 044-533 2074 **$$$$**
A grand hotel in English country-house style, with good food and sea views. Swimming pool.

TSITSIKAMMA

Storms River Mouth Rest Camp
Book through SANParks **$–$$$**
On the rugged coast of the Storms River estuary, this national-park rest camp has beachfront campsites and a variety of moderately priced chalets.

Tsitsikamma Lodge
N2 National Road,
Tsitsikamma, PO Box 10,
Storms River 6308
Tel: 042-280 3802 **$$$**
www.tsitsikamma.com
A hunting lodge with good-value log cabins in a forest setting. Honeymoon suites have spa baths and fireplaces.

PRICE CATEGORIES

Price categories are for a double room (some include breakfast):
$ = under R500
$$ = R500–1,000
$$$ = R1,000–2,000
$$$$ = over R2,000

A CTIVITIES

THE ARTS, NIGHTLIFE, CHILDREN'S ACTIVITIES, FESTIVALS, SHOPPING AND SPORTS

THE ARTS

Theatre

There is a whirlwind of mixed talent and energy that sweeps through Cape Town's theatre scene, from the City Bowl through to the townships. In addition to the established venues where big productions usually take centre-stage, there are also a number of privately owned theatres, nurturing the city's passion for the arts, that have proved to be a huge success over the years. Venues vary from old church halls to restaurants and small Victorian theatres. Going to the theatre in Cape Town is also an affordable night out on the town, in comparison to London's West End or New York's Broadway strip. There's something to suit everyone, from light-hearted comedy to serious drama.

Major theatre venues

Artscape Theatre Centre
DF Malan Street, Foreshore
Tel: 021-421 7839
www.artscape.co.za
Box office: Mon–Fri 9am–5pm, Sat 9am–12.30pm. Bookings can also be made one hour prior to performances on Sat and Sun. Bookings also available at Computicket or Dial-a-Seat. Expect to see anything from an Andrew Lloyd-Webber musical extravaganza to contemporary African dance, classical ballet or opera. Artscape is also home to the Cape Philharmonic Orchestra (tel: 021-410 9809, www.capephil harmonic.org.za), Cape Town City Ballet (tel: 021-650 4673, www.capetowncityballet.org.za), Cape Town Opera (tel: 021-410 9858, www.capetownopera.co.za) and the modern dance company Jazzart Dance Theatre (tel: 021-410 9848, www.jazzart.co.za).

Baxter Theatre Centre
Main Road, Rondebosch
Tel: 021-685 7880/680 3989
www.baxter.co.za
Box office: Mon–Sat 9am to start of performance. Tickets also available through Computicket. Special deals are available for pensioners, students and for block bookings over 10 people). Aside from its very ugly 1970s exterior, this theatre is always buzzing inside. You can enjoy a meal at the theatre restaurant before the show followed by a few drinks at the bar afterwards; you might even get to meet some of the cast. There are two main venues at the Baxter – the Main Theatre and Concert Hall. Productions include light musicals, heavy dramas and hilarious comedians.

Theatre on the Bay
1 Link Street, Camps Bay
Tel: 021-438 3301
www.theatreonthebay.co.za
Box office: daily 9.30am–5pm; show nights 9.30am–8pm. This vibey theatre definitely has the best setting in Cape Town. It's situated on the trendy strip on Camps Bay, where you can enjoy a light drink or supper before making your way to the show. It often hosts popular productions like Tim Plewman's hit show *Defending the Cave Man* – a new take on *Men are from Mars, Woman are from Venus*.

On Broadway
21 Somerset Road, Green Point
Tel: 021-418 8338
www.onbroadway.co.za
Box office: 9.30am–8pm. Booking essential.
A dinner theatre in the lively suburb of Green Point which features brilliant drag shows, cabaret and stand-up comedy shows. You're guaranteed to leave laughing. It's best to book well in advance as it's a popular venue and fills up quickly.

Independent Armchair Theatre
135 Lower Main Road, Observatory
Tel: 021-447 1514
Box Office: 9am–2am show nights.
A Bohemian-style venue filled with all sorts of comfy chairs and

TRANSPORT

sofas that you sit in to watch the show. Expect to see some excellent local comedy.

Kalk Bay Theatre
52 Main Road, Kalk Bay
Tel: 021-788 7257
The price of a tick (R75; R150) includes a three-course meal. Situated in an old church hall in the quaint village of Kalk Bay, this dinner-theatre puts on some hysterical interactive productions. It's most fun if you go in a big crowd.

Grand West Casino
1 Vanguard Drive, Goodwood
Tel: 021-505 7777
Box office: 6pm–11pm.
Even though it's not close to the city, you will probably catch a few good shows here, so it's worth calling to find out what's on. It's also the venue for the annual Cape Town International Comedy Festival, featuring some talented local stand-up acts.

Ballet/Dance

Cape Town City Ballet
Artscape Theatre Complex, DF Malan Street, Foreshore
Tel: 021-650 4673
www.capetowncityballet.org.za
Bookings: Computicket or Dial-a-Seat *(see box right)*.
This ballet company is the oldest of its kind in Cape Town. The company's dancers also perform at several other events in Cape Town, like the Spier Summer Festival (Jan–Feb) in Stellenbosch. Apart from staging some classical ballets, the Cape Town City Ballet is also exploring more contemporary-style productions, like *Queen at the Ballet*, which is a powerful mix of dance, opera and rock singers, and the Cape Town Philharmonic Orchestra.

Jazzart Dance Theatre
Artscape Theatre Centre, DF Malan Street, Foreshore
Tel: 021-410 9848
www.jazzart.co.za
Bookings: Computicket and Dial-a-Seat *(see box right)*.
While this dance company offers

training in African dance (gum-boot and contemporary) it's worth making a note of the fund-raiser production that they put together every year, called Dan-scape (tel: 021-410 9848). It features mostly community dance groups who are still in training, and gives them the chance to get some on-stage performing experience.

Cape Dance Company (CDC)
The Space, Bell Crescent, West-lake Business Park, Westlake Tokai
Tel: 021-712 9445
www.capedancecompany.bizland.com
This particular dance company runs in association with the Academy of Dance. It puts on performances annually at the Grahamstown Festival, and has also danced at the Artscape Theatre, as well as at the Edinburgh Festival.

Opera & Concerts

You'll be spoilt for choice in Cape Town with the range of opera productions, symphony concerts and chamber-orchestra events on offer. The Cape Town Philharmonic Orchestra is a full-time professional symphony orchestra that often hosts internationally known conductors and soloists. It's really been put on the map in terms of the growing global music culture, and has 45 permanent musicians performing over 100 concerts each year. In August 2005, the CPO took part in a production of *Show Boat* in Germany.

Artscape Theatre Centre
DF Malan Street, Foreshore
Tel: 021-410 9800
www.artscape.co.za
Box office: Mon–Fri 9am–5pm.
Bookings can also be made through Computicket and Dial-a-Seat *(see box right)*. Throughout the year you can enjoy the Cape Town Opera at the Opera House (which seats 1,200) and has excellent acoustics. The company is best known for its light classical pro-

ductions and opera in foreign languages (with subtitles displayed on an overhead digital screen).

Baxter Theatre Centre
Main Road, Rondebosch
Tel: 021-680 3989
www.baxter.co.za
Box office 9am–start of performance.
As part of the University of Cape Town, The Baxter Theatre Centre provides an exciting platform for live music that reflects a mix of cultural talents. It's an excellent venue for international and national productions that appeal to all devotees of fine music.

City Hall
Darling Street, opposite the Grand Parade (Cape Philharmonic Orchestra)
Tel: 021-410 9809
www.capephilharmonic.org.za
Bookings through Computicket or Dial-a-Seat *(see details below)*.
The Cape Philharmonic Orchestra performs here throughout the year, but Thursday nights are traditionally concert nights. The acoustics are excellent and the setting splendid.

ACCOMMODATION

BUYING TICKETS

Tickets can be booked at the relevant theatre box office, which is generally open during the week and on show days – either by telephone or in person. Alternatively, you can book through Computicket or Dial-a-seat:
Computicket: open Mon–Fri 9am–5pm, Sat 9am–6am. For credit card bookings, tel: 083-915 8000; for event information, tel: 083-915 8100. It's also possible to book online at www.computicket.co.za.
Dial-a-seat: For bookings tel: 021-421 7695 or 021-421 7839.
Prices vary according to the production, and can range from R60 to R500. Look out for specials on quieter nights (usually early in the week) or matinée performances.

ACTIVITIES

A – Z

ABOVE: Cape Town is known for its excellent jazz.

Outdoor concert venues

Kirstenbosch Botanical Garden Centre
Kirstenbosch Botanical Gardens, Rhodes Drive, Newlands
Tel: 021-799 8783
Bookings: through Computicket *(see box, page 217).*
During the summer, Kirstenbosch Botanical Gardens hosts summer concerts every Sunday evening, featuring everything from jazz to classics. For the best experience, pack a picnic and enjoy the music under the stars, with Table Mountain as the backdrop. The New Year's Eve concert with the Cape Philharmonic Orchestra is a delightful alternative to the celebrations in the city.

WHAT'S ON LISTINGS

The Friday editions of the *Cape Times* and *Cape Argus* newspapers have arts and entertainment sections that will keep you up to date with performances and events. The bi-monthly *Cape Etc* and monthly *SA Citylife* are also excellent sources for listings information. You can also get information online at www.tonight.co.za.

NIGHTLIFE

When the sun sets in the "Mother City", temperatures may start dropping, but the heat is on with bars and party venues that line up exciting events and shows all year round. Welcome to party town! Known for its varied and vibrant nightlife – a lot of clubs don't open until 11pm and are bound by law to close at 4am sharp. Many are open seven nights a week.

Start your evening early in Kloof Street or at a bar in Green Point/De Waterkant (which also has a string of gay and gay-friendly clubs and restaurants). After you've chilled out and absorbed the beautiful sunsets, you can hit the city and choose from an endless list of sizzling club venues to suit your taste in music. Long Street is the happening place for the young and hip, and you could spend all night wandering between the pubs and clubs. The dress code is almost always as casual as you wish, although shorts and trainers are not welcome at some venues.

Admission prices to clubs vary between R20–120, often free before 11pm. The legal drinking age is 18, although some clubs impose an age limit of 21 years.

Nightclubs

Rhodes House
60 Queen Victoria Street
Tel: 021-424 8844
www.rhodeshouse.com
Admission: Oct–Feb R80; Mar–Sept R50
In a converted Victorian mansion that was previously owned by Sir Cecil John Rhodes, this is the venue of choice for rock stars, celebrities, royals, models, millionaires and euro-trash. Dress up and make sure you have a lot of cash to hand, because drinks don't come cheap. What makes this club such a success story is the fact that you can either let yourself go on one of the two dance floors (one is in the central courtyard under a canopy of stars), or sit back and relax on a comfortable suede sofa in one of the private lounges. If you like R&B go on a Thursday.

The Fez
38 Hout Street, Greenmarket Square
Tel: 021-423 4889
www.fez.co.za
Open Wed–Sat 11pm–4am (Wed 9–11pm is Ladies' Night)
Admission: R40
Attracts a young, hip crowd, all dressed-up and ready to dance the night away. Commercial house and funky beats. Small dance floor with an upstairs VIP lounge. Very popular with tourists over the hot summer months. Check out monthly street parties

Mink
26b JDN House, Shortmarket Street, Greenmarket Square
Tel: 021-422 3262
www.minkcapetown.co.za
Open Thur–Sat 9pm–4am
Admission: R50
Slick-in-the-city is one way to describe this new kid on the block. During the week it's the perfect cocktail venue, and it doubles up as a club at weekends. R&B night every Thursday and funky house at weekends.

TRANSPORT

Ivory Room
196 Loop Street
Tel: 021-422 3257
Open Wed–Thur 5pm–2am;
Fri, Sat 10pm–4am
Admission: R30
A small but swish hang-out for an
older, sophisticated crowd who
can either chill out on the leather
sofas or take to the dance floor
for some all-night jamming.

Mercury Live and Lounge
43 De Villiers Street
Tel: 021-465 2106
www.mercuryl.co.za
Open Mon–Sat 8pm–4am
Admission: R10–80
A retro-style venue that feels like
you're dancing in a friend's living
room, except that the music is
better. Dance to resident DJ
Moodswing's range of classic,
pop, disco and house anthems.
Great monthly parties take place
upstairs every weekend over the
summer season. Also known for
students' special nights, with
great promotions.

The Gallery
84 Sir Lowry Road
Tel: 021-461 9649
Open Fri and Sat 9pm–8am
Admission: R40–80
If you're looking for all-night
dancing to hard house and trance,
look no further. There's nothing
glamorous about this nightclub
situated on the outskirts of town,
but you're sure to get your dance
fix, considering the impressive
line-up of well-known local and
international DJs.

Deluxe
Unity House, Cnr Long and
Longmarket streets
Tel: 021-422 4832
Open Fri, Sat 8pm–4am
Admission: R40
Decor is retro-glam, with an
outside patio and an intimate
lounge area for taking time out.
Here you'll find leggy models
drinking at the bar or shaking it
up on the dance floor.

Bossa Nova
43 Somerset Road, Green Point
Tel: 021-425 0295
www.bossanova.co.za
Open Tues–Fri 5pm–1am, Sat
8pm–4am
Admission: Fri, Sat men R50,
women R30. No admission
charge Tues–Thurs.
Because they specialise in tango
and salsa dancing, expect to
groove away the night to sexy
Latino beats, guaranteed to turn
up the heat on the dance floor.
The club also hosts salsa
classes twice a week.

Purgatory
8 Dixon Street, Green Point
Tel: 021-421 7464
www.purgatory.co.za
Open Wed–Sat 10pm–4am
Admission: R50
An exclusive clubbing experience
with one of the nicest VIP lounges
in Cape Town, perfect for private
parties. You'll feel like you're in a
1940s cinema, with its terraced
seating area overlooking the
dance floor. Mirrors, leather-clad
walls and shiny lacquered floors.

Opium
6 Dixon Street, De Waterkant
Tel: 021-425 4010
www.opium.co.za
Open Wed–Sun 9pm–4am
Admission: R40
A popular spot in Dixon Street
that can get very busy over the
weekend with a mixed crowd of
international models, tourists
and hip-hop students. With two
dance floors (one that's an open-
air venue over the summer
months) you have a choice of
music, depending on your mood.

Sutra Groove Bar
86 Loop Street
Tel: 021-422 4218
www.sutragroovebar.co.za
Open Wed–Sun 9pm–4am
Admission: R30–50
Situated in the middle of town,
this is a good-looking club filled
with good-looking people. Its
multi-level design means that you
can sit in the sleek bar downstairs or dance upstairs at the
disco den. Expect deep and tech
house music.

Music Venues

Jazz
Cape Town is big on jazz, with two
annual festivals, four jazz-only
venues and several jazz events
that take place during the year.
Venues vary from stylish restau-
rant-type supper clubs to more
relaxed pubs that get quite loud
and noisy. To stay informed on
the jazz scene, check out the jazz
column in the Wednesday Cape
Argus or visit www.tonight.co.za.
Tickets for the bigger jazz events
can be booked through Computicket (see box on page 217).

Dizzy Jazz Café
The Drive, Camps Bay
Tel: 021-438 2686
A pavement café bar in Camps
Bay that carries on into the early
hours of the morning. There are
usually live jazz performances
that get foot-stomping and very
festive every night of the week.

Green Dolphin
Victoria and Albert Arcade,
V&A Waterfront
Tel: 021-421 7471
www.greendolphin.co.za
Admission: R20–25
With live jazz sets seven days a
week, the Green Dolphin really
does uphold its motto, "Dedicated to the preservation of
jazz". High-quality line-ups feature unique collaborations of
local jazz artists. Sunday blues
nights are very popular, so book
in advance.

Manenberg's Jazz Café
102 Clock Tower Precinct,
V&A Waterfront
Tel: 021-421 5639
Admission: R40–80
You will find the best of the best
jazz musicians playing at this
popular seafront venue. Have a
few drinks at the bar, soak up
the atmosphere and prepare to
make a night of it.

ACCOMMODATION

ACTIVITIES

A – Z

ABOVE: music man.

Marimba Restaurant & Cigar Bar

Cnr Heerengracht and Coen
Steytler Ave, Entrance 5,
Cape Town International
Convention Centre
Tel: 021-418 3366
The place for world music, big
band, blues, soul and contem-
porary African sounds. Book
early, because on big nights the
restaurant is booked weeks in
advance. Catch the Tuesday night
"Marimban Big Band" in action.

Rock

Green Point Stadium
Fritz Sonnenberg Road,
Green Point
Tel: 021-434 4510; bookings at
Computicket *(see box page 217)*.
This is Cape Town's grand old
dame of rock concerts, which
has hosted Michael Jackson, U2
and the Mandela 46664 concert,
among other big names.
The Drum Café
32 Glynn Street, Gardens
Tel: 021-461 1305
www.drumcafe.co.za
Be there on a Saturday night for
"Rock Night", when the basement
venue fills up with shaggy hippies
and ageing wannabe rockers.
Jo'burg
218 Long Street
Tel: 021-422 0142.
Admission: free
A drinking den on the Long Street
strip where you'll find a mixed

bag of people, especially when
they're hosting a live band on a
Sunday night.
Acoustic Café
Main and Camp Road, Muizenberg
Tel: 021-788 1900
Admission: R20–30
A new venue that's really starting
to make some noise (in a good
way). There's a colourful mix of
surfers, hippies and laid-back
locals who gather here on
Thursday, Friday and Saturday
evenings for the live band.

Pubs and Bars

Whether you choose to sit inside
an old wood-panelled bar drinking a pint or two, or get dressed
up and schmooze the jet-set at a
seafront cocktail bar, you're
sure to find a watering hole to
suit your mood. Remember,
wherever you decide to spend
your evening, get a taxi home or
back to your hotel.

Atlantic Seaboard & Waterfront

Alba
Pierhead Building, V&A Waterfront
Tel: 021-425 3385
After a day's shopping at the V&A
Waterfront, this is where you'll
want to kick back on one of the
couches overlooking the harbour
and enjoy an icy cocktail as you
watch the sun go down. A chic
meeting spot before or after
dinner, often with a live band or
DJ playing at weekends.
Baraza
The Promenade, Victoria Road,
Camps Bay
Tel: 021-438 1758
Shake the sand off your toes
and chill out with a cocktail in
hand watching the sun go down.
After dark a DJ kicks in, and the
party usually goes on late into
the evening.
Bascule Whisky Bar & Wine Cellar
Cape Grace Hotel, West Quay,
V&A Waterfront, Cape Town
Tel: 021-410 7100
www.capegrace.com
Although you might break the

Gay Clubs and Bars

Cape Town's gay clubs are
mostly situated in De Waterkant and Green Point but
come and go depending on
the season – during peak
season (Dec and Jan) they
often reinvent themselves.

Club
Sliver, 27 Somerset Road,
Green Point, tel: 021-421
4799; www.sliver.co.za
Admission: R30.
Mostly male, with two dance
floors, beautiful bodies and
uplifting music that pumps
until the early hours.

Pubs and Bars
Bronx Action Bar, 35 Somerset Road, Green Point, tel:
021-419 9216; ww.bronx.co.za.
Admission: free.
An old favourite gay and
lesbian venue that's been
on the strip the longest.
Excellent music; karaoke
on Monday.
M Bar, The Metropole,
38 Long Street, tel: 021-424
7247; www.metropolehotel.co.za.
A sophisticated bar that
also has a strong straight
following. Versace sofas,
cocktails guaranteed to
make you blush and a sexy
crowd ready to party through
the night.

bank with a single glass of icy
Sauvignon Blanc, what better way
to enjoy it than with a bottomless
bowl of pistachio nuts, friendly
people, vibey music and breathtaking views of Table Mountain.
This place really buzzes on a
Friday evening after work, when
people spill out onto the hotel's
private marina.
Buddha Bar
39 Main Road, Green Point
Tel: 021-434 4010
www.buddhabar.co.za
A small, Eastern-themed bar with
a Zen fountain, silk cushions and
intricately carved wooden furnish-

ings. No relation to the famous Buddha Bar in Paris, but it's still stylish and sophisticated.

Buena Vista Social Café
81 Main Road, Green Point
Tel: 021-433 0611
www.buenavista.co.za
This is the closest you're going to get to a hot Havana night in Cape Town. Think *mojitas*, cigars and revolutionary images on the walls. There's a friendly atmosphere that happily unites the bar-restaurant-lounge areas.

Café Caprice
Victoria Road, Camps Bay
Tel: 021-438 8315
If you're looking for something to do on a Sunday night, this is where it all happens. Meet the tanned, pretty set that have walked off the beach and are ready to party (and pose) all night long. It's Ibiza meets Cannes in the summertime, but it's in a small space that spills out onto the pavement across from the beach. Spectacular sunsets, so arrive early to grab a table.

Eclipse
Victoria Road, Camps Bay
Tel: 021-438 0882
Part of the London chain of the same name, this bar-lounge transforms into a club later in the evening, and attracts a young

design-conscious crowd looking for a beach party, without the sand. A simple and luxuriously decorated space with great views and an excellent cocktail menu.

La Med
Victoria Road, Clifton
Tel: 021-438 5600
With the best views of the Atlantic Ocean, this is an institution for casual Sunday sundowners (as long as the wind isn't blowing). Come early to get a spot on the deck overlooking the ocean before hitting the late-night dance floor that opens later in the evening.

Paulaner Brauhaus
V&A Waterfront
Tel: 021-418 9999
An authentic traditional German *brauhaus* that brews the best beer in town. If you feel like a bite to eat, they have a comprehensive menu. On no account forgo the freshly made pretzels – they're delicious!

City Bowl & City Centre

Kennedy's
251 Long Street, Cape Town
Tel: 021-424 1212
www.kennedys.co.za
Open Mon–Fri noon–late,
Sat 7pm–late
Recently renovated to provide a

stylish bar, this is the place to enjoy single malts and Havana cigars.

Miam Miam
169 Long Street
Tel: 021-422 5823
For those in the know, Miam Miam is the latest hidden gem on Cape Town's Long Street. Forget about grungy backpackers sipping on beer – this minimalist bar-cum-restaurant-cum-gallery is pulling in a hip, sophisticated crowd for after-work cocktails and snacks. Either sit on the adjustable bucket stools around the bar, or sink into the large comfy leather sofas with one of their excellent Bloody Marys in hand. Also check out the monthly-changing collections of local art.

Planet
Mount Nelson Hotel,
76 Orange Street, Gardens
Tel: 021-483 1000
Open daily 5pm–late
Expect to find a mix of young and mature, locals and tourists, all sipping on a champagne cocktail and tapping their feet to the funky music. This hip new addition to the Mount Nelson Hotel is opulently decorated but still user-friendly, and you just might spot an international movie star or two when they are in town.

Raffiki's
13C Kloofnek Road,
Tamboerskloof
Tel: 021-426 4731
Join an easygoing mix of backpackers and locals to enjoy a beer on the long bamboo balcony.

Southern Suburbs

Foresters' Arms
52 Newlands Avenue, Newlands
Tel: 021-689 5949
Set in the leafy Southern Suburbs, this is the closest you're going to get to a traditional English pub – the smell of old leather, smoky nights and draught ales on tap. It's also a great venue for watching sport on a Saturday afternoon alongside the Newlands locals and university students.

BELOW: club time in Camps Bay.

Oblivion Wine Bar & Restaurant
Cnr 3rd Avenue and Chichester
Road, Harfield Village
Tel: 021-671 8522
Open 11.30am–late
This is a buzzing drinking hole
every night of the week, with an
excellent range of local, award-
winning wines and a small menu
for those who get a little peckish.

Peddlars on the Bend
Spaanschemaat River,
Constantia
Tel: 021-794 7747
Roaring fireplace in winters, an
alfresco area for hot summer
nights, an energetic bar and
restaurant serving fine country
cuisine – this place has it all.

Southern Peninsula

Polana
Kalk Bay Harbour, Main Road,
Kalk Bay
Tel: 021-788 7162
You just don't get closer to the
sea in Cape Town. Sip away the
afternoon gazing out across the
bay with a glass of wine in hand.
Later, move upstairs for a
seafood platter at the Harbour
House restaurant.

Cinemas

Cape Town's cinemas are of an
excellent standard, and show
international releases (both art-
house films and blockbusters)
with a minimum delay time. Keep
in mind the Tuesday half-price
screenings (if you're willing to
stand and wait for about 20
minutes). The choice of films on
mainstream cinema screens
remains international.

Cavendish Nouveau
Cavendish Square, Claremont
Tel: 0861-300 444; Ticketline
082 16789
Box office 11am–11pm.
Tickets R33 (half price Tues)
Not strictly an art-house theatre,
but they do screen the majority of
non-mainstream films released in
South Africa.

Cinema Nouveau Waterfront
Victoria Mall, V&A Waterfront
Tel: 0861-300 444;

Ticketline 082 16789
Box office 11am–11pm. Tickets
R33 (half price Tues).
International releases.

Cinema Prive
Canal Walk, Century City.
Tel: 021-555 2510
Box office 8.30am–11pm daily.
If you feel like catching an arty
movie, followed by some late-
night shopping, this is a good
choice. And you're almost guaranteed a seat everytime, as
most people there are going to
see more mainstream films.

Independent cinemas

The Labia and Labia on Kloof
Next door to Mount Nelson Hotel
Tel: 021-424 5927
Box office daily noon–midnight.
Tickets R25.
The Labia is a nice old cinema that
shows both mainstream and art-
house movies. Its sister cinema
around the corner is more modern.
Set inside a shopping centre, with
a good selection of restaurants
and coffee shops (and ample parking), the Labia on Kloof makes
going to the movies a real pleasure. And you can take your coffee, wine and beer that you can
take inside with you. The popcorn
comes in old-fashioned bags.

Casino

**Grand West Casino & Entertain-
ment Centre**
1 Vanguard Drive, Goodwood
Tel: 021-505 7777
www.grandwest.co.za
There are three casinos in the
Cape region and this is undoubtedly the best. A massive complex incorporating various
reconstructed historic buildings,
it has two hotels, an Olympic-
size ice rink, several restaurants
and, of course, the casino. This
features 1,750 slot machines
and 66 tables, plus bars, restaurants, lounges, a nightclub and
revue bar. Gambling areas are
open to those over 18 years,
dress is smart casual in the
gaming halls and a passport or
ID is required.

CHILDREN'S ACTIVITIES

Cape Ostrich Farm
Cape of Good Hope
Nature Reserve
Tel: 021-780 9294
www.capepointostrichfarm.co.za
Tour: R25 (under-16s R10)
Even though you won't be able to
ride on the ostriches, you can
take a tour of the breeding stations and see all the baby chicks
in incubators. Also a variety of
ostrich paraphernalia for sale,
like feathers, ostrich eggs and
leather accessories.

World of Birds
Valley Road, Hout Bay
Tel: 021-790 2730
www.worldofbirds.org.za
Admission: R45 (child 3–16 R30)
Walk-through aviaries that house
more than 4,000 birds and some
monkeys.

**Grand West Casino and
Entertainment Centre**
1 Vanguard Drive, Goodwood
Tel: 021-505 7777
www.grandwest.co.za
Games, rides, go-karting and
minigolf at the Magic Company.
The ice station has two rinks (one
for smaller children), and there's
a cinema complex and The Grand
Kids Corner crèche, where you
can leave the children while you
play the slots or tables.

Laserquest
Lower Level, Stadium on Main
Tel: 021-683 7296
Run around in the dark shooting
little points of light at your friends.
A good place to come when the
weather is wet. Exhausting, but
lots of fun.

Action Paint Ball
Tokai Forest
Tel: 021-790 7603
Children of 11 or older can play
this game. Strict safety rules and
regulations and first-aid standards are followed by the trained
managers and field marshals.

Thundercity
Tower Road, Cape Town
International Airport
Tel: 021-934 8007

ABOVE: Two Oceans Aquarium is one of the most popular attractions for children.

www.thundercity.com
Admission: R30
(seniors and students R25)
Largest collection of privately
owned ex-military aircraft.

Planetarium
South African Museum,
25 Queen Victoria Street
Tel: 021-481 3900
Admission: R20 (under 17s R6)
Sit inside a dark room and
watch the night sky appear
before your eyes. A variety of
shows cater for all age groups –
little ones love the interactive
"Twinkle" show, while teens
might enjoy "The Sky Tonight" to
check out what the sky will look
like that night. The reclining
seats are a comfortable bonus.

Two Oceans Aquarium
Dock Road, V&A Waterfront
Tel: 021-418 3823
www.aquarium.co.za
Admission: R60
(children 4–17 R28)
Everything that lives underwater
from kelp to sea horses. Seeing
the sharks being fed in the preda-
tor tank is especially popular.
Plenty of hands-on activities too,
as well as seals and penguins,
and lots of staff available to
explain what you're seeing.

Child-Friendly Shopping Centres

Cavendish Square
1 Dreyer Street, Claremont
Tel: 021-671 8042.
Children's activities in the central
courtyard, Zip Zap Circus, fashion shows and cinemas.

Canal Walk
Century Boulevard, Century City,
Milnerton
Tel: 0860 101 165
Children's promotional events,
cinema complex, fashion shows
and other activities.

V&A Waterfront
Tel: 021-408 7600
Concerts and events during the
holidays and children's entertainment monthly.

Science & Technology

MTN ScienCentre
407 Canal Walk, Century City,
Entrance 5
Tel: 021-529 8100
Admission: R24; under-16s R20;
pensioners and students R22.
An interactive educational science
centre that's fun for the whole
family. Workshops and programmes over school holidays.

FESTIVALS

January
Jazzathon
V&A Waterfront
Tel: 021-683 2201
www.jazzathon.co.za
Highly recommended festival
held over several days in mid-
summer. Free entry.

March
Cape Town Festival
Tel: 021-465 9042
www.capetownfestival.co.za
A wave of sizzling talent comes to
venues throughout the region
during March.

July
**Encounters South African Inde-
pendent Documentary Festival**
Cinema Nouveau, V&A
Waterfront
Tel: 021-461 1228
www.encounters.co.za.
An interesting programme of doc-
umentaries from top film-makers.

August
Nokia Cape Town Fashion Week
Cape Town International
Convention Centre
Tel: 021-422 0390
www.capetownfashionweek.com

Fashionistas gather to see the top African (and some international) designers showcase their garments. Early/mid-August.

V&A Waterfront Winter Food Fair
Market Square, V&A Waterfront
Tel: 021-556 8200.
A feast of hot and tasty local cuisine and wine. Mid-August.

September

Cape Town International Kite Festival
Zandvlei, Muizenberg
Tel: 021-447 9040
www.kitefest.co.za
Kites of all shapes and sizes fly high in the Cape's southeaster. Mid-September.

Cape Argus/ Woolworths Gun Run
Beach Road, Mouille Point
This popular half-marathon is run along the Atlantic seaboard on 25 September.

October

Cape à la Carte
Cape Town International Convention Centre
Tel: 021-426 0800
A feast of local flavours are provided by celebrity chefs, restaurant specials and stands devoted to food, drink and entertaining. Mid- to late October.

ABOVE: African textiles on Greenmarket Square.

November

Sithengi South African Film & Television Market
Artscape Theatre Complex
Taking its name from a Nguni word relating to buying and marketplaces, the Sithengi Film & Television Market has been going strong since 1996.

December–January

Cape Town Minstrel Carnival.
Cape Town's biggest and most raucous carnival sees the city celebrating the advent of the New Year with numerous festivals, competitions and extravagant parades.

SHOPPING

What to Buy

Food & wine

You can't go home without tasting South Africa's speciality, biltong (dried raw meat), available from PJ'S Biltong Bar kiosks, Pick'n Pay, Woolworths and most butchers. Visitors should know that importing biltong into some countries might be illegal. A case of wine might be a safer bet to take back home with you. Take a winelands tour through Stellenbosch, Paarl and Franschhoek and find quality, award-winning wines for as little as R20 a bottle. If you're a tea-drinker, take some Rooibos tea home with you, a herbal tea that's rich in antioxidants and delicious with honey.

African arts, crafts & curios

Cape Town is a Mecca for traders from all over Africa. At Greenmarket Square on Shortmarket Street in the city centre you'll find an eclectic range of goods including African jewels, tribal masks, wooden sculpture, intricate beadwork and handmade clothing. An excellent lightweight gift is one of the wire sculptures, ranging from R10–600, that you'll find on the side of the road from wire daisies to a life-size wire lion. For ethnic crafts, make a trip to the Montebello Design Centre in Newlands.

Antiques

Antique-lovers should take a leisurely stroll down Church Street, a short street off Long Street that's an arcade of antiques and bookshops, where you are guaranteed to find a real bargain.

TAX/VAT

VAT stands at 14 percent on all goods sold in Cape Town. Visitors can reclaim this on their departure for purchases over R250, provided all receipts have been kept and the appropriate tax invoices have been obtained and filled in. All your purchased goods should be declared to the VAT Refund Administrator at the Cape Town International Departures terminal. A refund is then paid after passing through Passport Control. For further information and paperwork queries, contact the VAT Refund Office, Victoria Wharf Shopping Centre, V&A Waterfront, tel: 021-421 1612; www.taxrefunds.co.za.

Fashion

Fashion junkies will probably be blown away by the impressive and growing range of vintage-clothing shops on Long Street, where you could probably pick up a "previously owned" Prada fur for next to nothing. Also look out for Yin, an eclectic clothing boutique that stocks handmade garments designed by a talented group of female African fashion designers. As you wander around the shopping malls you'll start to find familiar international brands and hot local labels, but even here they can be bought at surprisingly reasonable prices.

Where to Buy

Antiques & collectables

Le Brocanteur
Gardens Shopping Centre
Tel: 021-461 6805
Come here for classic rococo French country furniture, as well as French linen, crystal chandeliers and more.

Bruce Tait Antiques and Kitsch Collectables
Buitenkloof Centre, Kloof Street
Tel: 021-422 1567
The 1950s kitsch memorabilia here ranges from religious items to nasty glitter bangles and sputnik chairs.

Burr & Muir
82 Church Street
Tel: 021-422 1319
Owner Geoff Burr is extremely knowledgeable about glassware and ceramics from the art deco and art nouveau periods.

Delos
140 Buitengracht Street, Bo Kaap
Tel: 021-422 0334
A shimmering collection of crystal chandeliers and antique light fittings are on offer at Delos.

Deon Viljoen Fine Art
1 Palmboom Road
Newlands
Tel: 021-883 9730
Cape heritage furniture and collectables are the speciality here.

Pier Rabe Antiques
141 Dorp Street, Stellenbosch

Tel: 021-883 9730
Rusbanks and Tulbagh chairs.

Private Collections
66 Waterkant St
Tel: 021-421 0298
In the trendy design quarter of De Waterkant, this is a good place to look for Anglo-Raj antiques, including 19th-century Indian ebony or rosewood pieces, architectural antiques such as carved doors, beds and other Indian heritage furniture.

Books

Clarke's Book Shop
211 Long Street
Tel: 021-423 5739
www.clarkesbooks.co.za
Carries new and second-hand books on Cape Town and South Africa. Well worth a browse.

CNA
Victoria Wharf, V&A Waterfront
Tel: 021-418 3510
and Constantia Village
Tel: 021-794 5835
Another good chain, with maps and guidebooks as well as coffee table tomes, fiction and non-fiction.

Exclusive Books
V&A Waterfront
Tel: 021-419 0905
www.exclusivebooks.com
This is South Africa's national chain (there are five more in Cape Town), which keeps book-lovers coming back for more. You can spend the afternoon reading a book or the latest magazine glossies from around the world in the store's coffee shop.

Quagga Art and Books
Main Road, Kalk Bay
Tel: 021-788 2752
An interesting collection of art, artefacts and books. Lots of second-hand books too.

Ulrich Naumann
Burg Street (opposite Cape Town Tourism)
Tel: 021-423 7832
Wide selection of African and natural history titles.

Wordsworth Books
Gardens Centre, Gardens
Tel: 021-461 8464

One of the six Wordsworth shops in Cape Town, where friendly, well-read staff are happy to give you a review of the latest best-sellers or perhaps a discount for bulk purchasing.

Markets

Greenmarket Square
Cnr Shortmarket and Berg streets
Tel: 083-692 2864
Stalls here are filled to the brim with African masks, carvings, jewellery and clothing. Beware of pickpockets, as they're rife in this touristy area.

Green Point Flea Market
Green Point Stadium
Tel: 083-321 2072
This Sunday market has stalls which are mostly devoted to all things from the African continent. It has affordable curios and friendly traders who are willing to bargain, within reason.

Holistic Lifestyle Fair
Cnr Station and Lower Main roads, Observatory
Tel: 021-782 8882
The potions, lotions, crystals and chakra balancings, plus henna tattoos and hemp clothing on offer here are just a few of the

BELOW: shopping on the Waterfront.

things that give Cape Town its Bohemian-hippie reputation.

Wines

Caroline's Fine Wine Cellar
15 Long Street
Tel: 021-419 8984
A specialist wine store that stocks an excellent range of local and international wines. Caroline's also hosts daily wine tastings, sells fine Rosenthal crystalware and serves traditional Boland cuisine in the downstairs wine cellar.

Wine Concepts on Kloof
Lifestyles on Kloof Centre, 50 Kloof Street, Gardens
Tel: 021-426 4401
This is a showcase for lesser-known wines that are well priced and easy drinking, as well as more expensive bottles for special occasions.

SPORTS

Abseiling

Abseiling is a daring way of experiencing Table Mountain. Contact Abseil Africa, tel: 021-424 4760; www.abseilafrica.co.za.

Cricket

Newlands Cricket Ground in the Southern Suburbs is one of the finest in the world, not least on account of its magnificent location. If you fancy seeing a match while you are in town, contact Newlands Ticket Hotline, tel: 021-657 2099.

Golf

There are 18 golf clubs in the Cape Town area. Here are a few of the most central courses:
Mowbray
Raapenberg Road
Tel: 021-685 3018
Good central 18-hole course at the foot of Table Mountain.
Rondebosch
Klipfontein Road, Rondebosch,

Southern Suburbs
Tel: 021-689 4176
Another 18-hole course at the foot of Table Mountain.
Royal Cape Golf Course
174 Ottery Road, Wynberg, Southern Suburbs
Tel: 021-761 6551
Excellent 18-hole course used for professional tournaments.
Kenilworth Golf Academy
Rosemead Avenue, Kenilworth
Tel: 021-761 6007
Come here for a lesson with a professional if you want to brush up your golf skills.

Rugby

If you would like to watch a game of rugby at the Newlands Stadium, contact the Western Province Rugby Association (tel: 021-659 4600; www.wprugby.co.za) for fixtures and ticket information.

Surfing

The Cape Peninsula has several good beaches for surfing. Which beach is best will depend on the wind direction. A local radio station, KFM 94.7, broadcasts a daily surf report. Popular spots include Long Beach, Noordhoek, Fish Hoek and Muizenberg. Contact www.wavewatch.co.za.

SIGHTSEEING TOURS

Walking Tours

With its cosmopolitan buzz, street entertainment and markets, as well as a multitude of alfresco cafés and restaurants where you can take a rest, Cape Town is a great city for exploring on foot. **Cape Town Tourism** operate Wanderlust's "Cape Town on Foot" tours (tel: 021-426 4260; www.wanderlust.co.za), which take 2½ hours to cover the main sights and history of the city centre. These tours are very popular, so book in advance.

Grassroute Tours (tel: 021-706 1006; www.grassroutetours. co.za) and **Roots Africa Tours** (tel: 021-987 8330; www.rootsafrica. co.za) both offer tours of Cape Town's cultural sites and organise excursions to townships.

Boat Tours

Waterfront Boat Company (tel: 021-418 5806; www.waterfront boats.co.za) offers harbour tours, educational excursions and champagne cruises, all of which depart from Quay Five on the V&A Waterfront. Tours range from a one-hour cruise (R60) to a full day's fishing trip (R1,650).
  The Waterfront Information Office (tel: 021-408 750; www.waterfront.co.za) can provide information on a variety of other tours that are available from the V&A Waterfront.
  Boat trips to see the Cape seals on Duiker Island in False Bay can be arranged through **Drumbeat Charters** (tel: 021-438 9208). They depart from Hout Bay Harbour, and there is also a one-way trip from Hout Bay to the Waterfront Harbour.

Bicycle Tours

Daytrippers (tel: 021-511 4766; www.daytrippers.co.za) organise bicycle tours, including the popular full-day "Cape Point Tour". This scenic tour follows the Atlantic Coast to the Cape of Good Hope Nature Reserve. The cost is R323, and this includes bicycle rental, a picnic lunch and any admission charges. **Adventure Village** (tel: 021-424 1580; www.adventurevillage.co.za) operates a similar service.

Other Tours

Civair (tel: 021-419 5182; www.civair.co.za) offers breathtaking 20-minute, 30-minute and hour-long scenic helicopter tours along the Atlantic coast, with prices ranging from R2,000 to R6,000.

TRANSPORT

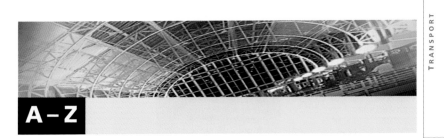

A–Z

ACCOMMODATION

A HANDY SUMMARY OF PRACTICAL INFORMATION, ARRANGED ALPHABETICALLY

A Admission Charges 227
B Budgeting for Your Trip 227
   Business Hours 228
C Climate 228
   Crime & Safety 228
   Customs Regulations 229
D Disabled Travellers 229
E Electricity 230
   Embassies/Consulates 230
   Emergency Numbers 230

Entry Requirements 230
G Gay & Lesbian Travellers 231
H Health & Medical Care 231
I Internet 232
L Libraries 232
   Lost Property 232
M Media 232
   Money 233
P Postal Services 233
   Public Holidays 233

R Religious Services 233
S Student Travellers 234
T Telephones 234
   Time Zone 235
   Tipping 235
   Tour Operators 235
   Tourist Information 235
W Websites 236
   Weights & Measures 236
   What to Bring 236

ACTIVITIES

A dmission Charges

Most museums and galleries charge admission fees but these are inexpensive by European and US standards, with most charging between R5 and R50. Some larger establishments are free of charge on certain days and offer special deals for large groups.

High-profile attractions are more expensive. The boat trip to and tour of Robben Island, for example, costs R150 for an adult (R75 for a child), and the cable-car ride up Table Mountain costs R110 return for an adult (R58 for a child).

Senior citizens and students are entitled to reduced-rate admissions at most museums

and galleries, although they may need to produce a student card or passport as proof of age. Children are usually admitted for half-price.

B udgeting for Your Trip

If you're looking for accommodation with an acceptable level of comfort, cleanliness and facilities (TV, en-suite bathroom and breakfast) at reasonable cost, your best bet is a bed-and-breakfast, where the price of a double room starts at less than R500. For budget hotels you'll pay anything from R500 to R1,000, while more luxurious or designer hotels in the city centre or on the seafront will have a much higher room rate.

For between R1,000 and R2,000 there's a range of good hotels, from boutique establishments to business-traveller favourites with luxury facilities and amenities. Anything over R2,000 is certainly in the de luxe league.

Food costs are very reasonable, and range from about R15 for a ready-made sandwich to R150 per head for a three-course meal with wine at a bistro-style eatery, and from R200–300 at a fine-dining restaurant (with good wine). A 1-litre bottle of mineral water will cost you between R5 and R10. Spirts are very cheap (as well as widely available: even modest cafés seem to have a licence), though the price of

A–Z

wine, will, of course, depend on the quality. Expect to pay about R60–70 for a bottle of house wine and R70–80 for an easy-drinking wine.

A hire car will cost from R170 per day (depending on special rental deals), and petrol costs about a R6 a litre. A city-centre bus ticket is around R4.

Taxi fares are relatively expensive at around R8–12 per kilometre, and a one-way ticket for the airport shuttle is around R150 per person. A taxi to, say, Kirstenbosch, from the city centre, will cost about R100.

Business Hours

Most shops in the city centre and suburbs are open 9am–5pm on weekdays and until 1pm on Saturdays. Activity in the city centre comes to an end around 1pm on Saturdays. However, shopping malls such as the V&A Waterfront, Cavendish Square in Claremont and Canal Walk at Century City keep much later hours, staying open from 9am–9pm throughout the week (from 10am Sunday). On public holidays the city centre is completely dead, but you will find plenty of life at the Waterfront.

Goverment agencies are open Mon–Fri 9am–5pm. Muslim-owned businesses close noon–1pm on Fridays for prayers. Most liquor stores close at 6pm (Mon–Sat). Supermarkets generally close at 6pm (according to the seasons) , until 5pm on Saturday and until 2pm on Sunday.

In mid-summer sunrise is around 5.30am and sundown at around 8.30pm. In mid-winter it gets dark at about 5.45pm and light at about 7.30am, depending on cloud cover.

C limate

The seasons in the southern hemisphere are, of course, the opposite to those in the northern hemisphere. Cape Town has a

ABOVE: the Clock Tower at the V&A Waterfront.

Mediterranean climate with four seasons. Winter runs from June to August, when temperatures range from 7–18°C (45–65°F), with pleasant, sunny days scattered between cold, wet ones. From September to November the weather is extremely unpredicatable, with anything from hot summer days to a howling south-easterly wind that blows at around 120 km/h (75 mph). December to March is considered mid-summer. The weather is often at its best in March and April, when there is little wind and temperatures are not too stifling. In the interior it becomes very hot in the summer months, and during winter snow falls on the mountain peaks.

For the weather forecast bureau, tel: 021-40881 or 021-934 0450, or consult the daily newspapers.

Clothing

South Africa used to be fairly old-fashioned in its attitude to what you should wear, with people dressing up for even quite modest social occasions and women opting for full make-up. This is no longer the rule, however, and Cape Town is informal, particularly in summer. That said, most

businessmen will wear a suit and tie except on hot days, when it is acceptable to go without the jacket. These days, for an informal lunch or shopping expedition you can get away with shorts and T-shirts.

In the evening most restaurants expect smart-casual attire, but more exclusive places prefer men to wear a jacket and tie.

It rains quite often in Cape Town between May and August, so bring a raincoat. Summers are long and dry, which calls for light clothing and a swimsuit, but bring a warm jacket or sweater for trips up Table Mountain, boat trips or for travelling around the Peninsula.

Crime & Safety

Even though South Africa's crime statistics are notoriously high, most of the crime is concentrated in Cape Town's townships, or occurs late at night in the quieter, darker areas of the city. In the downtown areas closed-circuit TV cameras have been installed on most street corners, keeping an electronic eye on the city, and these have proved to be an effective deterrent.

Avoid walking alone after dark in unpopulated streets and do not draw attention to your money and jewellery. If you are dining out, ask the restaurant staff to call a taxi for you. Be extra careful with your belongings wherever you go, whether it's a restaurant, inner-city flea market or nightclub. Keep your handbag and wallet close by at all times. Petty theft such as pickpocketing is especially prevalent at flea markets. If you're parking in town at night, try to find a well-lit area near busy restaurants, with a car guard close by.

When drawing money from an ATM machine do not accept help from any person or stranger that offers assistance, as it's likely they'll clean out your account. Some banks employ a guard to watch over their ATM machines.

Credit cards are welcome at most shops and restaurants, so it is not necessary to carry around a lot of cash. Lost/stolen credit cards should be reported to the following 24-hour services:
American Express, tel: 0860-003 768
Diners Club, tel: 0860-346 377
MasterCard, tel: 0800-990 418
Visa International, tel: 0800-990 475

Police

If you've been subjected to a serious crime such as mugging, robbery, rape or assault, contact the Flying Squad on 10111. For petty crime (such as pickpocketing), call the local police station (look under Regional Offices of National and Governmental in the blue section of the Yellow Pages directory). If you have a problem with finding the right number, contact Directory Enquiries on 1023.

To claim for theft or loss on an insurance policy it is necessary to notify the local police, usually within a specified time limit.

Useful contact numbers

Main Police Station, tel: 021-467 8077
The Tourist Safety Unit, tel: 021-421 5115, 021-421 5116
Poison Crisis Centre, tel: 021-689 5277, 021-931 6129

Police Tourist Unit, tel: 021-418 2852

Customs Regulations

Money

Visitors are permitted to import a maximum of R5,000 in South African banknotes, but can bring unlimited quantities of Traveller's Cheques denominated in South African rand. Large amounts of foreign currency should be declared on arrival.

On departure, visitors can export a maximum of R500 in South African notes. It is advisable to keep bank-exchange receipts.

Goods

Travellers (aged 18 and over only in the case of alcohol and tobacco) are allowed to import the following items duty-free:
• **Alcohol** – 2 litres of wine, 1 litre of spirits.
• **Tobacco** – 200 cigarettes, 20 cigars, 250g tobacco.
• **Perfume** – 50 ml perfume, 250 ml eau de toilette.
• **Gifts** up to the value of R3,000 per person.
Duty is levied at 20 percent on anything over these limits. The following are prohibited: drugs and narcotics; pornographic

materials; plants, seeds, bulbs, raw cotton; uncooked meat and poultry; uncut diamonds; unwrought gold, ammunition.

Reclaiming VAT

VAT (value-added tax) is charged at 14 percent, but foreign visitors can reclaim the VAT on goods that cost more than R250. This must be done within 90 days of purchase. To make a claim, it is necessary to request a tax invoice for the goods from the sales assistant when you make your purchase. This must include a tax-invoice number, the seller's VAT registration number, the date of issue, the seller's name and address, the buyer's name and address, a description of the goods, the cost of the goods and the amount of VAT charged. On your departure from South Africa this should be presented, along with the goods, at the airport's VAT Goods Inspection Desk prior to check-in (allow plenty of time for this). An administration charge of 1.5 percent is made. For further information, contact: www.taxrefunds.co.za.

Disabled Travellers

Hotels and tourist attractions in Cape Town have a good reputation for meeting the needs of travellers with disabilities. SAA provides Passenger Aid Units (PAU) at all major airports, and larger car-rental companies can provide vehicles with hand controls. For further information, contact the Johannesburg-based Association for the Physically Disabled, tel: 011-646 8331; the visually impaired can contact the SA National Council for the Blind, tel: 012-346 1190.

Several tour operators provide services for travellers with disabilities, including suitable hotels and itineraries. These include Titch Tours (tel: 021-686 5501, www.titchtours.co.za) and Flamingo Tours (tel: 021-557 4496, www.flamingotours.co.za).

BELOW: flying the flag for South Africa.

ABOVE: you may be a long way from home, but your consulate is at hand.

E lectricity

The supply is 220/230 volts AC at 50 cycles per second. Three-pronged round-pin plugs are universal, so to use UK or US appliances you'll need to take a plug adaptor, sold at airport terminals in your home country, but also available at electrical appliance stores in Cape Town. Most rooms have 110-volt outlets for electric shavers.

Embassies & Consulates

Most of the major consulates and embassies are situated in Johannesburg, but several countries do have representatives or consulates in Cape Town. If your consulate isn't listed below, consult the Yellow Pages or call Directory Enquiries (tel: 1023). *For South African embassies in your own country, see Entry Requirements, right.*

Australian Consulate
292 Orient Street,
Arcadia, Pretoria
Tel: 012-342 3740
British Consulate
Southern Life Centre,
8 Riebeeck Street
Tel: 021-405 2400

Canadian High Commission
SA Reserve Bank Building,
60 St George's Mall
Tel: 021-423 5240
New Zealand Consulate
2 Lente Road, Sybrand Park
Tel: 021-696 8561
American Consulate General
Monte Carlo Building, Heerengracht Street, Foreshore
Tel: 021-421 4280

Emergency Numbers

Ambulance, tel: 1017
Fire, tel: 021-461 5555
General emergencies, tel: 107 (mobile-phone users dial 112)
Flying Squad, tel: 10111
Mountain Rescue Services, tel: 10111
Sea Rescue, tel: 021-405 3500

Entry Requirements

All visitors need a valid passport to enter South Africa. Travel agencies and South African Embassies *(see below)* can provide visa application forms for those who require them.

Visas

Nationals from the EU, Australia, Canada, the USA and Japan do not require a visa for stays of less than 90 days, though they will need to provide a return ticket (or the means to purchase one) at their point of entry.

If you are subject to visa requirements, you will need to apply for your visa at least four weeks before your intended departure. You can apply at your nearest South African Embassy, High Commission or Consulate. Visas are issued upon completion of the necessary forms, payment of a fee, proof of sufficient financial means and possession of a return ticket (or proof of the means to purchase one). You will also need to supply two identity photographs. Your passport must be valid for at least 30 days after the expiry date of your intended visit.

Arriving with children

If your child's passport shows a different surname to your own, you will need to provide evidence that the child is yours, such as a birth certificate.

South African Embassies abroad

Visa requirements are subject to change, so it is important to check with the South African High Commission in your own country before travelling.

UK

South African High Commission
South Africa House
Trafalgar Square
London WC2N 5DP
www.southafricahouse.com
Consular section:
15 Whitehall
London SW1
Tel: 020-7925 8900

Australia

South African High Commission
Cnr Rhodes Place and
State Circle
Yarralumla
Canberra, ACT 2600
Tel: 02-6273 2424
www.rsa.emb.gov.au

USA

Embassy of South Africa
3051 Massachusetts Avenue,
NW, Washington, DC 20008
Tel: 202-232 4400
www.saembassy.org

Etiquette

South Africa has an informal
atmosphere, and people usually
introduce themselves by their
first name, including in business
relationships. However, punctu-
ality is the order of the day, and
visitors are expected to be on
time for meetings, tours,
restaurant bookings, hotel
check-in and check-out, etc.

G ay & Lesbian Travellers

If South Africa is the rainbow
nation, then the Mother City is
definitely the reigning queen. The
Cape gay scene is lively and
friendly, whilst continually making
a cultural, political and economic
contribution to the city. It attracts
both local and international gay
visitors.

The gay scene is most
pronounced in De Waterkant gay
village in Green Point, which is a
popular meeting spot thanks to a
number of gay-friendly cafés,
clubs, steam rooms, restaurants,
hotels and designer shops. However, if you travel further along

the Atlantic Seaboard you'll
find a colourful array of smaller,
intimate restaurants, boutique
hotels and cafés also catering for
the gay market.

Cape Town's gay scene is
noted for certain annual festivals and parties, including the
Mother City Queer Project which
takes place in December (a drag
ball hosting up to 8,000 people),
destination parties throughout
the year and relaxed (but very
social) beach time recreation
over the summer. The lesbian
scene is less extensive, confined to organised parties and
selected gay bars around the
Green Point area.

Contact Information

For further information on the gay
scene contact Cape Town
Tourism, tel: 021-426 4260. Also
visit www.gaydar.co.za for safe,
online dating to see who's out
there for friendship and relationships. For further information on
the Mother City Queer Project
visit www.mcqp.co.za for details on
themes and venue. Also check
out www.capetownpride.co.za for
details on the Gay Pride parade
and other activities taking place
around the city. Lesbians should
visit www.lushcapetown.co.za to find
out more about the lesbian party
circuit.

H ealth & Medical Care

Precautions

No special precautions are necessary unless you are also travelling to Mpumalanga Province
(including the Kruger National
Park), the Northern Province or
northeastern KwaZulu-Nata,
where you will need to take
malaria tablets, especially from
May–October.

You can drink tap water anywhere in Cape Town unless a
notice warns you otherwise. The
sun in South Africa is much
stronger than in Europe, and it is
essential for visitors to use a
good sun screen for protection,

and wear a hat when out and
about. Poisonous snakes and
spiders are present in many
places, especially in lush, mountainous areas (like Table Mountain and Twelve Apostles
Mountain range), so be careful
when tramping around. Watch
where you are walking, and wear
protective footwear rather than
open sandals.

Aids

HIV infection and Aids have
become huge problems in South
Africa, so it is especially
important to exercise caution
and take necessary precautions
in any sexual relations. Hospitals
are extremely vigilant in ensuring
that HIV does not spread during
medical procedures.

Medical facilities

Cape Town has excellent medical
facilities. Indeed, the first heart
transplant was conducted here
by Christiaan Barnard in
1967 (see page 122). The city
also has an international reputation for excellent, low-cost cos-
metic surgery.

Visitors are advised to take
out medical insurance for the
duration of their trip, as all medical care must be paid for.

Most hospitals have a 24-hour
accident and emergency department with highly trained doctors
and fully equipped operating theatres. Hospitals are classified as
government hospitals or private
hospitals/clinics. The latter are
better equipped. Outpatient treatment may be obtained at hospitals for a nominal fee.

For further information,
consult Directory Enquiries on
1023 or call:
**Christiaan Barnard Memorial
Hospital**, tel: 021-480 6111
Red Cross Children's Hospital,
tel: 021-449 3500

Doctors and dentists

For a list of doctors or dentists
consult Directory Enquiries on
1023 or speak to your hotel
receptionist or concierge. You

TRANSPORT

ACCOMMODATION

ACTIVITIES

N I A

might have to call in advance to organise an appointment. Also, as a tourist you will have to pay cash for medicines and consultation fees, so be sure to keep receipts for insurance purposes.

Late-night pharmacies

Glengariff Clicks Pharmacy
2 Main Road, Sea Point
Tel: 021-434 8622
Open Mon–Sat 8am–11pm,
Sun 9am–9pm
Lite-Kem
24 Darling Street
Tel: 021-461 8040
Open daily 7.30am–11pm
SAA-Netcare Travel Clinic
The Fountainhead Medical Centre, Heerengracht
Tel: 021-419 3172
Open Mon–Fri 8am–5pm,
Sat 9am–1pm
Offers traveller's vaccinations, first-aid kits and travel medical advice, especially on malaria which occurs in northern areas. Credit cards accepted.

Helplines

These lines are available 24 hours a day, seven days a week:
Alcoholics Anonymous, tel: 021-592 5047
Childline, tel: 0800-055 555
Lifeline, tel: 021-461 1111
Narcotics Anonymous, tel: 0881-30 03 27
Rape Crisis Centre, tel: 021-447 9762

Internet

Most ISPs (Internet Service Providers) will provide a programme that allows you to connect to the internet and email services anywhere in the world. Many of the better hotels provide an internet point in bedrooms or, failing that, a business centre. If you intend to stay in South Africa for an extended period, you may want to contact a local ISP which will provide you with a user name, password and internet dial-up. Some well-known and reliable service providers include:

iAfrica, tel: 021-426 5252, www.iafrica.com
M-Web, tel: 0860-032 000, www.mweb.co.za
Telkom Internet, tel: 10219, www.telkomsa.net
World Online, tel: 0860-001 177, www.worldonline.co.za

Internet cafés

There are a number of internet cafés in Cape Town, especially around Long Street. Look out for: the weird and wonderful **Purple Turtle**, conveniently situated on Greenmarket Square (with a tattoo parlour and body piercing upstairs); **Computer Junction** at 12 Main Road Sea Point (tel: 021-439 6772); and the **Infocafe** (tel: 021-426 4424), which is located inside the Cape Town Information Centre on the corner of Burg and Castle streets. You will also find internet access in most public libraries, backpacker hostels, hotels and guest lodges.

Libraries

Visitors may register as temporary members at any Cape Town City Library branch. For information contact the City Main Library (tel: 021-467 1567).

Centre for the Book (62 Queen Victoria Street, tel: 021-423 2669, www.centreforthebook.org.za) aims to promote reading by making books accessible to everyone. Visitors to the centre will find a range of contemporary South African literature or can surf the web at the in-house internet café. Browsing is encouraged, and reading books in the central reading room is free of charge.

Lost Property

Report your loss at the local police station and leave your contact details and address. Missing items of luggage can be located at the Lost and Found division of the Cape Town International Airport, tel: 021-937 1200. It may also be worth checking the "lost

and found" section in the classified section of the local daily newspapers.

Media

Newspaper and magazines

The *Cape Argus*, an afternoon newspaper, and *Die Burger*, an Afrikaans-language morning newspaper, are the most widely read daily papers in the area. They provide general interest news with a dash of politics and an emphasis on human-interest stories. The *Cape Times*, a morning newspaper, carries more international news and provides readers with greater depth of information on South African and international political developments.

The three major Sunday newspapers, the *Sunday Times*, *Weekend Argus* and *Rapport*, include a mix of detailed analyses of political developments, summary of the week's news and saucy sensation. The *Mail & Guardian*, published on a Friday, is an excellent read, and focuses on South African, African and international politics. It is read by business people and decision-makers throughout southern Africa.

The two major newspaper houses also have excellent online versions:
Independent On-Line, www.iol.co.za
Media24 (English), www.media24.co.za
Beeld (Afrikaans), www.news24.com
Die Burger (Afrikaans), www.news24.com

South Africa also offers a wide range of local and international magazines, ranging from fashion to fishing. You will find them at leading newsagents, supermarkets and bookstores throughout the Western Cape.

You can also pick up a copy of the *Big Issue* magazine at most traffic intersections. Proceeds from the sales go to the vendors, who are usually homeless people in need of an income.

Radio

The Western Cape has a range of local, regional and national radio stations. Most broadcast in English. KFM (94.5 FM), the most popular radio station in the Western Cape, plays a mix of '70s, '80s, '90s and current hits. Good Hope FM and P4 Radio are two of the most popular radio stations in Cape Town. Community radio stations have boomed in South Africa in recent years. Stations such as Christian station CCFM in Cape Town and the Muslim community station Voice of the Cape are among the community stations aimed at serving the Western Cape's diverse population.

Television

The South African Broadcasting Corporation (SABC) provides three television channels: SABC 1, 2 and 3. SABC 1 and 2 broadcast programmes in English, Afrikaans and Xhosa, while SABC 3 broadcasts only in English, and includes many award-winning American and British hit TV shows. Privately owned free-to-air e-TV broadcasts a mix of local and international programmes. M-Net, a pay station, shows good movies, live sport and chat shows, while DSTV (a satellite channel) shows BBC, CNN, MTV, Discovery and National Geographic, among others. Most hotels and guest houses and even backpacker's hostels provide DSTV channels.

Money

Most banks are open Mon–Fri 9am–3.30pm, Sat 8–11am. The unit of currency in South Africa is the rand (R), divided into 100 cents (c). Notes are issued in R200, R100, R50, R20, R10; coins R5, R2, R1, 50c, 20c, 10c, 5c, 2c and 1c. Currency-exchange rates are available at banks and are published in the daily press, or contact your closest bureau de change. In the last year or so rates have been around R11 to £1 and R6.7 to $1.

For information on taking money in and out of South Africa, and also on obtaining VAT refunds, see page 229.

Credit cards

Credit cards (Visa, MasterCard, Eurocard, Diners Club and American Express) are widely accepted for goods and services. However, they cannot be used to buy petrol.

ATMs

ATMs are common in the downtown areas. Some have on-site security guards outside normal hours. The machines accept most major credit cards and some debit cards. Though convenient, ATMs can be quite an expensive way of changing money, as you are likely to be charged a fee by your bank as well as incur interest on the sum. Beware when using ATMs, especially of "helpful" strangers, who try to involve themselves in your transaction.

Postal Services

You'll find that sending mail from South Africa to anywhere in the world is relatively inexpensive. A postcard to Europe or the United States costs around R2, while letters cost about R3 for a standard envelope weighing about 50 g (1.7 oz). Postage stamps are sold at the Post Office and selected newsagents and retail outlets. The Post Office (tel: 0860 111 502, www.sapo.co.za) handles local and international post and offers 24-hour door-to-door (Speed) services, including insurance, between major cities. Opening times are: weekdays 8.30am–4.30pm, Saturday 8am–noon. Cape Town's General Post Office (tel: 021-464 1700), is a huge art deco building in Darling Street.

Courier and freight services

The Post Office and local courier companies can help you ship your purchases home and deal with the formalities. There are

ABOVE: Christianity is the dominant religion.

many freight companies in Cape Town that will assist you with the shipping of goods and you'll find them in the Yellow Pages under "Courier Services".

Public Holidays

New Year's Day 1 January
Constitution Day 27 February
Human Rights Day 21 March
Good Friday March/April
Family Day 17 April
Youth Day 16 June
Workers' Day 1 May
Women's Day 9 August
Heritage Day 24 September
Day of Reconciliation 16 December
Christmas Day 25 December
Day of Goodwill 26 December

Public Toilets

The best bet are the toilets in shopping malls, which will include toilets for disabled and baby-changing facilities. Most garages also have clean toilets.

R eligious Services

Most South Africans are Christians. The largest denominations

ABOVE: if you are travelling on a budget, head for Long Street which has several backpackers' hostels.

are Anglican (Church of England), Roman Catholic and Dutch Reformed. There are also large Jewish and Muslim communities living in the Western Cape. To find the place of worship of your choice, consult your hotel staff or the weekend press.

Otherwise contact these places of worship for information on services:

Baha'i Centre
2 Vine Street, Woodstock
Tel: 021-448 1102

Buddhist Information
Plumstead
Tel: 021-671 7443

Central Methodist Mission
Cnr Longmarket and Burg streets, Greenmarket Square
Tel: 021-422 2744

Dutch Reformed Church
Groote Kerk, Adderley Street, Cape Town
Tel: 021-461 7044

Evangelical Lutheran Church
98 Strand Street
Tel: 021-421 5854

Jewish Cape Town Hebrew Congregation
88 Hatfield Street, Gardens
Tel: 021 465 1405

Palm Tree Mosque
185 Long Street
Tel: 021-447 6415
or 021-448 4723

St George's Anglican Cathedral
Cnr Queen and Wale streets
Tel: 021-424 7360

St Mary's Roman Catholic Cathedral
Roeland Street
Tel: 021-461 1167

S tudent Travellers

Young people under the age of 26 are entitled to many concessionary rates, including air fares, hostel accommodation and admission to museums and galleries, although a valid passport or international student card may be required (visit www.isic.co.za for information on internationally recognised student cards).

STA Travel is the world's largest travel company specialising in the needs of young people and students, ranging from travel insurance to discount cards, budget travel packages and more. For further information visit www.statravel.co.za.

A popular student magazine in South Africa is *SL Magazine* (www.slmagazine.co.za), which is available from most newsagents and bookstores. It's a hip and funky read that's filled with information on current movies, exhibitions, music concerts and all cultural events.

T elephones

The dialling code for South Africa is 27 followed by the local regional codes. These include Cape Town (0)21, Johannesburg (0)11, Pretoria (0)12 and Durban (0)31. Telephones have direct dialling to most parts of the world. If you have a problem getting through to an international number contact Directory Enquiries on 1023.

Public phones

International calls from hotel rooms are often very expensive (be sure to check the rates before dialling). It is usually considerably cheaper to buy a phone card and use a call box. You will find telephone booths all over town, particularly near shopping malls and hotels.

Public phones are either coin- or card-operated. Phone cards of varying values (R10, 20, 50, 100 and 200) are available from newsagents, post offices and Telkom offices.

To phone abroad from South Africa, dial 09 followed by the relevant country code:
Australia 61
US and Canada 1
UK 44
Ireland 353

TRANSPORT

Mobile/cell phones

South Africa's booming mobile-phone industry is served by three service providers: MTN, Vodacom and Cell C. All three operate on GSM digital. It may be that your phone is compatible, so speak to your network provider about international roaming. Alternatively, you can hire a cell phone at the airport or from tourist information centres. It's also relatively inexpensive to purchase a local SIM card (some international cell phones will work here if you purchase a local SIM card). All of the following network providers deliver excellent service that allows you to call or exchange text messages at any time. The number prefixes for the networks are: Vodacom (082 and 072), MTN (083 and 073) and Cell C (084).

Telegrams

These can be telephoned by calling 1028 or sent from any post office.

Time Zone

Standard time is two hours in advance of Greenwich Mean Time, one hour in advance of Central European Winter Time and seven hours in advance of United States Eastern Standard Time throughout the year.

Tipping

Gratuities are the norm in South Africa because of the very low wages of service staff. You'll be expected to tip hotel porters up to R5 per item, registered taxi drivers 10 percent, petrol attendants get around R3 for washing your windscreen and car guards are usually happy with about R3–5. Waiters or service attendants in restaurants should be tipped a minimum of 10 percent of the total bill (also subject to quality of service), but check your bill to ensure a service charge hasn't already been included.

Tour Operators & Travel Agents

There are a huge number of tour operators in the Eastern Cape. The tourist information centre on the corner of Castle and Burg streets or near the Clocktower on the Waterfront are stuffed with leaflets advertising every kind of tour, from township tours to horse-riding tours through the Peninsula. As a rule, prices are quite high, and it may work out cheaper to hire a car and undertake excursions independently.

Here is a selection of the many and varied options on offer:

African Pathfinder
9 Summerly Road,
Kenilworth 7700
Tel: 021-762 4335
Tailor-made honeymoons, holidays, safaris, etc.

180 Degree Adventures
19 Clare Street, Gardens
Tel: 021-462 0992
A range of fun-filled adventure tours around the Cape Peninsula.

Cape Rainbow Tours
PO Box 51372, Waterfront
Tel: 021-551 5465
This company has a fleet of luxury, air-conditioned microbuses, offering day tours, Garden Route tours and country tours.

Cruise Sub Aqua
14 Jefferson Road, Noordhoek
Tel: 021-785 6994
As the name suggests, they can organise an underwater adventure amongst shipwrecks or a swim with dolphins and seals.

Embassy Travel
17 Wale Street
Tel: 021-424 1111
This is one of the leading travel agencies. Exellent arrangements for car hire, air travel, conference organising, day tours, etc.

Mike Bosch Tours
PO Box 27365, Rhine Road,
Cape Town 8050
Tel: 021-434 1956
For the discerning traveller wanting mountain, coastline, beach and vineyard tours.

ACCOMMODATION

Tourist Information Offices

Once you've arrived, your first stop should be the impressive Cape Town Tourism Visitor Centre at The Pinnacle (tel: 021-426 4260, www.capetown.org), located on the corner of Castle and Burg streets in the city centre. Opening times are Mon–Fri 8.30am–5.30am, Sat 8.30am–1pm and Sun 9am–1pm. This is a one-stop information centre that will provide you with everything you need to know, from maps and brochures to accommodation, tours and events.

There is another Cape Town Tourism office, conveniently situated near the Clocktower at the V&A Waterfront (tel: 021-405 4500). This one is open until about 8.30pm.

ACTIVITIES

Other useful addresses

South African Tourism
Bojanala House, 90 Protea Road, Chislehurston, Sandton 2196
Tel: 011-895 3000
Fax: 011-895 3001
Email: info@southafrica.net
www.southafrica.net

A – Z

BELOW: Cape Town calling.

ABOVE: departing on a sunset cruise around Table Bay.

Western Cape Tourism Board
Tel: 021-426 5639
Fax: 021-426 5640
Email: info@capetourism.org
www.capetourism.org

South African Tourism international offices

Australia
Level 1, 117 York Street, Sydney, NSW 2000, Australia
Tel: 02-9261 5000
Fax: 02-9261 2000
United Kingdom
Nos 5 & 6 Alt Grove, Wimbledon, London SW19 4DZ
Tel: 020-8971 9364
Fax: 020-8944 6705
USA
500 Fifth Avenue, 20th Floor, Suite 2040, New York NY 10110
Tel: 212-730 2929
Fax: 212-764 1980

W ebsites

One of the best websites to look to for information on Cape Town is the official Cape Town Tourism site www.cape-town.org, which has plenty of useful travel related information and news from the city, and includes details of attractions, sites, accommodation, entertainment, getting around, tours and day trips, activities, shopping and more.

Other useful websites offering lots of current information are www.tourismcapetown.co.za, www.westerncape.co.za and www.capetourism.co.za.

For a wider view of South Africa visit www.southafrica.net, which also gives worthwhile information on Cape Town and the rest of South Africa. A smaller, independent site worth checking out is www.capetown.gopassport.com – a directory that covers Cape Town accommodation, restaurants, property, car hire, tour operators and nightlife, among other specials and travel deals.

Weights and Measures

1 metre (m) = 100 cm
1 centimetre (cm) = 0.394 in
1 kilometre (km) = 0.621 miles
1 hectare = 10,000 sq metres
= 2.471 acres
1 litre = 0.22 UK gallon
1 litre = 0.26 US gallon
1 kilogram (kg) = 1,000 g
1 gram (g) = 0.035 oz
1 kilogram = 2.2 lbs

What to Bring

If you take a prescription drug on a regular basis be sure to bring supplies with you; as an added precaution, bring a copy of your prescription too. In winter bring a warmish waterproof coat and an umbrella. Also bring a pair of flat, comfortable shoes, and possibly walking boots if you are planning to hike (though trainers will suffice for most hikes in summer). If you are planning to extend your trip with a safari, or even if you just want to enjoy the amazing bird life of the Cape, bring a pair of binoculars.

A towel is also necessary if you plan to spend time on the beach, as hotels may not supply these. Other essentials include sun block (minimum factor 15) and a sun hat, although these can easily be bought in Cape Town. Camera film is cheaper in South Africa than in many other countries.

If you bring a laptop make sure that it can operate on 240 volts or that you have the necessary transformer. You will also need to purchase an adaptor plug *(see electricity, page 230)*, though these can also be bought in electrical stores in South Africa. Make sure that your laptop and any other electronic equipment you bring along is adequately insured against loss or theft and be vigilant about protecting your property at all times.

FURTHER READING

History & Biography

Long Walk to Freedom by Nelson Mandela. A compelling, must-read autobiography for anyone coming to South Africa.

Desmond Tutu: A Biography by Steven D. Gish. Inspiring life story of the tireless anti-apartheid campaigner Archbishop Desmond Tutu.

My Traitor's Heart by Rian Malan. An outstanding autobiography of a white South African coming to terms with his heritage and the future of his country.

Tomorrow is Another Country by Allister Sparks. Follows the transition from an apartheid state to a rainbow nation.

Beyond the Miracle by Allister Sparks. Sparks delves into various aspects of Mbeki's South Africa, identifying its challenges and successes.

Biko by Donald Woods. Portrait of the Black Consciousness Movement leader killed in police custody in 1977.

A Rainbow Nation Revisited by Donald Woods. Following years of exile the white activist, journalist and champion of Steve Biko, revisits his native South Africa during the 1990s.

Every Secret Thing: My Family, My Country by Gillian Slovo. Fascinating memoir by the daughter of white activists Joe Slovo and Ruth First.

South Africa: A Modern History by Rodney Davenport. An excellent general history of South Africa.

A History of South Africa by Frank Welsh. A comprehensive and readable history from colonial times until democracy.

The Boer War by Thomas Packenham. Masterly and thorough account of the protracted Anglo-Boer hostilities.

Of Warriors, Lovers and Prophets by Max du Preez. A fresh, lively look at South Africa's history.

Culture

Magnificent South Africa by Elaine Hurford and Peter Joyce. A fascinating visual record of South Africa that covers the geographical areas, historical perspectives and the people.

The Vanishing Cultures of South Africa by Peter Magubane. Coffee table tome illustrating many dying aspects of South African culture.

The Lost Word of the Kalahari by Laurens van der Post. A poetic interpretation of the San culture.

Indaba My Children by Vusamazulu Credo Mutwa. An extraordinary compilation of history, legend, folk tales, customs and beliefs by an author who grew up in the province of Natal.

Fiction

The Conservationist by Nadine Gordimer. 1974 Booker Prize winner, by one of South Africa's highly acclaimed fiction writers.

Disgrace by J.M. Coetzee. A cynical look at South African society which won the 1999 Booker Prize.

Cry, The Beloved Country by Alan Paton. A classic, profoundly compassionate tale of a Zulu pastor and his son, set in the 1940s.

Power of One by Bryce Courtenay. A moving story of a young English boy's search for love and friendship.

Architecture

Cape Dutch Houses & Other Old Favourites by Phillida Brooke Simons. A beautifully illustrated guide to the vernacular architecture of the Cape.

Natural History & Hiking

Best Walks in the Cape Peninsula by Mike Lundy. Highly recommended guide with walks to waterfalls, viewpoints, caves and other special features.

Southern African Birds by Ian Sinclair. An excellent guide with colour photographs.

Mammals of Southern Africa by Charles and Tilde Stuart. A useful guide for wildlife spotters.

Food & Wine

Cape on a Plate by Tony Jackman. A comprehensive guide to eating out in the Cape.

Mixed Case by Jean-Pierre Rossouw. An off-beat guide to touring the Cape Winelands.

Modern South African Cuisine by Garth Stroebel. Encapsulates the culinary heritage of South Africa and its modern influences.

Special Interest

The Bigfoot Family Guide to Cape Town by Andre Plant. A small book with lots of fun ideas for families.

Holistic Holidays in South Africa by Janine Nepgen and Sharyn Spicer. Life-changing holidays to rejuvenate body, mind and soul.

The Art of African Shopping by Adam Levin. A useful guide to buying African crafts, artefacts, jewellery, etc.

Other Insight Guides

Insight Guides

The 190-title Insight Guides series is the main series in the Insight stable, known for its superb pictures, detailed maps excellent coverage of sights and comprehensive listings section. *Insight Guide: South Africa* makes an excellent companion to this *City Guide: Cape Town*, especially if you are planning to travel beyond the Cape regions. In addition to the expected coverage of history and sights, it includes essays on the compelling history and culture of South Africa as well as a wildlife gazetter.

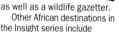

Other African destinations in the Insight series include Morocco, Tunisia, Kenya, Namibia and Tanzania and Zanzibar.

Insight City Guides

Other cities included in Insight's highly successful City Guide series include Amsterdam, Barcelona, Beijing, Boston, Brussels, Hong Kong, Las Vegas, London, Madrid, New York, Paris, Prague, Rome, Singapore, Tokyo and Washington DC.

Insight Pocket Guides

Cape Town is covered in the complementary Insight Pocket Guide series, designed for visitors with a limited amount of time to spend in a destination. Written by a locally-based author, they comprise a series of tailor-made itineraries linking the essential sights, supported by a detailed practical information section highlighting recommended restaurants, hotels and travel tips. The books come with a pull-out map.

Insight FlexiMaps

Insight FlexiMaps have a tough, laminated rainproof finish making them ideal for heavy use on the ground. They feature a list of the top 10 sites in a city or area, and a detailed gazetteer for easy location of streets. The series includes *FlexiMap Cape Town*.

Berlitz Guides

The handy Berlitz Pocket guides are useful on-the-spot reference guides covering all the main places of interest at a destination, as well as providing a comprehensive A–Z of practical information and hotel and restaurant recommendations Look out for *Berlitz Pocket Guide: Cape Town* and *Berlitz Pocket Guide: South Africa*.

CAPE TOWN STREET ATLAS

The key map shows the area of Cape Town covered by the
atlas section. An index of street names and places of interest
shown on the maps can be found on the following pages. For
each entry there is a page number and grid reference.

Map Legend

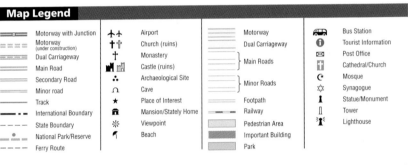

Motorway with Junction	✈ ✈	Airport		Motorway	🚌	Bus Station
Motorway (under construction)	✝ ⛪	Church (ruins)		Dual Carriageway	❶	Tourist Information
Dual Carriageway	✝	Monastery		Main Roads	✉	Post Office
Main Road	🏰	Castle (ruins)			✝	Cathedral/Church
Secondary Road	∴	Archaeological Site		Minor Roads	☪	Mosque
Minor road	∩	Cave			✡	Synagogue
Track	★	Place of Interest		Footpath	🛉	Statue/Monument
International Boundary	🏠	Mansion/Stately Home		Railway	⛫	Tower
State Boundary	☀	Viewpoint		Pedestrian Area	🛉	Lighthouse
National Park/Reserve	⚑	Beach		Important Building		
Ferry Route				Park		

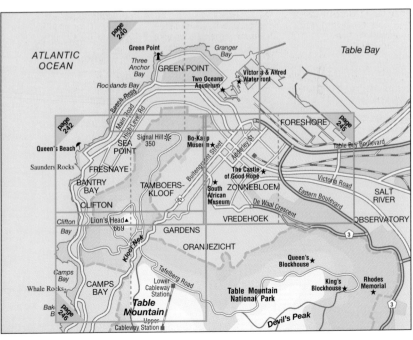

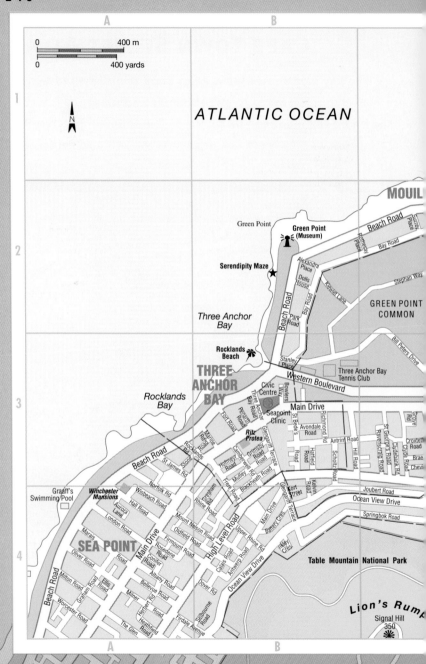

ATLANTIC OCEAN

MOUIL

Green Point

Green Point (Museum)

Beach Road

Surrey Place

Bay Road

Pottinsky Place

Serendipity Maze ★

Alexandra Place

Dolls House

Park Road

Kewler Lane

Stephan Way

Three Anchor Bay

Beach Road

Bay Road

GREEN POINT COMMON

Bill Peters Drive

Rocklands Beach 🌴

Stanley Place

Three Anchor Bay Tennis Club

THREE ANCHOR BAY

Western Boulevard

Rocklands Bay

Civic Centre

Bowlers Way

Main Drive

Three Anchor Bay Way

Seapoint Clinic

St Bede's Road

Avondale Road

Richmond Rd

Grove Rd

Ritz Protea

Fort Road

Marina Rd

Pepiam

Glengariff Terrace

Antrim Road

Hatfield Road

Scholtz Road

Hill Road

St George's Road

Ravenscraig Road

Clydebank Rd

Clyde Road

Croxteth Road

Brae

Chevi

Rocklands Road

Stone

Homeyr Road

Campbwell Rd

Grimsich Road

Mutley Rd

Beach Road

St James Rd

Tree Road

Blackheath Road

Main Drive

Barent Cres

Glengariff Terrace

Fort Street

Kelvin Road

Joubert Road

Ocean View Drive

Graaff's Swimming Pool

Norfolk Rd

Winchester Mansions

Wisbeach Road

Graham

Rhine Road

Springbok Road

Aurora Lane

Hall Road

London Road

Mount Nelson Road

Oldfield Road

Upper Rhine Rd

Ilkley Cres

Marais

Main Drive

Firmount Road

Rosedene

Calais Road

Antwerp Road

Ocean View Drive

Table Mountain National Park

SEA POINT

Oliver Road

Road

Conifer Road

Albany Road

Dover Rd

Beach Road

Milton Road

Ellis Road

Bellevue Rd

Milner Road

Herbert Road

Firdale Avenue

Selbourne Road

Worcester Road

The Glen

Heathfield Road

Lion's Rump

Signal Hill 350 ❋

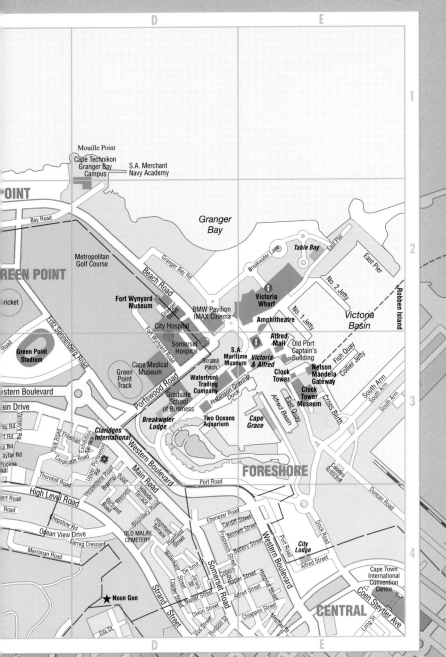

D

E

1

Mouille Point

Cape Technikon
Granger Bay
Campus

S.A. Merchant
Navy Academy

POINT

Bay Road

Granger
Bay

Table Bay

East Pier

East Pier

2

Metropolitan
Golf Course

Granger Bay Rd

Breakwater Lane

No. 2 Jetty

GREEN POINT

Beach Road

Robben Island

Cricket

Fritz Sonnenberg Road

Fort Wynyard
Museum

Granger Street

BMW Pavilion
IMAX Cinema

Victoria
Wharf

No. 1 Jetty

Victoria
Basin

Green Point
Stadium

Fort Wynyard Road

City Hospital

Somerset
Hospital

Amphitheatre

S.A.
Maritime
Museum

Alfred
Mall

Old Port
Captain's
Building

Fish Quay

Collier Jetty

Green Point Track

Cape Medical
Museum

Portswood Road

Scratch
Patch

Victoria
& Alfred

Clock
Tower

Nelson
Mandela
Gateway

South Arm

South Arm

Western Boulevard

Waterfront
Trading
Company

Robinson Graving Dock

Clock
Tower
Museum

Cross Berth

Main Drive

Graduate
School
of Business

Alfred Basin

East Quay

Breakwater
Lodge

Two Oceans
Aquarium

Cape
Grace

Claridges
International

Exhibition Road

Upper Portswood Road

Western Boulevard

FORESHORE

Labia Crescent

Duncan Road

Dock Road

3

Ney Rd

St Johns Rd

Freeman Road

York Road

Braemar Road

Cavalcade Road

Bay Rd

Main Road

Hillside Terrace

Boundary Road

Port Road

Port Road

Dock Road

Varnaylor Rd

Rodena Rd

Thornhill Road

Yesterday Road

Belford Road

Wessels Road

Broomfield Terrace

Ebenezer Road

Cardiff Street

Bennett Street

Western Boulevard

City
Lodge

4

High Level Road

Chepstow Rd

Ocean View Drive

Carreg Crescent

OLD MALAY
CEMETERY

Highfield Street

Prestwich Street

Battery Street

Alfred Street

bert Road

Road

Merriman Road

Waterkant Street

De Smit Street

Cobern St

Jarvis St

Napier Street

Hospital Street

Cape Town
International
Convention
Centre

★ Noon Gun

Strand Street

Loader Street

Napier Street

Dixon Street

Vos Street

Hudson St

Chiappini Street

Macduff St

CENTRAL

Coen Steytler Ave

Long St

Ella St

Somerset Road

D

E

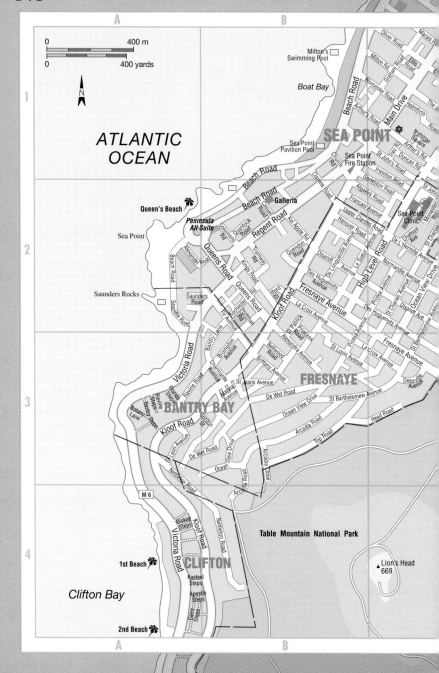

Table Mountain National Park

Signal Hill
350

Lion's Rump

Signal Hill Road

SCHOTSCHE KLOOF

St Mary Maternity

Military Road

Military Rd

TAMBOERSKLOOF

Leeukloof

Queens Road

Brownlow Road

Kenmore Road

Poyser Road

Milner Road

Devonport Road

Carstens Street

Brunswick Road

Leeuwenvoet Road

Hillside Road

Bennington Road

Miljov Manor

Frederick Close

Burnside Road

Woodside Road

Gilmour Hills

Belle Ombre Road

Upper Buitengracht

Tamboerskloof Road

New Church Street

Park Lane

Park House Road

Park Road

Kloof Road

Hildene Road

Albert Road

Bond Street

Camden Street

Warren Street

Kloof Road

New Road

Wilkinson Street

Faure Street

Upper Albert Road

St Michael's Rd

Bay View

Hastings Street

Eaton Road

Upper Union St

Mount Nelson

Union Street

Welleveden Street

De Hoop

Rael Street

Cambridge Avenue

Conradie Recreation Ground

Vansby Street

Regent Square

Leeuwendal

Cape Swiss

Nicol Street

Burnaba

De Lorentz Street

Kloof Avenue

Union Street

Kynsteyn Street

Vine Street

Mackail Street

Camp Street

Quarry Hill

Avenue

Kelvin St

Bath St

Derwent Road

Milan St

Stephen Road

Welgemeend Street

Pingen Street

Newport

Tuin St

Quarry Hill

Hofmeyr Road

Cotswold Ave

Firdale Road

Kloof Road

Ivanhoe Street

Yolfre Road

Kloof Nek Road

Constantia Road

Bellevue Street

Hof Street

GARDENS

Volks Hospital

Rasden Street

Molteno Road

DE WAAL PARK

Leeuwenhof & Bo-Tuin

High Level Road

Ocean View Drive

Freshaye Sports Club

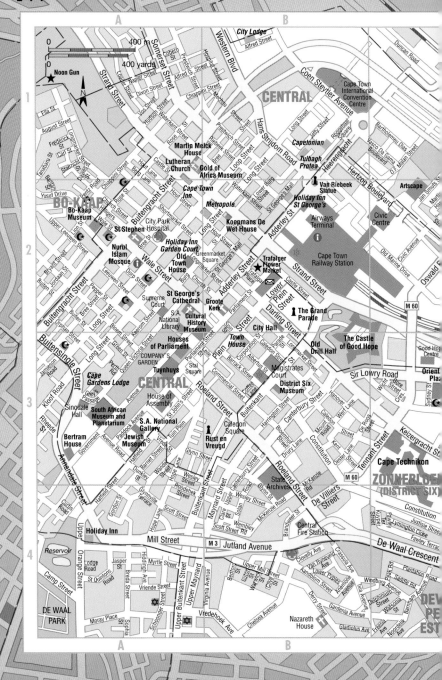

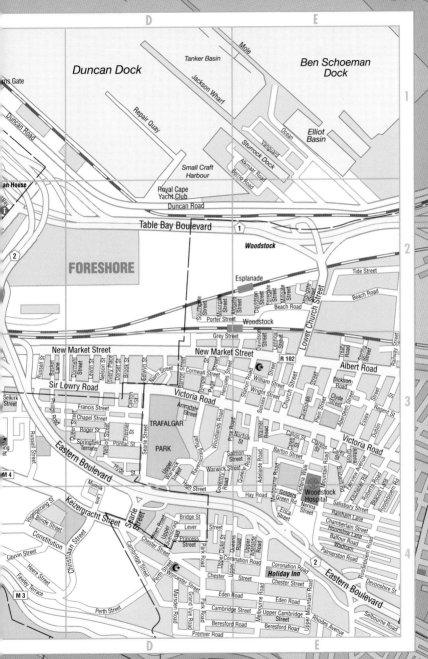

Duncan Dock

Tanker Basin

Mole

Ben Schoeman Dock

ms Gate

Jackson Wharf

Repair Quay

Ocean

Elliot Basin

Duncan Road

Vanguard

Sturrock Dock

Akmaar Road

Berrio Road

an House

Small Craft Harbour

Royal Cape Yacht Club

Duncan Road

Table Bay Boulevard ①

Woodstock

2

FORESHORE

Esplanade

Tide Street

Southome Street

Mongan Street

Davidson Street

Alidgate Street

Beach Road

Foreghan Street

Milligate Street

Highgate Street

Lower Church Street

Beach Road

Porter Street

Woodstock

Grey Street

Davidson Street

Lennox Street

New Market Street

New Market Street

Russell St

Basket Lane

Dorman St

Lewin St

Nelson St

Dorset St

Brook St

Selvin St

Nairn St

Carron St

Cornwall Street

Byrne St

Hercules St

Pade St

William Street

Station Road

Sussex Street

Wright Street

R 102

Albert Road

Treaty Street

Spring Street

Railway Street

Sir Lowry Road

Selkirk Street

Francis Street

Chapel Street

Queen Street

Roger St

Nelson St

Premier St

Pontlac St

Caxton St

Victoria Road

Armadale Street

Woodlands Road

Pine Road

Norfolk St

Walmer Road

Church Street

Dickson Road

Cavendish St

Clyde Street

Aberdeen Street

Essex Street

Victoria Road

Dublin St

Regent St

Springfield Terrace

TRAFALGAR

Ravensden Road

Salmon Street

Adelaide Road

Calvin St

Carcens St

Barton Street

Crang St

Carey St

Brabant Rd

Fairview Avenue

Xitchener Rd

Roberts Road

Bascon Lane

M 4

Eastern Boulevard

PARK

Upper Warwick Street

Warwick Street

Queen St

Golden Green Rd

Mountain Road

Victoria Walk

Woodstock Hospital

Salisbury Street

Roodebloem Road

High Street

Hay Road

Nerina Street

Rainham Lane

Devonshire St

Keizergracht Street

Seale St

Munnik St

Railey St

Bridge St

Lever

Street

Erica Street

Chamberlain Street

Hounslow Lane

Balfour Road

Wadham

Palmerston Road

Voghezang Street

Blinde Street

Christiaan Street

Upper Canal Street

Canal Road

Chester Street

Princess Street

Park Street

Upper Duke St

Upper Adelaide Street

Queens Street

Coronation Road

Coronation Road

Holiday Inn

②

Eastern Boulevard

Constitution

Cauvin Street

Heere Street

Fawley Terrace

Cambridge Street

Worcester Street

Marsden Road

Grand Vue Road

Chester

Street

Eden Road

Melbourne Road

Chester Street

Eden Road

Rhodes Avenue

Selbourne Road

M 3

Perth Street

Cambridge Street

Beresford Road

Upper Cambridge Street

Beresford Road

Premier Road

D

E

Woodstock

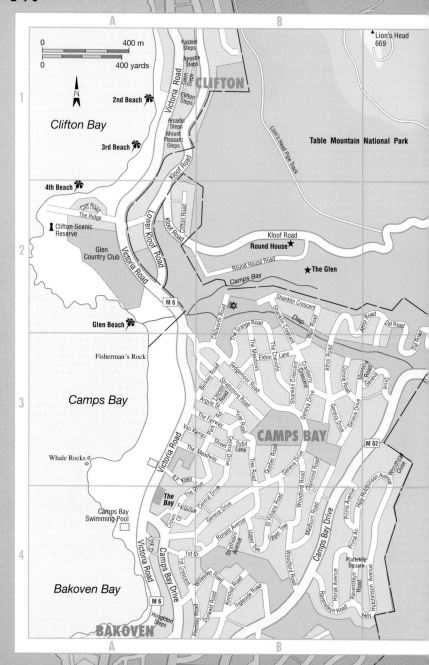

D **E**

Cotswold Ave

Firdale Road

Kloof Nek Road

Constantia Road

Kloof Road

Ivanhoe Street

Kotze Street

Hof Street

Hofmeyr Street

Lingen Street

Hope Street

Volks Hospital

Leeuwenhof & Bo-Tuin

GARDENS

Rayden Street

DE WAAL PARK

Molteno Reservoir

1

Bellevue Street

Buxkale Road

Westmore Road

Leeuwenhof Road

Dalkeith Crescent

Kensington Road

Rosmead Avenue

Burton Avenue

Molteno Road

Belvedere Avenue

Alexandra Avenue

Belmont Avenue

Forest Road

Signal Hill Road

M 62

Higgo Crescent

Higgo Avenue

Summerseat

Close Rustic Road

Higgo Lane

Glen Crescent

Glen Avenue

Glen Crescent

Glen Crescent

Montrose Avenue

Marmion Road

Forest Road

Higgo Lane

Higgo Lane

Trek Road

Glencoe West

Invermark Crescent

Glen Avenue

Glen Crescent

Woodburn Crescent

Cairnmount Avenue

Garfield Road

Roseberry Avenue

Kloof Nek

Kloof Nek Road

Invermark Crescent

Glencoe East

Chesterfield Road

Glencoe East

Egremar Road

Strathcona Road

2

Road

Drive

Tafelberg Road

Mocke Reservoir

Rugby Road

Posset Lane

Upper Contour Path

Tafelberg Road

Lower Cableway Station

Tafelberg Road

3

Pipe Track

Table Mountain National Park

4

Upper Cableway Station

Western Table

Table 1073 ▲ **Mountain**

D **E**

Schoonder Street **244** A4
Scott Street **244** A4–B4
Sea Point Clinic **242** C2
Sea Point Fire Station **242** B1
Sea Point Pavilion Pool **242** B1
Seacliffe Road **242** A2
Seapoint Clinic **240** B3
Searle Street **245** D4–D3
Sedgemoor Road **246** B3
Selbourne Road **240** B4
Selkirk Street **245** C3
Selwyn Street **245** D3
Serendipity Maze **240** B2
Shanklin Crescent **246** B2–B3
Shortmarket Street **244** A2
Signal Hill Road **243** C4–C3–D2–D1, **247** C1
Sinodale Hall **244** A3
Sir Lowry Road **244** B3–C3, **245** C3
Solan Road **244** B4
Solomons Road **242** B2
Somerset Hospital **241** D3
Somerset Street **241** D4
Sophia Street **244** A4
South African National Library **244** A2
South African Maritime Museum **241** D3
South African Museum **244** A3
South African National Gallery **244** A3
South African Navy Academy **241** D1
South Arm **241** E3
Southgate Street **245** D2
Sparta Road **243** C1
Spin Street **244** B2
Spring Street **245** E3
Springbok Road **240** C4
Springfield Terrace **245** D3

St Bartholomew Avenue **242** B3–C3
St Bede's Road **240** B3
St Charles Avenue **242** C2
St Denis Road **243** C2
St Fillians Road **246** B4
St George's Mall **244** B2
St George's Road **240** C3
St George's Cathedral **244** A2
St James Road **240** A3
St Jeans Avenue **242** B3
St John's Road **242** C1–C2
St John's Street **244** A3
St Leon Avenue **242** A3
St Louis Avenue **242** B3
St Mary Maternity **243** E2
St Michael's Road **243** D3
St Patrick **242** B2
St Quintons **244** A4
St Stephen **244** A2
Stadzicht Street **244** A1
Stal Square **244** A3
Stanley Place **240** B3
State Archives **244** B3
Station Road **245** E3
Stephan Way **240** C2
Stephen Road **243** E4
Stone Road **240** A3
Strand Street **244** B2
Strathcona Road **247** E2
Strathearn Avenue **246** B4
Strathmore Road **246** B3
Summerseat Close **247** D1
Supreme Court **244** A2
Surrey Place **240** C2
Sussex Street **245** E3
Sybil Lane **246** B3
Sydney Road **241** C3
Sydney Street **244** C3

T

Table Bay **241** E2
Table Bay Boulevard **245** D2

Tafelberg Road **247** C2–D3–E3
Tamboerskloof Road **243** E3
Tanabaru Street **243** E2–E1
Tennant Street **244** B3
Thornhill Road **241** C3
Three Anchor Bay Road **240** B3
Three Anchor Bay Tennis Club **240** B3
Tide Street **245** E2
Top Road **242** B3
Torbay Road **241** C3
Town House **244** B3
Trafalgar Place **244** B2
Trafalgar Square **242** C1
Tramway Road **242** B2
Treaty Road **245** E3
Tree Road **246** B3
Trek Road **247** D2
Tuin Plein **244** A3
Tuin Street **243** E4
Two Oceans Aquarium **241** D3

U

Union Street **243** E4
Upper Adelaide Road **245** E4
Upper Albert Road **243** D3
Upper Bloem Street **243** E2
Upper Buitengracht **243** E3
Upper Buitenkant Street **244** A4–A4
Upper Cambridge Street **245** E4
Upper Canterburry Street **244** B4–B3
Upper Contour Path **247** D3
Upper Clarens Road **242** B2
Upper Duke Street **245** D4
Upper Leeuwen Street **244** A2
Upper Maynard **244** A4
Upper Mill Street **244** B4

Upper Mountain Road **245** E4
Upper Orange Street **244** A4
Upper Pepper Street **243** E2
Upper Portswood Road **241** D3
Upper Queens Road **245** D4
Upper Ravenscraig Road **245** D4
Upper Rhine Road **240** B4
Upper Tree **246** B4
Upper Union Street **243** E3
Upper Warwick Street **245** D3

V

Van Kampz Street **246** A3
Van Riebeek Statue **244** B2
Van Ryneveld Avenue **244** B4
Vanguard **245** E1
Varney's Road **241** C3
Varsity Street **243** D4
Vasco Da Gama Boulevard **244** C1
Vesperdene Road **241** D4
Victoria & Alfred **241** E3
Victoria Road **242** A4–A3, **245** D3, **246** A1–A2–A3–A4,
Victoria Street **243** E3
Victoria Walk **245** E4
Victoria Wharf **241** E2
Viktoria Road **245** E3
Vine Street **243** E4
Virginia Avenue **244** A4
Vlei Road **241** C3
Voetboog Road **243** E1
Vogelgezang Street **245** C4
Volks Hospital **243** E4
Vos Street **241** D4
Vrede Street **244** A3
Vredehoek Ave **244** A4–B4
Vriende Street **244** A4

W

Wadham **245** E4
Wale Street **244** A2
Walmer Road **245** E3
Wandel Street **244** A3
Warren Street **243** D3
Warwick Street **244** B4 **245** D3
Waterkant Street **241** D4, **244** A1–B1
Watsonia Street **244** C4
Welgemeend Street **243** E4
Weltevreden Street **243** E3
Wembley Road **244** B3
Werf Lane **244** B3
Wesley Street **244** A3–B4
Wessels **241** D4
Western Boulevard **240** B3, **241** C3–D3–E4
Westmore Road **247** D1
Whitford Street **243** E2
Wicht Crescent **244** C3
Wigtown Road **241** C3
Wilkinson Street **243** E3
Willesden Road **246** B4
William Street **245** E3
Winchester Mansions **240** A4
Windburg Avenue **244** C4
Wisbeach Road **240** A4
Woodburn Crescent **247** E2
Woodford Road **246** B4–B3
Woodhead Close **246** C3
Woodlands Road **245** D3
Woodside Road **243** E3
Woodstock Hospital **245** E4
Worcester Road **240** A4
Worcester Street **245** D4
Wright Street **245** E3

Y

York Road **241** C3
Yusuf Drive **243** E1

ART & PHOTO CREDITS

Shaen Adey/Struik Image Library/Images of Africa 7CL, 123
AKG-images London 23
Anthony Bannister/Gallo 190, 198T
Daphne Barew 193
Bodo Bondzio 182, 194, 230
Gerald Cubitt 7BR, 14, 83R, 90, 94T, 95, 95T, 98T, 142T, 195, 195T, 199
Thomas Dawson 81
Jerry Dennis 194T
Nigel J. Dennis/Gallo 192T
Nigel J. Dennis/Struik Image Library/Images of Africa 128T
Rudi van Elst 196
Mary Evans Picture Library 18, 19
William Fehr Collection 16, 20, 32
Franz-Marc Frei/Corbis 168/169
Gold of Africa Museum/Barbier-Mueller Collection 86T
Roger de la Harpe/Africa Imagery 56, 204
Roger de la Harpe/Gallo 180T
Holler (Schirmer) Hermanus 180
Hein Von Horsten/Gallo 128
Hein Von Horsten/Struik Image Library/Images of Africa 119
Hulton Archive/Getty Images 21, 28
Mike Hutchings/Reuters/Corbis 30
Walter Knirr/Struik Image Library/Images of Africa 144
Stefan Lindblom/Corbis 55
Link Picture Library 200
Mothalefi Mahlabe/South

Photographs/African Pictures 57
Pieter Malan/iAfrika/African Pictures 220
Rita Meyer/Struik Image Library/Images of Africa 145T
Richard Nowitz 4B, 6CL, 8TR, 40, 71, 80, 81T, 91, 93, 97, 97T, 107T, 108, 115, 132, 141, 143, 149, 153T, 157T, 158, 179
Alain Proust/Cephas 109
Clive Rose/Getty Images 124
Trevor Samson/AFP/Getty Images 22
David Sanger 3B, 6BR, 8BL, 37, 47, 51, 59, 66, 98, 104, 111, 115T, 131T, 137, 140, 142, 151, 152, 154T, 159T, 175, 176, 176T, 214, 218, 229, 233
Dorothy Stannard 72T, 89, 127
Selwyn Tait/Corbis Sygma 29
Erhardt Thiel/Struik Image Library/Images of Africa 107, 122, 130
Topham Picturepoint 25, 26, Lisa Trocchi/Gallo 109T
David Turnley/Corbis 27
Dieter Vogel 197
John Warburton-Lee 198
Bill Wassman/Apa all back cover images, 2/3, 4T, 6TR, 7TR, 9TR, 9CL, 8CL, 10/11, 12/13, 34/35, 36, 41L&R, 42, 43, 48, 50, 54, 58, 60/61, 62/63, 68, 69, 72R, 74, 75, 75T, 76, 77, 78, 78T, 79, 79T, 82, 82T, 83L, 84T, 85, 85T, 86, 93T, 96, 99, 100, 116, 120, 121, 125, 128T, 131, 134/135, 145, 148, 153, 154, 155, 156, 157, 158T, 160, 161, 162, 163, 164, 164T, 165, 166, 167, 170,

171, 173, 173T, 175T, 177, 178, 181T, 183, 185, 187, 202, 203, 205, 207, 209, 212, 216, 221, 224, 227, 234, 235
Paul Weinberg/South Light 33
Ariadne Van Zandbergen 5B, 72L, 73, 76, 84, 105, 110, 113, 114, 117, 126, 129, 136, 139, 156T, 159 181, 182T, 184, 184T, 188/189, 223, 225, 228, 236

PICTURE SPREADS

Pages 44/45 Top: Roger de la Harpe/African Pictures. Bottom left to right: David Rogers/Getty Images, Anna Zieminski/AFP/Getty Images, Touchline/Getty Images, Shaen Adey/Struik Image Library/Images of Africa
Pages 102/103 Top left to right: David Sanger, Hulton Archive/Getty Images, Alain Proust/iAfrika Photos/African Pictures. Bottom left to right: Ariadne Van Zandbergen, David Sanger, Ariadne Van Zandbergen, Bill Wassman/Apa
Pages 146/147 Top left to right: Gerald Cubitt, Bill Wassman/Apa. Bottom left to right: Gerald Cubitt, Nigel J. Dennis/Gallo, Bill Wassman/Apa, Gerald Cubitt

Map Production: James Macdonald and Stephen Ramsay

©2005 Apa Publications GmbH & Co. Verlag KG, Singapore Branch

Production: Linton Donaldson

GENERAL INDEX

A

accommodation
Alphen (Constantia Valley) 131
Cape Grace Hotel *93*
Mount Nelson Hotel *83–4*
Steenberg (Constantia Valley) 130–31
Table Bay Hotel 94
Victoria and Alfred Hotel 94–5
Adderley Street *23*, 74
admission charges 227
African Music Store 85
Alfred Mall 94–5
Alto Winery 177
Amphitheatre 94
architecture 59, 76, 106
Arniston 182–3
art and crafts 57–8
rock art 17, *81*, 185, 195
arts and entertainment 53–8, 216–18
Auwal Mosque 108
Avontuur Winery 176–7

B

Baartman, Saartjie *19*
Bain's Kloof Pass 179
Bantry Bay 151–2
Barrydale 196
Bertram House 83
Betty's Bay 181
Biko, Steve 29
Birds of Eden 199
Bishopscourt 125
Bloubergstrand *183*–4
BMW Pavilion *92*
Bo-kaap 21, 77, **105–9**
Bo-kaap Museum 106, **108**
Bontebok National Park 183
Boschendal Estate *178*
Botha, Louis 24
Botha, P.W. 31, 193
Boulders Beach *158*, *159*
Bredasdorp 182
Shipwreck Museum 182

business hours 228
Buthelezi, Mangosuthu 30

C

Camps Bay 149, *153*–4
Cape Agulhas 171, **181–2**
Cape Care Route 114
Cape Floral Kingdom *147*
Cape Grace Hotel *93*
Cape of Good Hope 17, 142, **157**
Cape of Good Hope Nature Reserve 147
Castle of Good Hope 18, *71–2*
Military Museum 72
William Fehr Collection *32*, 72
Cape Peninsula 149–67
Cape Peninsula National Park 121
Cederberg Wilderness Area *185*
Chavonnes Battery 97
children 222–3
churches
Dutch Reformed Church (Swellendam) 183
Groote Kerk *78*
Holy Trinity Church (Knysna) *197*
Lutheran Church *86*
Moederkerk (George) 193
Moederkerk (Worcester) 180
Old Slave Church 85–6
St George's Cathedral 59, **76–7**
St Saviour's Church (Claremont) 125
City Hall *68*, 72
Clanwilliam 185
Claremont 124–5
Cavendish Square 124–5, 223
Herschel Monument 125
St Saviour's Church 125
Clifton 152–3

climate 228
Clock Tower 95
Clock Tower Centre 95
Clovelly 163
Coetzee, J.M. *55*
Company's Garden 18, 20, **79–81**
Constantiaberg 156
Constantia Valley 128–30
Alphen 131
Groot Constantia *129–30*, *131*
Pollsmoor Prison 131
Steenberg 130–31
crime and safety 31, 74, 112, 143, 156, 228–9
Cullinan diamond 24
Cultural History Museum 77–8
customs regulations 229

D

dance 56–7
Darling 184
Evita se Perron 184
Darwin, Charles 151
da Gama, Vasco 17–18, 157
De Hoop Nature Reserve 183
de Klerk, F.W. 30–31, *33*
Dias Bartolomeu 17, 157, 191
disabled travellers 229
District Six 27, 28
District Six Museum 27, 28, **73–4**
Drake, Sir Francis 157
Duiker Island 155
Du Toitskloof Pass 179

E

eating out 48
Bo-kaap 109
Cape Peninsula 166–7
City Centre 87–9
Garden Route 201
Overberg 187
Southern Suburbs 132–4

Table Mountain 145
Victoria and Alfred Waterfront 100–101
West Coast 187–8
Winelands 186–7
ecology and conservation 140, 147
economy 31
electricity 230
Eli 182
embassies and consulates 230, 231
emergencies 230
entry requirements 230
etiquette 231

F

False Bay *157*
festivals and events 96, 223–4
Cape Argus Cycle Tour *45*
Cape Gourmet Festival 47
Cape Town Marathon 45
Navy festival (Simon's Town) 161
New Year 107
Out in Africa: Gay and Lesbian Film Festival 58
Penguin Festival (Simon's Town) 161
Pink Loerie Mardi Gras 197
South African World Film Festival (Sithengi) 58
film industry 58
Fish Hoek *162*–3
Fish Hoek Valley Museum 163
Heritage Museum in Amlay House 163
food and drink 47–51
wine 51, 128–31, 173–80, 185
Franschhoek 51, 177–8
Huguenot Memorial Museum *177*
Franschhoek Valley Wine Route 178

G

Garden Route 191–201
gardens
  Abalimi Bezekhaya
    Peace Park and
    Community Garden
    (Khayelitsha) 115
  Botanical Garden
    (Stellenbosch) 174
  Company's Garden 18,
    20, **79–81**
  Harold Porter National
    Botanical Gardens
    181
  Karoo National
    Botanical Garden
    (Worcester) 180
  Kirstenbosch National
    Botanical Gardens
    116, 125–8
gay scene 151, 153,
  197, 220, 231
geology 137–8, 151
George 193
  George Museum 193
  Moederkerk 193
  Outeniqua Choo Tjoe
    193, 196
  Public Library 193
  Slave Tree 193
getting around 71, 203–4
  Cape Town Explorer 71,
    139, 204
getting there 202–3
Gold of Africa Museum
  86
Gouritz Bridge bungee-
  jump 192
Grand Parade 72–3
Great Synagogue 82
Great Trek 21
Greenmarket Square 69,
  75–6
Green Point 98, 99
Green Point Common 99
Groot Drakenstein 175
Groote Kerk 78
Groote Schuur 21, 59,
  121, **122–3**
Guguletu 114
  Sivuyile Tourism Centre
    114

H

Harold Porter National
  Botanical Gardens
  181

health and medical care
  231–2, 236
  Aids 31, 231
Helderberg 175
Helderberg Nature
  Reserve 177
Helderberg Wine Route
  176–7
Helshoogte Pass 177
Hermanus 180–81
  Fernkloof Nature
    Reserve 181
  Old Harbour Museum
    180
Herschel, Sir John 125
hiking 140–42, 143,
  175, 181
history 17–33
  Anglo-Boer War 22, 23
  apartheid 22-31
  British occupation
    20–24
  Dutch settlement
    18–20
  slavery 19–20, 77–8
Hottentots Holland
  Nature Reserve 175
Hout Bay 155–6, 156
  East Fort 155–6
  World of Birds 155,
    222

I

IMAX Theatre 92
International Slave
  Route Project 78
internet access 232

J

Jewish Museum 82–3
  Holocaust Centre 82–3
  Old Synagogue 82
Jonkershoek Nature
  Reserve 175
Joseph, Helen 28

K

Kadalie, Clements 24
Kalk Bay 163–4
Karoo 147
Keurbooms Nature
  Reserve 198
Keurboomstrand 198
Khayelitsha 111,
  114–15
  Abalimi Bezekhaya

Peace Park and Com-
  munity Garden 115
Khayelitsha Craft
  Market 115
Lookout Hill 115
Oliver Tambo Hall 115
Khoi 19
Kirstenbosch National
  Botanical Gardens
  116, 125–8
Knysna 197–9
  Featherbed Nature
    Reserve 197
  Holy Trinity Church 197
  Knysna Elephant Park
    199
  Knysna Lagoon 197
  Mitchell's Brewery 198
  The Heads 197
  Thesen House 197
Kogel Bay 156
Kogelberg Biosphere
  Reserve 181
Kommetjie 156–7
Koopmans-De Wet House
  71, **75**
Koopmans-De Wet, Mrs
  Marie 71, 75

L

Lambert's Bay 184–5
  Bird Island 184–5
Langa 113–14
  Guga S'Thebe Cultural
    Centre 110, 113–14
  Tsoga Environmental
    Centre 114
Langebaan Lagoon 184
language 106, 109, 179
literature 54–5
Little Karoo 194
Llandudno 154–5
Long Street 59, 84–5
Long Street Baths 85
Lutheran Church 86
Lwandle Migrant Labour
  Museum 115

M

Malan, Dr D.F. 26, 174
Malmesbury 185
Mandela, Nelson 28,
  30–31, 72, 78, 95,
  102–3, 131, 179
  Long Walk to Freedom
    102
Market Square 94

Masjid al Borhan 109
Masjid al Jami 109
Masjid Boorhaanol Islam
  109
Mbeki, Govan 102
Mbeki, Thabo 31
media 232–3
Michael Stevenson
  Contemporary 57
Mineral World 98–9
money matters 227–8,
  233
  taxes and refunds 224,
    229
Monkeyland 199
Montagu Pass 196
mosques
  Auwal Mosque 108
  Masjid al Borhan 109
  Masjid al Jami 109
  Masjid Boorhaanol
    Islam 109
  Nurul Islam Mosque 109
  Palm Tree Mosque 85
Mossel Bay 191–2
  Bartholomeu Diaz
    Museum Complex
    191
  Seal Island 192
Mouille Point 99
Mount Nelson Hotel
  83–4
Mowbray 119
  Groote Schuur Hospital
    museum 122
Muizenberg 164–5
  Joan St Leger Lindbergh
    Arts Foundation 165
  Natale Labia Museum
    165
  Posthuys 165
museums and galleries
  Bartholomeu Diaz
    Museum Complex
    (Mossel Bay) 191
  Bertram House 83
  Bo-kaap Museum 106,
    108
  C.P. Nel Museum
    (Oudtshoorn) 194
  Cultural History
    Museum 77–8
  District Six Museum 27,
    28, 73–4
  Dorp Museum
    (Stellenbosch) 173–4
  Fish Hoek Valley
    Museum (Fish Hoek)
    163

George Museum (George) 193
Gold of Africa Museum 86
Groot Constantia (Constantia Valley) 129–30
Groote Schuur Hospital museum (Mowbray) 122
Heritage Museum in Amlay House (Fish Hoek) 163
Huguenot Memorial Museum (Franschhoek) 177
Irma Stern Museum (Rosebank) 58, 119–20
Jewish Museum 82–3
Kruithuis (Stellenbosch) 174
Lwandle Migrant Labour Museum 115
Michaelis Collection 76
Michael Stevenson Contemporary 57
Military Museum 72
Natale Labia Museum (Muizenberg) 165
Old Harbour Museum (Hermanus) 180
Paarl Museum (Paarl) 178
Rugby Museum (Newlands) 124
SA Maritime Museum 98, 157
SA Naval Museum (Simon's Town) 162
Sasol Art Museum (Stellenbosch) 174
Sendinggestig Museum 85–6
Shipwreck Museum (Bredasdorp) 182
Simon's Town Museum (Simon's Town) 157, 159–62
South African Museum 80, 81–2
South African National Gallery 57, 58, **82**
Warrior Toy Museum (Simon's Town) 162
William Fehr Collection 72 (museum)
music 56, 58

N

Napier 182
national parks and nature reserves
Bontebok National Park 183
Cape of Good Hope Nature Reserve 147
Cape Peninsula National Park 121
Cederberg Wilderness Area *185*
De Hoop Nature Reserve 183
Featherbed Nature Reserve (Knysna) 197
Fernkloof Nature Reserve (Hermanus) 181
Helderberg Nature Reserve 177
Hottentots Holland Nature Reserve 175
Jonkershoek Nature Reserve 175
Keurbooms Nature Reserve 198
Kogelberg Biosphere Reserve *181*
Nature's Valley 199
Paarl Mountain Nature Reserve 178–9
Robberg Nature Reserve 198
Silvermine Nature Reserve 140
Simonsdam Nature Reserve 182
Table Mountain National Park 18, 121, **137–45**
Tsitsikamma National Park 199–200
West Coast National Park 184–5
Wilderness National Park *195*, 196–7
Nature's Valley 199
Nelson Mandela Gateway 95
Newlands 123–4
Newlands Cricket Ground 44, 123–4, *124*
Newlands Rugby Stadium 44, 123, **124**
Rugby Museum 124
South African Breweries 124

Sports Science Institute 124
nightlife 218–22
Noon Gun 109, 118
Noordhoek 156
Noordhoek Peak 156
Nurul Islam Mosque 109

O

Observatory 119
Old Mutual Building 76
Old Slave Church 85–6
Old Slave Lodge *see* **Cultural History Museum**
Old Town House *75*
Michaelis Collection 76
Oudekraal 154
Olifants River Valley *185*
ostrich farms 194–5, 222
Oudtshoorn 194–5
Cango Caves *194*, 195
Cango ostrich farm 195
Cango Wildlife Ranch 195
C.P. Nel Museum 194
Highgate ostrich farm 195
Le Roux Townhouse 194
Safari Ostrich Farm 195
Outeniekwa Mountains 194
Overberg 180–83

P

Paarl 51, 178–9
Afrikaans Taal *179*
Drakenstein Prison 179
Strooidakkerk 178
Paarl Museum 178
Paarl Mountain Nature Reserve 178–9
Paarl Wine route 179–80
Palm Tree Mosque 85
Pan Africanist Congress (PAC) 26
Pan-African Market 85
Parliament *78*, 79
Paternoster 184
Plaatje, Sol 24
plantlife 18–19, 126, 127–8, 138, 143–4, 146–7
Plettenberg Bay 198

politics and government 25–31, 78
postal services 233
Prince Albert 195
public holidays 233
public toilets 233

R

Red Shed Craft Workshop *94*
religion 233–4
Christianity 113
Dutch Reformed Church 25
Islam 20, 105-6
Rhodes, Cecil John *21*, 120–21, 126, 165
Rhodes Memorial *117*, *120–21*, 141
Riversdale 191
Robben Island 18, 28, 95, 97, ***102–3***
Robberg Nature Reserve 198
Robinson Pass 196
Rondebosch 122
Rosebank 119
Irma Stern Museum 58, 119–20
Mostert's Mill *119*
Rustenberg Estate 176
Rust-en-Vrede Winery 177
Rust en Vreugd *83*

S

SA Maritime Museum 98, 157
St George's Cathedral *20*, 59, **76–7**, *77*
St George's Mall 74
St James 164, *165*
Saldanha Bay 184
Salt River 118–19
San bushmen *17*, 81, 195
Sandy Bay 155
Scarborough 157
Scratch Patch 98
Sea Point 150–51, *151*
Graaff's Pool 151
Sea Point Public Pool 151
Sendinggestig Museum 85–6
Seweweekspoort Pass 195–6

shopping 93–5, 224–6
sightseeing tours 226
Silvermine Nature
    Reserve 140
Simonsberg 175
Simonsdam Nature
    Reserve 182
Simon's Town 157,
    158–62
    Jubilee Square 159
    Mineral World &
        Topstones 162
    Navy festival 161
    Penguin Festival 161
    SA Naval Museum 162
    Simon's Town Museum
        157, 159–62
    Warrior Toy Museum
        162
Sisulu, Walter 28
Slangkop Lighthouse
    157
Slave Lodge 20
Sobukwe, Robert 26,
    27–8
Somerset West 176
South African Museum
    80, 81–2
    Planetarium 81–2, 223
South African National
    Gallery 57, 58, 82
Southern Suburbs
    117–34
Spier Estate 176
sport and activities
    44–5, 145, 173,
    197–8, 226
    bungee jumping 192,
        200
    kloofing 152
    surfing 154

Smuts, Jan 25, 26, 141,
    174
Stanford 182
Stellenbosch 51, 173–7
    Blettermanhuis 174
    Botanical Garden 174
    Burgerhuis 174
    Die Braak 174
    Dorp Museum 173–4
    Grosvenor House 174
    Kruithuis 174
    Murray House 174
    nightlife 174–5
    Oom Samie's se Winkel
        173
    Sasol Art Museum 174
    University of
        Stellenbosch 174
Stellenbosch Mountains
    175
Stern, Irma 119–20
Stormsvlei 183
Strand Street 74
student travellers 234
Swartberg Pass 195
Swellendam 182, 183,
    191
    Drostdy 183
    Dutch Reformed Church
        183
    Town Hall 183

T

Table Bay 18
Table Bay Hotel 94
Table Mountain National
    Park 18, 121, 136,
    137–45
Tanu Baru 106
telephones 234–5

theatre 55–6
Theuniskraal Estate 180
time zone 235
tipping 235
Townships 53–4,
    111–15
Trafalgar Place Flower
    Market 74
tourism 140
tourist information 95,
    235–6
tour operators 235
Tsitsikamma National
    Park 199–200
Tuan Guru 108–9
Tulbagh 179–80
    Oude Drostdy 180
Tutu, Archbishop
    Desmond 30, 31, 125
Tuynhuys 79
Twelve Apostles 148,
    153
Two Oceans Aquarium
    97–8, 223

U/V

University of Cape Town
    121–2, 123
Uys, Pieter-Dirk 56,
    184
van Riebeeck, Jan 18,
    19
Vergelegen 176
Vergenoegd Estate 176
Verwoerd, Hendrik 28
Victoria and Alfred Hotel
    94–5
Victoria and Alfred
    Waterfront 91–101
Victoria Wharf 93

Vredendal 185
    Bredendal Estate 185

W

Waalburg 76
websites 236
weights and measures
    236
Wellington 51, 179
West Coast 183–5
West Coast National
    Park 184–5
Wilderness 196
Wilderness National
    Park 195, 196–7
wildlife and birds 128,
    144–5, 155, 156, 158,
    159, 181
    sharks 162, 163, 192
    whale-watching 162,
        171, 180, 181
wildlife parks and zoos
    Birds of Eden 199
    Cango Wildlife Ranch
        (Oudtshoorn) 195
    Knysna Elephant Park
        (Knysna) 199
    Monkeyland 199
    Two Oceans Aquarium
        97–8, 223
    World of Birds (Hout
        Bay) 155, 222
Woodstock 118
Worcester 180
    Drostdy 180
    Karoo National
        Botanical Garden 180
    Moederkerk (Worcester)
        180
Wynberg 128

Paths and Tracks

① Diagonal Track
② Hoerikwaggo Trail
③ Kasteelspoort Path
④ Lion's Head Pipe Track
⑤ Lower Traverse Path
⑥ Middle Traverse Path
⑦ Pipe Track
⑧ Saddle Path
⑨ Smuts Track
⑩ Upper Countour Path
⑪ Upper Traverse Path
⑫ Woodcutters Track

This map is for illustrative purposes only
Use a dedicated hiking map while climbing or exploring within the Table Mountain National Park

◄ Downtown
Orange Street
Upper Buitenkant St
VREDEHOEK
De Wall Park
Highlands Avenue
Molteno Road
Molteno Reservoir
Upper Orange Street
GARDENS
◄ Downtown
ORANJEZICHT
◄ Signal Hill
TAMBOERSKLOOF
Kloof Nek Road
Signal Hill Road
Lions Head 669
Kloof Nek
Tafelberg Road
Mocke Reservoir
Tafelberg Road
Lower Cableway Station
Kloof Road
Camps Bay
Water Filtration Centre
⑩
⑩
Venster Buttress
India Ravine
Arrow Face Buttress
African Ravine
Kloof Buttress
Union Ravine
Platteklip
Diep
Camps Bay Drive
African Ledge
Upper Cableway Station 1073
Western Table
CAMPS BAY
Cairn Ravine
Cairn Buttress
Fountain Ledge
War Memo
Sea Point
Fountain Buttress
Fountain Ravine
Fountain Peak 1061
Table
Victoria Road
Grotto Revine
Grotto Buttress
Blinkwater River
Blinkwater Ravine
Blind Gully
Blinkwater Peak 990
Bakoven Bay
Camps Bay Drive
Porcupine Ravine
Ta N
Barrier Buttress
Valken Buttress
Valley of Isolat
BAKOVEN
Valley of the Read Gods
OUDEKRAAL
③
Kasteels Buttress
Kasteelspoort
Kastelspoort River
Postern Buttress
Kasteelsberg Peak 780
Disa Gorge
Orange Kloof (Restricted Area)
B

Table Mountain

0   600 m
0   600 yds

Wood Buttress
Twelve Apostles